1

MITHRAS

THE FELLOW IN THE CAP

MITHRAS

THE FELLOW IN THE CAP

*

ESMÉ WYNNE-TYSON

CENTAUR PRESS LTD.

First published 1958
This edition 1972

© Esmé Wynne-Tyson 1958, 1972

ISBN 0–900000–79–1

This edition first published 1972
by Centaur Press Ltd., Fontwell,
Sussex and printed in Great Britain by
Unwin Brothers Limited
The Gresham Press, Old Woking, Surrey, England
A member of the Staples Printing Group

To

HENRY BAILEY STEVENS

ACKNOWLEDGEMENTS

FOR permission to use copyright material, the Author gratefully makes the following acknowledgements:

To Messrs Routledge and Kegan Paul Ltd. for permission to quote from *The Mysteries of Mithra* by Franz Cumont.

To Messrs Longmans Green and Co. Ltd. for permission to quote from *The Rise of Christianity* by E. W. Barnes.

To Trinity College, Cambridge, and Messrs Macmillan and Co. Ltd. for permission to quote from *The Golden Bough*, by Sir James Frazer.

To Messrs Macmillan and Co. Ltd. London and to the Macmillan Company of Canada and Mrs George Bambridge, for permission to use *A Song to Mithras*, from *Puck of Pook's Hill*, by Rudyard Kipling.

To Messrs Hutchinson and Co. Ltd. for permission to quote from *The Paganism in our Christianity* by Arthur Weigall.

To Messrs Putnam and Co. Ltd. for permission to quote from *Constantine the Great* by J. B. Firth and from *Julian* by Alice Gardener.

To Messrs Faber and Faber, Ltd. for permission to quote from *Plotinus: The Enneads*, translated by Stephen MacKenna.

I remember that the priests of the fellow
in the cap used at one time to say,
'Our Capped One himself is a Christian'.

St. Augustine. (John 1. Disc. 7.)

A SONG TO MITHRAS

Mithras, God of the Morning, our trumpets waken the Wall!
Rome is above the Nations, but Thou art over all!
Now as the names are answered, and the guards are marched away,
Mithras, also a soldier, give us strength for the day!

Mithras, God of the Noontide, the heather swims in the heat,
Our helmets scorch our foreheads; our sandals burn our feet.
Now in the ungirt hour; now ere we blink and drowse,
Mithras, also a soldier, keep us true to our vows!

Mithras, God of the Sunset, low on the Western main,
Thou descending immortal, immortal to rise again!
Now when the watch is ended, now when the wine is drawn,
Mithras, also a soldier, keep us pure till the dawn!

Mithras, God of the Midnight, here where the great bull dies,
Look on thy children in darkness. Oh, take our sacrifice!
Many roads Thou hast fashioned: all of them lead to the Light,
Mithras, also a soldier, teach us to die aright!

RUDYARD KIPLING

CONTENTS

PREFACE TO SECOND EDITION

AT the present time, when the words Imperial or Empire are among the most defamatory that can be used in an otherwise permissive age, it would be wise to pause in the heated arguments that such use engenders and learn how the idea of Empire building originated, thus coming to the roots of what is today regarded as the chief international and political crime. This would involve a study of the religious beliefs of the pre-Christian world that played such a large part in engendering and fostering the fierce national-ism that inevitably resulted in ideas of racial *grandeur* which, in turn, produced the persistent wars of conquest that have brought the world to its present unenviable state.

By far the most important of these influences on the West was the ancient cult of Mithras which, as an offshoot of Zoroastrianism, was based on the perpetual warfare of Light and Darkness, Good and Evil, in which Mithras was the chief warrior who inspired and aided the most worthy rulers of the world, ensuring them victory. His patronage of the sovereign gave birth to the dangerous concept of the Divine Right of Kings which has plagued humanity through-out the ages. If, instead of blaming and hating humanity of the present day for its Imperialism, critics of our present condition would seek to learn where the original blame lay, they would undoubtedly find it in the religious indoctri-nation of the past eras, which has so befuddled, bewildered and bemused the human mentality that it seems incapable of thinking rationally on the subject of war and has come to accept it as being an inevitable phenomenon of nature, like earthquakes and floods.

It was the identification of the sun-god with the rulers of antiquity which bestowed on them the "Divine Right" to govern mankind and rule by violence and war; and this concept was inseparable from a universal solar worship which had many names for the one Supreme God. Mazda, Attis, Apollo, Helios, Zeus, whatever they were called, their votaries were paying allegiance to the King of Heaven.

In the translated abridged version* of his monumental work *Textes et monuments figurés relatifs aux mystères de Mithra*, which after more than half a century is still the principal source book on Mithras, Franz Cumont tells us of this practice—which was known from earliest times in Egypt where God was worshipped in the persons of its Pharaohs—that the royal race derived its origin "from the sun-god Ra, but the soul of each sovereign was a double detached from the sun-god, Horus. All the Pharaohs were thus successive incarnations of the great day-star." And further on, he writes:

> The Archaemenides, who became masters of the valley of the Nile, and after them also the Ptolemies, inherited the homage that had been paid to the ancient Egyptian kings, and it is certain that Augustus and his successors, who scrupulously respected all the religious usages of the country as well as its political constitution, there suffered themselves to be made the recipients of the same character that a tradition of thirty centuries had accorded to the potentates of Egypt. From Alexandria, where even the Greeks themselves accepted it, this theocratic doctrine was propagated to the farthest confines of the empire. The priests of Isis were its most popular missionaries in Italy.

This was the priesthood of course, which Pythagoras acknowledged as the source of his wisdom.

Cumont writes that in 31 B.C. for the Asiatic People the monarchical memories had never faded: "For them a sovereign was always a king and a God. This transformation of the imperial power was a triumph of the Oriental genius over the Roman mind, the triumph of the religious idea

* *The Mysteries of Mithra*, by Franz Cumont (Constable & Co. Ltd.)

over the conception of the law." We need go no further than the Old Testament for evidence of this conflict and for verification of the antiquity and importance of the sun-cults of which Roman Mithraism was the last overt manifestation in the West.*

To Bible students living under a Monarchy, the grave displeasure evinced by both Samuel and his God when the Elders of Israel demanded a king (1 Samuel 8), must often have been puzzling. The sons of Samuel had proved corrupt as Judges, and Samuel himself was too old to continue such work much longer; it was therefore quite natural that the Jews should look towards the more successful and aggressive government by Monarchy practised by other nations.

The true reason for Samuel's displeasure is to be found in verse 7 where God is said to have reminded him that the people by demanding a king "have not rejected thee, but they have rejected me, that I should not reign over them"; and in verses 19 and 20 where it is recorded that the people said: "Nay, but we will have a king over us; that we may be like all the nations."

This was indeed the core of the trouble, for kingship was, as we have seen, from the first inextricably involved with the worship of the Sun who, whether he was known as Mithras, Shamash, Merodach, Baal or Thammuz was always the hated rival of Jehovah who, according to Deut. 4:19,20, (Moffatt's Translation), had allotted the sun and moon to be objects of worship to all nations, but had taken the Jews and lifted them from "the iron furnace of Egypt to be a people of his own", so that they must never bend the knee to the celestial orbs or their representatives, for Jehovah, a jealous God, would not be likened to anything else in heaven or on earth. Theocracy, therefore, with the law of God being taught and dispensed by priests and judges, was the government for Israel, who had been favoured with the knowledge of the One True God. And this was indeed the Rule of the Highest for those with a transcendental view of deity.

---

* Japan, of course, the Land of the Rising Sun, continued to perpetuate this myth until the present century.

The idea of Kingship, then, belonging as it did to pagan worship, was obviously the thin end of the wedge and must inevitably lead Israel back to the very ideas they had learnt in the land of Egypt, and from which Moses had hoped to wean them. As Samuel realized, it was worse than a rejection of himself; it was the demand for leadership lower than that of the One True God and His law. The conflict was acutely ideological. The Leaders of the Jews were convinced that their invisible God was greater and more perfect than the nature God of the sunworshippers; and they instinctively felt that a return to the lesser concept of the God-idea would be devolutionary.

But the identification of the earthly ruler with the Solar Majesty was as old as recorded history. We read of its origins in Biblical and historical accounts of Nimrod, the mighty hunter whose prowess in destroying the predatory beasts of his neighbourhood evidently won him fame, and a devoted following which soon became the only trained pack of human hounds in the world; for before his time, men were said to have gone unarmed and observed a law of boundaries which Nimrod, so tragically for the future peace of humanity, broke. Trogus Pompey writes of this that "Ninus of Assyria was the first that followed the lust of government in breaking the old hereditary law of nations. He first warred on the adjoining countries subduing the people (as yet unacquainted with arts military) as far as Libya."

That Ninus was but another name for Nimrod seems evident from the fact that everything ascribed to Ninus is also written of the mighty hunter. In Moffat's translation of the Bible we are told that Nimrod was an Ethopian and the the first man on earth to be a despot, being a mighty hunter before the Eternal; and that his empire began at Babylon and other places in the land of Shinar, but that afterwards it extended to Assyria where he built the great city of Nineveh and other places, as well as the Tower of Babel. As all this is attributed to Ninus, and after his post-mortem deification Nimrod was known as Nin, there can be little doubt that these were two names of the same builder of Babylon.

Nimrod, as we know, was the son of Cush who was the son of Ham, and in a footnote found in Herodotous, Book 11:181, we read:

> The Chaldeans . . . appear to have been a branch of the great Hamite race of Accad, which inhabited Babylonia from the earliest times. With this race originated the art of writing, the building of cities, the institution of a religious sytem, and the cultivation of all science and of astronomy in particular.

From the first this great Founder of civilization appears to have been against the governments of the flood-sending God of his ancestor Noah. In Ant. Book 1. Ch. IV:2, Josephus tells us that:

> It was Nimrod who excited them (the people) to such an affront and contempt of God. He was the grandson of Ham, the son of Noah—a bold man and of great strength of hand. He persuaded them not to ascribe to God, as though it were through his means they were happy, but to believe that it was their own courage which produced that happiness. He also gradually changed the government into a tyranny—seeing no other way of turning men from the fear of God but to bring them into a constant dependence on his power. He also said he would be revenged on God if he should have a mind to drown the world again; for that he would build a tower too high for the water to be able to reach! And that he would revenge himself on God for destroying their forefathers.

In fact it sounds as though Nimrod may have been the first recorded scientific materialist, and the damage he did to the human race by instigating the practice of war may be assessed from a study of history.

Fortunately for his subjects, he had a remarkable and accomplished wife, the Ethiopian Semiramis, who, after his death, assumed the reins of government and was renowned for the beneficence of her rule. She was evidently a deeply religious as well as highly intelligent woman and, according to Hesiod (*Theogonia* V. 453 p. 36), had a chief hand in forming the Mysteries which were soon to spread throughout the civilized world. She and her husband were known as Bel and Beltis, the Lord and the Lady, and when Nimrod died, she had him deified and worshipped as Bel or Baal, the Sun-God—hence the common belief that Babylon was founded by Bel.

After her own death, Semiramis, too, was deified as "the Mother of God". In images that were set up everywhere, and adored, she was depicted carrying her son in her arms. Together they were worshipped as Rhea and Nin, and from these two the worship of Mother and Child, the Moon and the Sun, spread throughout the earth. Wisdom, the Mother of the Gods, was depicted as Isis with Horus in Egypt, Ishtar with Thammuz in Assyria, Rhea-Cybele with Attis in Phrygia, Tara with the Buddha in India, and so on. In Egypt where, as we have seen, the Pharaoh was worshipped as the God incarnate, Semiramis, or Rhea, was known as Isis. That the two were identical seems obvious from St. Augustine's description of the Egyptian Goddess in *The City of God* (Book 14. ch.3) where he says:

"Some write that she came out of Ethiopia to be Queen of Egypt and because she was mighty and gracious in her reign, and taught the subjects many good arts, they gave her this honour after her death, and that with such diligent respect, that it was death to say she had ever been mortal."

But all this had previously been written of Semiramis, the Ethiopian. Moreover, Isis ,too, claimed to be the mother of the Sun-God. An inscription found in one of her temples reads:

I am all that has been, or that is, or that shall be. No mortal has removed my veil. The fruit which I have brought forth is the Sun.

Wherever we turn in ancient history we find accounts of the identification of the Sun with the earthly ruler. The Persians made a slightly different approach to the subject. Darius and Xerxes worshipped Ormuzd, and Mithras as his first "ray", or Amshaspand, and the latter with his brightness invested them with an aura of divinity so that they were worshipped as his representative. Mithras was known as the friend and protector of Emperors and Kings, but they were not fully identified with him, like the Pharaohs. It was this idea that the Persians brought to the West where rulers, such as Alexander the Great, claimed at one time to be identified with God, and worshipped as gods, and at another to be the sons of God.

A letter that survives from Olympias, the mother of Alexander, shows what embarrassment such claims were to the mothers of those deified men. Her son claimed to be the son of Zeus, a snake—the form in which the king of heaven visited the daughters of men—having been found in her bed some months before his birth: "My dear son", she implored, "I must entreat you to be quiet, and not cast aspersions on me, or bring accusations against me before Hera. She will certainly bring some great calamity upon me if you suggest in your letter that I have been her husband's mistress".

With the introduction of sun-worship into Italy (by, as some now think, Aeneas), the identification of the ruler with the God inevitably made its appearance. Romulus, the founder of Rome, was said to be the son of Mars—the King of Heaven in his martial aspect. Julius Caesar traced his ancestry to Iulos, the son of Aeneas, around whose infant head tongues of fire were said to have played—always the sign of the Sun-god or of the God.

It is not surprising that the sun-cult known as Mithraism found its way to, and persisted in, Gaul, so long a province of Rome, and in which the last Mithraic Emperor, Julian the Apostate, resided for so long. We cannot be certain how it was that the religious Toilet Ceremonies performed by the deified Pharaohs, evidently to symbolize the rising of the Sun ("he who riseth up"), came to be revived by Henri II of France under the name of *Les Affaires du Matin*, but undoubtedly there was a connection, as the likeness of the two ceremonies testifies. According to Dr. G. W. Kitchin (*A History of France*)," a definite body of the king's friends, very exclusive. . . . waited on him every morning. When he woke. . . . the proper officer brought him his shirt: then the nobles of the Court trooped into the room to salute their Monarch. He rose, and before them all knelt at a faldstool and prayed. . . . This use long continued in France; it was in full operation under Louis XIV."

St. Simon gives a description of the *Grande Levée* in the reign of Louis who, until this day, is alluded to as The Sun King. It is quite possible that the learned Diane de Poitiers, scholar and neoplatonist, knowing a great deal about the pagan religion, originated this custom. An ardent advocate of the Divine Right of Kings, she may well have suggested to her pupil and lover, Henri II, that he should revive a rite that called attention to both the dignity and divinity of the monarchical system; and Louis prided himself on being spiritually related to the House of Valios.

He was the last Western ruler to be surrounded by any illusions of divinity, and his reign was followed by the revolt against kingship, for which the exercise of the sovereign's Divine Right to wage continual wars, and levy iniquitous taxes, was to a great extent responsible. But the revolt was against something more than the injustice and tyranny of earthly kingship. It was primarily the revolt, instigated by the Encyclopaedists, against the idea of Rulership by the Highest, i.e., against the God represented by the Monarch. M. Camus in *L'Homme Revolté* described this rebellion as "the desanctification of history and the disincarnation of God". It represented mankind's determination to replace Rule by the Highest with the Rule of the People, and, as Camus put it, "Justice in order to establish itself amid Equality must give God his death-blow by attacking his representative on earth;" and, "Once you deny God, you must kill the King."

You cannot retain the symbol of a higher state than you wish to have manifested. You cannot at the same time have quality, i.e., a transcendental evolutionary goal to which to aspire, and equality. Mankind, therefore, when it revolts against the Rule of the Highest, impedes and frustrates its own evolution. Thus, in spite of the untold misery and suffering that militaristic monarchism has brought upon the human race, solar worship was not entirely without merit; for when rationalised by the great humanitarian pagan thinkers, such as Pythagoras and Plutarch, its philosophy did foster and encourage reverence for the Highest Good, and the way of self-perfectioning essential if the human race is ever to evolve to a higher state. The idea of self-government by God-government was perpetuated in the Mysteries that were also known as *The Perfections*, and, given a good enough concept of God (which Christians believe was found in the nature of Jesus Christ), this way of the philosophers presents an urgently needed alternative to the now universally threatened *devolution* of mankind to permissive, atheistic egalitarianism.

NOTES TO SECOND EDITION

Page 55. Paragraph 1.

St. Augustine in The City of God, Book i, ch. 3, confirms this when he quotes Juno as saying:

"The nation that I hate in peace sails by
With Troy and Troy's fallen gods to Italy."

And of Aeneas:

"Panthus, a priest of Phoebus and the Tower,
Burdened with his fallen gods. . . ."

Phoebus, the sun-God, was certainly he who stood forth "clear in a flood of light. . . ."

Commenting on the line from Virgil: "To thee doth Troy commend her gods, her all", St. Augustine comments: "If Virgil then calls them fallen gods, and conquered gods, needing man's help for their escape after their overthrow and fall, how mad are men to think that there was any wit shown in committing Rome to their keeping, or that it could not be lost, if first it lost not them?"

Page 58. Paragraph 4.

In his *First Principles*, when writing of the Threefold Wisdom (Book III, Ch.III), Origen refers to the three kinds of wisdom mentioned by Paul in I.Cor.,2;6,7., describing the first as being that which deals with the things of this world, such as the arts and sciences, and then goes on to say:

"As for the wisdom of the 'rulers of this world', we understand this to be what they call the secret and hidden philosophy of the Egyptians and the astrology of the Chaldeans and Indians who profess a knowledge of high things. . . . Accordingly we find in the holy scriptures that there are rulers over individual nations, as for instance, we read in Daniel of a certain 'prince of the kingdom of the Persians', and another 'prince of the kingdom of the Greeks', who, as is clearly shown by the sense of the passage itself, are not men but powers. Moreover, in the prophet Ezekiel 'the prince of Tyre' is most plainly pictured as a certain spiritual power. When these, therefore. . . . saw our Lord and Saviour promising and proclaiming that he had come into the world for the purpose of destroying all the doctrines whatever they might be, of the 'knowledge falsely so called', they immediately laid snares for him."

This passage obviously refers to the pre-Christian pagan religion, the sun-worship which included the deification of monarchs, or the identification of them with the Supreme Ruler, especially as practised in Egypt (where Pharaoh was the very personification of the sun-god), and Persia. The reference to the Indians is particularly interesting as India was undoubtedly the cradle of sun-worship, the name Mitra being found in the oldest Hindu Scriptures before it appeared in the West.

Page 114. Paragraph 2.

That spiritual healing was an essential and much commented upon characteristic of the Christian Faith until at least the third century, is proved by the evidence of Origen who in the *contra Celsum* deals with the accusation of Celsus that Jesus's miracles, which he, living probably in the previous century to Origen does not deny, were done by magic and sorcery. One of the best points Origen makes is that if Jesus and his followers were magicians and sorcerers they would not attempt to improve the moral character of those they cured, for sorcerers never attempted any such thing. The means whereby the Christians effected their cures, i.e. by the Holy Spirit and the Word, are suggested in the following citations:

contra Celsum 1. Book 1:46 "Traces of that Holy Spirit who appeared in the form of a dove are still preserved among Christians. They charm daemons away and perform many cures and perceive certain things about the future according to the will of the Logos."

Book 111: 24. "Some display evidence of having received some miraculous power because of this faith, shown in the people whom they cure; upon those who need healing they use no other invocation than that of the supreme God and of the name of Jesus together with the history about him. By these we also have seen many delivered from serious ailments, and from mental distraction and madness, and countless other diseases, which neither man nor daemons had cured."*

Origen also suggests very strongly that Christian healing of physical complaints necessarily involved a previous or simultaneous mental or moral healing; for speaking of the healings of the pagan Asclepius, he writes, "many who are not worthy even to live are said to have been healed; and no wise doctor would have consented to cure those who live in immorality."

In *The Decline and Fall of the Roman Empire* Gibbon writes: "The miraculous cure of diseases of the most inveterate or even supernatural kind can no longer occasion any surprise, when we recollect that in the days of Irenaeus, about the end of the century, the resurrection of the dead was very far from being esteemed an uncommon event."

---

*ORIGEN: *contra Celsum*, translated by Henry Chadwick (Cambridge University Press. 1953)

Page 114. Paragraph 6. Stone.

According to Aulus Gellius (i,21 : p.192), the most sacred form of an oath in pagan Rome was "Per Jovem Lapidem", "By Jupiter the Stone." As Hislop points out, by translating *Lapidem* back into the sacred tongue, or Chaldee, the oath becomes "By Jove, the Son," or "By the Son of Jove." Whether Peter's acknowledgement of the Master as the "son of God" elicited the play on the word "Petra" by the Master, or whether the passage was written in by a Gentile well aware of the pagan oath, it would certainly seem possible that the passage in Matthew 16:18,19, bore some relationship to the well-known Roman oath, which appears to have referred to the Sun-God who, as Ovid testifies, was worshipped in pagan Rome under the title of the "Eternal Boy", as Dionysos, or the ever-youthful Mithras.

The oath also seems to refer to an extraordinary story found in Hesiod's *Theogonia* ii, 485: pp. 38–41 when, to stop Saturn devouring his children, their mother Rhea brought him a round stone in swaddling clothes which cured him of his cannibal practice. According to Maurice in *Indian Antiquities* vol. ii, p. 348, this stone was said to be "preserved near the temple of Delphi, where care was taken to anoint it daily with oil, and to cover it with wool." Hislop suggests that this stone was the symbol of the "sin-bearing Son", and that the daily anointing points to it as symbolising the "Lord's Anointed", or dreamed of "Messiah". Priscian (Vol.1, *Religion of Greece*, ch. v., p. 208) says that the Greeks called this stone "Baitulos", and Hislop pointed out that this word derives from "B'hai-tuloh"—"the Life-restoring child." And the sacrificed swaddled stone is said by Hesiod (*Theogonia* i,495, p.41) to have restored the children of Saturn to life.

In his *Metamorphoses* Vol. ii, p. 486, Ovid tells us of Olenos who bore the guilt of another voluntarily, but petrified by the horror of it was turned into a stone which was taken to the holy mount of Ida where Cybele, the mother of the gods, was worshipped. Both these stories, which are based on the idea of vicarious suffering, may well have been known to the writer of the passage in Matthew.

Page 155. Paragraph 1.

Philo Judaeus,* referring to the pagan religion of his day, writes: "It is the Mark of a Beast to imagine that there are many gods." The author of *The Revelation* of St. John the Divine may well have known of this description. Both he and Philo obviously had access to esoteric, or what has come to be known as Kabbalist, Judaism.

Page 155. Last Paragraph. The Lion. The Bee. Wax Candles.

In his book, *Le Culte de Mithra*, M. Lajard tells us that there were twelve degrees in the Mithraic initiation divided into four stages. The first, under the heading of TERRE-STIAL, consisted of the Soldier, the Lion and the Bull.

If we are to judge by the Mithraic remains so far excavated, it was Mithras the Bull-slayer that was particularly emphasized in his cult that was so popular with the Roman legionaries; but in his role of Sun-God it was inevitable that he should, in his long and varied career, have frequently been presented in his aspect of the Lion, the astrological sign of Leo, or the sun at its height. It is in this guise that we find him in Hyde's *De Vetere Religione Persarum*, where he is depicted with a star above his back and a bee in his mouth.

In the Chaldean languages—and it was from Chaldaea and Babylon that the astrology so much a feature of Mithraism was derived—the word DABAR signifies both a Bee and a Word. Mithras was known as the logos, or Word. (Compare John 1:1-4) Mithras was also believed to have created all good things. In *De l'Origine des tous les Cultes* Dupuis speaks of Mithras as the Lion with the Bee. Muller in *Dorians* vol. 1: pp 403, 404 (Oxford 1830) writes of Diana

---

* *The Works of Philo Judaeus*, translated by C. D. Yonge, (Vol. IV. "Questions and Solutions".)

of the Ephesians (yet another aspect of the Queen of Heaven, identified with Cybele, Isis, Hecate and Juno): "Her constant symbol is the Bee, which is not otherwise attributed to Diana."

In his recently published book, *Animal Societies, from the Bee to the Gorilla*, Remy Chauvin, writing of the history of the bee, asks: "Who can say why Artemis of Ephesus is sometimes shown as a bee?" Muller appears to have answered the question. He goes on to tell us that the chief priest of her cult was called "Essen", or the *King-Bee*. In other words, DABAR, the enlightener of the souls of men. This may well be the derivation of the so-far unexplained name of "Essenes", the holy men from whom Jesus appears to have learnt so much; for this sect was renowned for its wisdom. It is interesting also to note that the priest of the cult of Diana of the Ephesians always had to kill his predecessor in order to arrive at this honour, in imitation, perhaps, of the order of the Hive. In those early times, Remy Chauvin tells us, it was believed that a King, not a Queen as it is now known, ruled the Hive.

It is from the wax of the Bee that the tapers and candles were made for the pagan religious ceremonies, symbolising the Light that shineth in the darkness and enlightens the world. (John i.)

The following passage is found in *Review of Epistle* of Dr. Gentianus Harvet of Louvaine, pp. 349b and 350a, otherwise known as *The Beehive of the Roman Church:*

"Forasmuch as we do marvellously wonder, in considering the first beginning of this substance, to wit, wax tapers, then must we of necessity greatly extol the original of Bees, for. . . . they gather the flowers with their feet, yet the flowers are not injured thereby; they bring forth no young ones, but deliver their young swarms through their *mouths*, like as Christ (for a wonderful example) is preceded from his Father's mouth."

Although this analogy is based on the false assumption that a King, and not a Queen, replenished the bee-hive, it is a clear identification of Christ, the Logos, with the ancient Bee-bearing Lion symbol of the sun-god. Two rare Roman Missals contain this passage, one printed in Vienna (1506) fol. 75. p. 2. The other printed at Venice (1522). In the *Pancarpium Marianum* cap.29: p.122. occurs the following:

"In this Paradise, this celestial Bee, that is, the *incarnate Wisdom*, did feed. Here it found that dropping honeycomb, with which the whole bitterness of the corrupted world has been turned into sweetness."

The waxen candles of the altars of the Romish Church therefore keep their maker, *Dabar*, the Bee or the Word, constantly before the attention of the Faithful. This would explain the prominent part they play in the Catholic ceremonial, and why their burning is believed to expiate sins. I.e., they are destroyed during the consumption of Wisdom, or the Word, although this symbolism may well have been forgotten, or never known, by modern priests. The practice of burning lighted candles and tapers in honour of the God was, however, a late innovation in the Catholic Church, for in the fourth century, Lactantius (*Institut.*, lib.VI, cap. 2: p.289) mocked the Romans for "lighting up candles to God, as if He lived in the dark."

It is interesting to note from Eusebius, *Vita Constantini* lib. 11:5: p.183, that before going to battle, Constantine's enemy, Licinius the pagan, threatened his gods that if they did not secure his victory he would light up no more "wax tapers to their honour."

Another connection of Mithras with the Bee is suggested by Porphyry who, in *Deantro Nympharum*, p.18, tells us that the ancients called the Moon "Melissa" and that the priestesses of Demeter were known as Melissae. The word Melissa means a "Bee"—the producer of sweetness—and, as Hislop points out, the Hebrew word denoting "to be sweet", i.e. Mltz, is derived from Melitz, the Mediator or interpreter. As we have seen, the feminine aspect of Mithras was Mylitta, the Mediatrix; the feminine of Melitz is Melitza, whereby we come to Melissa the Bee, or sweetener. Mithras being the Mediator, both Melitz and Mylitta are identified with the Bee. Further to confirm the identification Hislop writes that Melissa is "a common name of the priestesses of Cybele."

It should also be noted that long before the cult of Mithras vied with Christianity for supremacy in the West, there was a female prophet in Israel (the only one on record) called "Deborah"—the Hebrew word for Bee!

Page 166. Final Paragraph.

Considered by some to have been "the greatest teacher of the Church after the Apostles," (Jerome. Praef. in Hom. Orig. in Ezeck.) Origen had already rationalized this teaching in his *First Principles* when he wrote (Ch.IV, Book IV):

"God the Father, since he is both invisible and inseparable from the Son, generated the Son, not. . . . by an act of separation from himself. For if the Son is something separated from the Father, and if this expression signifies something resembling the offspring of animals and human beings, then both he who separated and he who is separated are of necessity bodies. For we do not say. . . . that a part of God's substance was changed into the Son, or that the Son was procreated by the Father out of no substance at all, that is, from something external to God's own substance, so that there was a time when the Son did not exist; but setting aside all thought of a material body, we say that the Word and Wisdom was begotten of the invisible and incorporeal God apart from any bodily feeling, like an act of will proceeding from the mind. Nor will it appear absurd seeing that he is called the "Son of his love", that he should also be regarded in this way as the "Son of his will."

Origen had not departed from his Master's definition of God as "Spirit" (John 4:24.), and saw the incorporeal Christ rather than the visible Jesus, as the Son of God, reminding his hearers that this Son is the "image of the invisible God", as eternal as the Father. He writes:

"If he is the 'image of the invisible God', he is an invisible image; and I would dare to add that as he is a likeness of the Father there is no time when he did not exist. For when did God, who according to John is said to be 'light'. . . . have no effulgence of his own glory, that we should dare to lay down a beginning for the Son, before which he did not exist? And when did the image of the unspeakable, unnameable, unutterable substance of the Father, his impress, the Word who knows the Father not exist? Let the man who dares to say, "There was a time when the Son was not', understand that this is what he will be saying, 'Once wisdom did not exist, and Word did not exist, and life did not exist.'"

Unfortunately, by the time of the Nicene Council, so much confusion had arisen in the Church by the deifying of the human Jesus, and regarding the physical Teacher as the Son of God, the Saviour, rather than his wise and saving Word, i.e., his teachings, that this was precisely what the Arians did dare to say. And indeed this was the logical conclusion to be deduced from the premise enunciated by the Nicene Creed which started with the declaration that God, who is Spirit, made what was visible as well as what is invisible, and was the Father of the perishable flesh— which "profiteth nothing"—as well as of the Eternal Spirit in man.

Page 170. Final Paragraph.

The first evidence of this wavering, together with a firm declaration of the original non-violent Christian policy, is found in Origen's *contra Celsum*. This revered Father of the Church, who lived in the century before that in which the Council of Nicaea assembled (A.D. 185–253), writes (Book III, sects. 7 & 8) in answer to the charge made by Celsus that Christianity was merely the result of a revolt from the orthodox Jewish community:

"If a revolt had been the cause of the Christians existing

as a separate group (and they originated from the Jews for whom it was lawful to take up arms in defence of their families and to serve in the wars), the lawgiver of the Christians would not have forbidden entirely the taking of human life. He taught that it was never right for his disciples to go so far against a man even if he should be very wicked; for he did not consider it compatible with his inspired legislation to allow the taking of human life in any form at all. . . . Concerning the Christians. . . . we say that they have been taught not to defend themselves against their enemies; and because they have kept the laws which command gentleness and love to men, on this account they have received from God that which they could not have succeeded in doing if they had been given the right to make war. . . ."

We have here a clear statement of the pacifist policy of the Early Church, but in Book II, section 30, there occurs a passage setting forth a most illogical attitude for a pacifist, evincing the belief that the *Pax Romana*, established by means of the sword, was the right atmosphere for the dissemination of Christianity, with more than a suggestion that it might prove to be the end of all wars. It runs:

"Righteousness arose in his days, and abundance of peace began with his birth. It was quite clear that Jesus was born during the reign of Augustus, the one who reduced to uniformity, so to speak, the many kingdoms on earth so that he had a single empire. It would have hindered Jesus' teaching from being spread through the whole world if there had been many kingdoms. . . . also because men everywhere would have been compelled to do military service and to fight in defence of their own land. This used to happen before the times of Augustus, and even earlier still when a war was necessary, such as that between the Pelopennesians and the Athenians. . . . Accordingly, how could this teaching which preaches peace and does not even allow men to take vengeance on their enemies, have had any success unless the international situation had everywhere been changed and a milder spirit prevailed at the advent of Jesus?"

This authorative approval of the unethically established *status quo* was a first step towards taking up arms to preserve it; and, as we have seen, in the course of the next century this is exactly what happened.

Page 173. Paragraph 11.

The Cross can make no pretension to being an exclusively Christian symbol. Justin Martyr seems to have believed that it originated with the ancient Jews, and identified it with the old form of TAW, the last letter in the Hebrew alphabet. He believed that it was the mark referred to in Ezekiel 9:4, and also that which the Israelites made with the blood of the Paschal lamb on the doorsteps of their houses in order to avoid the plague. In fact, he sees the Passover as a pre-figuration of the sufferings of Christ, and writes in the *Dialogue with Trypho* (XL.3):

"The sheep of the Passover which was commanded to be roasted whole was a figure of the suffering of the Cross, by which Christ was to suffer. For when the sheep is being roasted it is roasted arranged in a fashion like the fashion of the Cross, for one spit is pierced straight from the lower parts to the head, and one again at the back, to which also the paws of the sheep are fastened."

He also attributed magical power to the sign which he said was what Moses made of himself when he stretched out his hands on either side when praying for Joshua's victory in battle:

"Hor and Aaron supported them the whole day long lest he should be weary and they should fall down. For if any of this figure that imitated the form of a cross had given way, the people . . . were defeated . . . he prevailed by the cross." (**XC.**4)

But Justin either did not **know, or** did not care to tell, of the origins of this belief in the power of the cross, which was, according to Dr. Alexander Hislop,* the mystic Tau of the Chaldeans and Egyptians, the original form of their letter T, and the initial of the sun-god, Tammuz. It was originally represented with an *ansa* or handle, that was afterwards dispensed with, and was called the *Crux Ansata*. Quoting from Sir G. Wilkinson, Dr. Hislop writes:

"The first form of that which is called the *Christian Cross*, found on Christian monuments" (in Egypt) "is the un-equivocal Pagan Tau, or Egyptian Sign of Life." This makes Justin's idea that this sign was placed on the doorposts of the captive Israelites of Egypt, both plausible and probable. The Babylonian Messiah, Bacchus, is pictured with a head-band adorned with crosses. In his *Indian Antiquities* (vol.VI: p. 49), Maurice writes:

"The Druids in their groves were accustomed to select the most stately and beautiful tree as an emblem of the deity they adored, and having cut the side branches, they affixed two of the largest of them to the highest part of the trunk, in such a manner that those branches extended on each side like the arms of a man, and, together with the body, presented the appearance of a huge cross, and on the bark in several places, was also inscribed the letter THAU".

By means of ancient Egyptian monuments, Wilkinson was able to trace the use of the cross by barbarian tribes back to the 15th century B.C. Hislop tells us that it was worn by the Vestal Virgins, and was used by the Buddhists. In fact, as the sign of life, or Tree of Life, and, as such, a great charm, it was known almost universally throughout the ancient world. But it was also used, as we know, as the tree of death for sacrificial victims and criminals, thus becoming the opposite of its original, beneficent nature—the accursed tree.

It was on this age-old symbol of the sun-worshippers and ancient Judaism (the tree of the knowledge of good *and* evil

The Two Babylons, by Alexander Hislop (A & C Black Ltd.)

forbidden in Genesis 2:17) that one who brought to earth a higher vision of deity than either of the older Faiths possessed—a perfect God of unvarying goodness and love—was crucified. Ironically it is by this sign of Tammuz that children are admitted by baptism into a Church primarily designed to commemorate a Teacher who came to overthrow the former imperfect deific concepts of paganism and nature-worship.

INTRODUCTION

The recent discovery of a Mithraic temple in the City of London calls to mind one of the strangest mysteries in the history of religion, that of the complete disappearance of an ancient and persistent Faith which was Christianity's most serious rival during the first three centuries of our era.

Mithraism, as the Western world knew it, was an adaptation of an age-old Faith to the needs and outlook of the Occident. In this form Mithras, worshipped as a Sun-God long before the advent of Zoroaster, appeared in the guise of warrior, the special protector and friend of kings and soldiers, demanding in his worshippers the discipline, courage and non-attachment necessary if the armies of the monarchs who worshipped him were to be victorious. Possibly like the modern cults of Nazi-ism, Fascism and Communism, it was the immensity of the demands made upon the followers of this God that ensured their loyalty and devotion, calling as it did for self-sacrifice, and giving the psychological satisfaction of a sense of enlargement, of belonging to and being part of something greater than the human self. In fact Cumont, writing before the days of Mussolini, in his authoritative work, *The Mysteries of Mithra*, provides a certain basis for the supposition that Fascism might have been in some sense a revival of the older cult when he informs us that the Mithraic priests, while offering libations, held in their hands the *bundle of sacred twigs*. But the possibility of this connexion will become more apparent as the nature of Mithraism is better understood. One thing is certain, whatever inspired their fervour, it was undoubtedly the Roman legions who were chiefly responsible for spreading the Mithraic religion in the countries of their occupation, although merchants and captured slaves also played a

15

considerable part in its propagation, and at one time it had headquarters in all the Mediterranean ports. It was welcomed both by war-like barbarians—its chief success being in Germany where more Mithraic remains have been found than anywhere else in the Western world—and by the Celts whose druidical priests were already familiar with the occult rites of sun-worship. And while no monumental signs have ever been found of any Roman profession of the Christian faith in the countries occupied by its legions, innumerable architectural remains in Germany, France and England give proof of the militarists' devotion to Mithras. Caves known as *Mithraea,* or *Specus Mithraeum,* containing sculptures of Mithras-worship have been found in many parts of Britain. C. W. King after telling us of the Mithraic bas-reliefs that still abound in the former Western provinces of the Roman Empire, cites those found in this country "along the line of the Picts' wall, and a remarkably fine example at York, the station of the Sixth Legion". He speaks of the famous "Arthur's Oon", which was destroyed in the nineteenth century, as being "unmistakably a *Specus Mithraicum*—the same in design as Chosroes' magnificent Fire Temple at Gazaca."[1]

Yet despite its antiquity and its influence on the Roman conquerors at a time when they swayed the thought and policies of mankind, at the end of the fourth century this tremendously popular cult seems suddenly to have disappeared.

Obviously there is something very curious here. The ancient gods do not so easily die, or disappear leaving no trace, especially when their altars have been so firmly and widely established as those of Mithras. It is true that ancient religions have often been superseded by a newer faith built on the old foundations, as in the case of Judaism from which both Christianity and Islam sprang; and Hinduism which fathered Buddhism; but in none of these cases was the parent Faith eliminated. There is something unnatural about this sudden and total disappearance of one to

[1] *The Gnostics and Their Remains.* C. W. King, M.A. (David Nutt, 1887.

whom St. Augustine referred (as though his true designation had been prohibited) as "the fellow in the cap". Zoroastrianism, the parent Faith, still claims its followers and may be studied through the pages of the Zend-Avesta, while even the religion of Ancient Egypt is preserved in *The Book of the Dead*, and other sacred writings. But of Mithras, except from the architectural remains of his *Mithraea* and an occasional reference to him and his cult in ancient writings, we can find no trace. Yet it is known that there was once a considerable Mithraic literature, despite the fact that Mithraism was a mystery-religion and jealously guarded its rites and secrets from the eyes of the infidel.

There seems something both sinister and conspiratorial about it all, like a murder story in which the body is never found, especially when we learn of the bitter enmity that existed between the Early Church Fathers and the priests of Mithras, who were incidentally also known as Fathers by their followers, but were regarded by the Christians as devils; and also of what was apparently the final deathblow to the Mysteries of Mithras when their last great champion, Julian the Apostate, came to such an untimely end.

What methods were used by the Christian victors, secure by then in the fact that their Faith was the established State religion, to annihilate so completely their ancient foe?

And, above all, since no god ever wholly and finally dies, what happened to Mithras?

It is at the answer to these and similar questions that we shall seek to arrive in the course of our inquiries; and, as a start a reply must be given to the many who, since the discovery of the City Temple, have heard the name of the deity for the first time, and are interestedly inquiring: "Who *was* Mithras?"

I

Who was Mithras?

THOSE of us who have lived in one of the many towns of
Britain and the Continent that still bear traces of Roman
occupation must have often wondered at the persistent
portrayal of the sun in the various bas-reliefs and monuments
that bear witness to what is thought of in a general way as
"some pagan form of worship".

This is particularly evident in Bath where the Roman
influence has always been perpetuated. On buildings,
frescoes and monuments we find ourselves constantly
confronted with round sun-faces surrounded by floating,
flame-like locks, or plain discs with petal-rays resembling a
sun-flower. In all of this we find hints as to the nature of
the deity, who, as history relates, commanded such loyalty
and devotion among the Roman legions—Mithras, the Sun-
God! And Mithraism, his cult, a form of oriental heliolatry
adapted to the needs and outlook of the Occident, was the
last overt sun-worship in the Western world.

The age of this cult has always been the subject of much
controversy. The Fathers of the Early Church, embarrassed
by the similarity of certain features of Christianity and
Mithraism, oscillated between the explanation that those of
the former were imitated by the latter, and, when this
obvious fallacy could not be maintained, that the Mithraic
devils had anticipated the Christian rites in order to discredit them. But the plain, unquestionable fact is, that

Mithras, under one name or another, has haunted religious history since its first records were made.

This is understandable in the Sun-God who is, by nature, ubiquitous, and the manner of his worship differs little from one country to another. It was inseparable from the age-old fecundity religions, and it is difficult, therefore, to say where he first made his definite appearance as a Deity; where, in other words, men first saw in the shining glory above them, something deserving of worship.

But the actual name of Mithras appears to have been first enshrined in the oldest of all known scriptures, the Rig-Veda, long before he appeared in the Persian Zend-Avesta with which he is principally identified. As Professor Franz Cumont, the most authoritative writer on Mithraism, puts it:

> The tribes of Iran never ceased to worship Mithra from their first assumption of worldly power till the day of their conversion to Islam.[1]

In the old Vedic writings, he is referred to as "God of the Daylight"; in the Zend-Avesta as "Lord of the Pastures", while inscriptions found by Winckler at Boghazkeui, in 1907, indicate that as early as the fourteenth century B.C. Mithra, or Mithras, was worshipped among the Mitanni of Northern Mesopotamia. And, as we shall see in a later chapter dealing with his Phrygian origins, his connexion, as Atys, with Cybele, by which he gained his best-known title, the Phrygian God, may also be traced to somewhere near this date.

An even greater antiquity is suggested by his constant identification with the Bull, from whose blood and limbs, when he had been slain by the God, emanated all beneficent creatures and edible herbs. For if, as John M. Robertson suggests in his learned article on Mithraism, found in *Religious Systems of the World*, this symbolized the Sun

---

[1] *Mysteries of Mithra* by Franz Cumont. (Kegan Paul, Trench, Trubner and Co.)

entering the Sign of the Bull at the vernal equinox, such a symbol must date back to more than 3,000 years before the Christian era, since the constellation of the Ram had taken the place of the Bull about two thousand one hundred years before the reign of Augustus. He goes on to say, "It has been variously suggested that the Bull slain by Mithras is the symbol of the earth, the symbol of the moon, the Bull of the Zodiac, and the cosmogenic Bull of the Magian system," and that, "for the ancients the Bull of Mithras could represent all four of these things."[1]

Over 300 years B.C. Artaxerxes Mnemon was using "By the Light of Mithras" as a great oath, and was known to be an ardent devotee of this deity. This famous warrior, the conqueror of Cyrus, lived to be a nonagenarian, and even then was said to have died for the psychological reason of grief over the shortcomings of his son.

Mithras was identified with many other of the Sun-Gods, including Shamas of the Assyrians who perfectly answers to the description of the Roman Mithras, having been known as "the warrior of the world", "the judge of heaven and earth", "the light of the gods", the "ruler of the day, who vanquishes the king's enemies" and "casts his motive influence" over the monarchs, going forth with their armies and enabling them to extend their dominions. As we shall see, this might well be a description of the Sun-God so beloved by the legionaries of Rome. In the West he is known as Atys, Bacchus, or Apollo, and, in 47 B.C., he is found in the form of Helios-Dionysos upon the medallion of Pharnaces II, son of Mithridates, King of Pontus, where Mithras reigned as the chief God from the days of Alexander. Pontus was one of the main gates from which the cult spread into the Western world. C. W. King refers to this expansion in the following statement:

Mithraism was originally the religion taught by Zoroaster, although somewhat changed and materialized

---

[1] *Religious Systems of the World.* (Sonnenchien.)

so as better to assimilate itself to the previously established nature-worship of the West. Under this grosser form it took its name from Mithras, who in the Zend-Avesta is not the Supreme Being (Ormuzd) but the chief of the Subordinate Powers, the seven Amshaspands. Mithras is the Zend name for the sun, the proper mansion of this spirit, but not the Spirit himself.[1]

From the first Mithras was equated with the Sun and with Light. In the subordinate position to which he was relegated by the monotheistic Zoroaster, he became known as the Mediator between man and the Supreme Being, "a humane and beneficent God, nearer to man than the great Spirit of Good, a Saviour, a Redeemer, eternally young, son of the Most High, and preserver of mankind from the Evil One. In brief, he is a pagan Christ." (*Ibid.*)

His name, in Persian, MIHR, meant both "the Sun" and "the Friend", symbolizing an all-beneficent power, or God of Love. But when this high, spiritual conception degenerated, and he became, like Shamas, the special patron and protector of Kings and Emperors, his war-like attributes were accentuated, and he emerged finally as an invincible warrior-god. After fighting Mazda's battles for him against the Powers of Darkness on the spiritual plane, he descended to earth, and fought, in a very real sense, the wars of the Persian and Pontine Kings, the Macedonian Princes and Roman Emperors.

In his transformation from Zoroaster's concept of him as a lesser Genius, or Yazata, a lower category than that of his former one of Amshaspand who shared the government of the universe with the Supreme Being, he became, as he journeyed Westward, especially in places like Pontus, Commagene and eventually Rome, identified with the Sun-God himself.

The legendary life of Mithras is as fragmentary and confused as that of most deities of the primitive faiths, and

[1] *The Gnostics and Their Remains*, by C. W. King, M.A. (David Nutt 1887.)

it seems to be a mixture of both his Eastern and Western origins.

We are asked to believe that, at the beginning of time, before the earth was inhabited, certain shepherds, whose existence in the circumstances is rather puzzling, observed, as the sun rose, the young and naked Mithras emerging from a rock, wearing a Phrygian cap and carrying in one hand a knife and in the other a flaming torch; at which the shepherds came and worshipped, bringing him gifts. They testified that, being cold, he climbed into a tree and made himself a garment of fig leaves.

Early showing his warrior-like nature, he strove with the Sun, and vanquished him, after which he replaced the radiant crown on his defeated rival's head, shook hands with him, and they became allies for ever afterwards. Next he conquered the Primeval Bull, mounted and subdued it, and dragged it back to the cave in which he lived; this difficult task symbolizing the sufferings of mankind. The Bull, the name for which, in Persian, is the same as Life, escaped from the cave and the Sun commanded Mithras to find and kill it. Helped by his faithful dog, but reluctantly and much against his will, Mithras succeeded in doing this, plunging his knife into the animal's side; and from the beast's blood was created all the useful plants and herbs, while from his spinal cord sprang the grain, an event symbolized by the three wheat ears that are attached to the Bull's tail in Mithraic sculpturings. Thus Mithras indirectly provided the Bread of Life. From the blood also came the harmless animals and sentient creatures.

Thereby Mithras became the creator of all good living things through his reluctant immolation of the beast. From death had come the resurrection to more abundant life.

In Mithraism, the race of men is said to have begun from a single couple, and over this race Mithras mounts guard, defending it from the persecutions of Ahriman, the Prince of Darkness, the Father of Lies, the antithesis of Light (Ahura Mazda) and so also of the Sun-God. This spirit of evil first caused a great drought, and when the in-

habitants of the earth appealed to Mithras, he pierced a rock
with his golden arrows and water gushed forth. At another
time Ahriman sent a flood to engulf mankind, but one man
was inspired by Mithras to make an ark, and so escaped with
his family and cattle. Finally, a fire threatened to consume
mankind, but again the followers of the Sun-God were
saved. After these tasks were accomplished. Mithras ascended
to heaven in a chariot, having partaken of a Last Supper
with those who had helped him in his labours, a communion
meal which afterwards became one of the chief rites of the
Mithraists.[1]

As we have seen, Mithras was not only the Sun-God,
but the Mediator between mankind and the Supreme
Being, known as Boundless Time (equivalent to the Hebraic
Eternal). His birthday was celebrated in the Mithraic
calendar on 25th December. Sunday, the seventh day of
the week—for seven was his number—was consecrated to
him, and known as the Lord's Day long before the Christian
era. His rebirth was commemorated at Easter. In *De
Errore Profanarum Religionum*, that staunch Christian, Firmicus,
informs us that at the time of the vernal equinox the
Mithraic worshippers "lay a stone image by night on a
bier and liturgically mourn it, this image representing the
dead God. This symbolical corpse is then placed in the
tomb, and after a time is withdrawn from it, whereupon
the worshippers rejoice, exhorting one another to be of
good cheer . . . murmuring, 'be of good cheer; you have
been initiated in the Mysteries, and you shall have salvation
from your sorrows!' "

Mithras presided over the Last Judgement, and guided
the souls of the faithful to the heavenly spheres where he
welcomed them into his golden habitation as a father
would his children. By their at-one-ment with him and his
qualities, his followers became immortal.

---

[1] In the *Mysteries of Mithras* by Franz Cumont, there is an illustration of a
fragment of a Mithraic bas-relief depicting this Last Supper. In the centre is
a trivet bearing four cakes, each marked with a cross. The cakes are round,
symbolizing the sun, and look exactly like our Hot Cross Buns. They may well
be the small cakes made and eaten by Egyptians and Persians in honour of the
Queen of HEAVEN and marked with the Southern Cross worshipped by them.

The qualities most stressed in the character of this God as he appeared in the Occident, were those of invincibility, fortitude, austerity, courage, endurance, loyalty, strength, power, non-attachment, and strange as it may seem at such a period, and among militarists who are not as a rule given to asceticism, purity.

This qualification is understandable, however, when taken in conjunction with a certain teaching of the ancient Gnosis, of which, as we shall see, the Mysteries of Mithras were a branch. Chastity was not, as with the Christians, sought for itself alone as being the inevitable result of putting on the Mind of Christ, an essential part of the spiritual life. For the Mithraists, accepting the Gnostic teaching, it was a source of physical strength, a conservation of energy that could be better expended on feats of endurance on the field of battle. According to this belief, women became a temptation to be avoided, and this is almost certainly one of the reasons for their exclusion from the Mithraic brotherhood, although the most obvious explanation for this omission is that no woman could be expected to have the requisite physical courage and endurance to undergo the initiatory rites known as the Twelve Tortures.

It will have been noticed that all the qualities listed above were essentially of the masculine variety, with no hint of the gentler attributes of love, mercy, compassion, tenderness, intuition, that may be considered to constitute the "feminine" qualities necessary to a balanced nature whether of God or man. The later Occidental Mithraists undoubtedly worshipped a wholly male God.

As the Phrygian God, in which guise Mithras was originally known in the West, this deficiency was compensated for by his alliance as Atys, with Cybele and her cult, first in Phrygia, then in Greece, where Cybele became Ceres, and their cults flourished together in the famous Eleusinian Mysteries. It was only after Darius had introduced the Sun-God in his Persian form, as the friend of Monarchs, that it became the militaristic cult of such notable warriors as Alexander the Great and Mithridates VII, and, after its acceptance by the Roman Emperors, the favourite cult of their legionaries, which is the aspect of this deity with which we are primarily concerned. This aspect, according to Cumont, took shape after the conquest of Macedonia by Darius I, King of Persia (521–485 B.C.) "It was then," he writes, "that Mithraism received approximately its definitive form of imperialistic religion in which it has been known to the West." From that time, Mithras became, beyond all things, the God of warriors, and friend of Kings; the God that ensured them victory, the invincible power worshipped by common soldiers and officers alike; in a word, the reincarnation of his former manifestation as Shamas, the God beloved of the predatory Assyrians.

Yet there was evidently a time in his history when Mithras was represented as a bi-sexual God, portrayed with a beautiful, serene, feminine face surmounting a virile body; a fact which led to some confusion. Herodotus (485–425 B.C.), for instance, evidently believed him to be a goddess, and wrote of the worship of Urania that this female deity was "borrowed from the Arabs and Assyrians. Mylitta is the name by which the Assyrians know the Goddess, whom the Arabians call Alitta, and the Persians Mithra."[1]

But undoubtedly no trace of the "woman" can be found in the unconquerable Bull-Slayer of Roman times.

After many battles following the death of Alexander the Great, dynasties were established by his generals in Cappadocia, Commagene, Armenia and Pontus, their rulers later becoming Kings who claimed kinship with the earlier monarchs, and adopted their gods, especially Mithras, who was devotedly worshipped in all these places. He was honoured, above all, in Pontus whose Kings took the name of Mithridates, believing that their authority to rule was "given of Mithra", who endowed them with the divine Light which made them at one with, or an emanation of, his own brightness, and therefore worthy to be worshipped with him.

---

[1] *Herodotus* Book I. Chapter 131.

This was a belief peculiar to the Persian religion, although it originally had its roots in the Indian belief of the Universal Monarch whose rule on earth is the reflection of the heavenly rule; and, on it, Mithraism was based, making it a most suitable Faith for Empire builders, and rulers who wished to claim absolute obedience, allegiance and loyalty from their fighting services.

This concept of the Sun-God was, of course, far removed from that of Mithra, the Friend, the giver of all good gifts whose beneficent rays blessed all upon whom they rested, and whose battles against evil thoughts were confined to the consciousness of men, not fought on earthly battlefields; for homicide, like other evils, would be the work of Ahriman and his Devas, and far from the will of the beneficent Ormuzd.

Mithras, on the other hand, by no means restricted his warfare to spiritual spheres. We have to look no further than Kipling's *Song to Mithras* to discover that, in the eyes of the Roman legionaries, their God was "also a soldier", the strong and manly Slayer of the Bull, the disciplined Spartan that the soldiers of Rome strove so slavishly to emulate to the infinite satisfaction of the founders of an Empire that was continually increased by the reckless bravery of her armed forces, direct spiritual descendants of the heroes of Troy.

In the story of *The Winged Hats* in *Puck of Pook's Hill*, Kipling depicts the loyalty and devotion of the legionaries to the Mithraic cult that, like Freemasonry, which is its distant connexion and still perpetuates some of its ceremonialism, bound its members together as strongly as it bound them to their God. The brotherhood of the worshippers of Mithras was, in fact, a closer bond than that of brothers of the flesh. Like the Freemasons, it had its Mysteries, pass-words, rites, orders and degrees known only to its initiates, and the close-guarding of its secrets may have been a contributory, though by no means the main factor in its strange disappearance. The Mithraists, as well as the Christian Bishops, had reasons for keeping the

Mysteries hidden from the common gaze. Those who adopted this esoteric creed could feel that they were a spiritual *élite*, having access to a wisdom beyond that of ordinary humanity, as became members of a nation of world-conquerors.

But although Mithras was "also a soldier", even primarily a warrior, in the eyes of the legions, he was also the supreme Sun-God: "Rome is above the Nations, but Thou art over all!" and, like every other Sun-God, he was immortal and able to impart immortality to his followers. He descended into hell and rose from the dead: "Thou descending immortal, immortal to rise again."

His degeneracy as a God, though not as a power, lies in his complete masculinization after he had become specifically the God of the Imperialists, the upholder of violence and power-politics. In this connexion, one of the chief reasons given by Cumont for the failure of Mithraism to become the universal religion dreamt of by Mithridates VII, and later by Julian the Apostate, lay in its esoteric and exoteric exclusion of women. As he writes, "a religion which aspired to become universal could not deny a knowledge of divine things to one half of the human race."

Nevertheless, Mithras' male quality of invincibility was essential in a God designed for world-conquerors. *Soli Deo Invicto Mithrae* is found on monuments and coins minted in the rein of Constantine, proving that this Emperor still hoped for favours from the older God, despite his championship of the new.

Is it possible that a God so deeply enshrined in the hearts of Emperors and warriors, slaves, merchants, freemen and freedmen, whose temples and monuments are found throughout the wide area of Roman occupation, could have been so finally and completely vanquished as the ruins of his altars and the disappearance of his name would lead us to believe?

Throughout his age-old history, Mithras was, as we have seen, always adaptable. He cared little for a change of name so long as his worship was ensured and his rites perpetuated. We have shown that, in his role of Goddess, he was worshipped under several names; and that as Shamas, he ruled in Babylon and Assyria as surely as in Persia. As Dionysos and Apollo he was known to the Greeks and Romans, and his ability to adapt himself to the conditions and needs of the environment in which he found himself may well account for his long survival. Why should it have been imagined that such an infinitely resourceful God had been finally overthrown simply because he disappeared from the eyes of men? Gods do not so easily die, but sometimes the clouded vision of mankind fails to perceive them. When we clear the sight and examine more closely the God and his cult that were believed to have been exterminated, we shall, I think, find irrefutable evidence of his resurrection, although the names under which he now suffers himself to be worshipped may surprise and shock many.

The first step to this recognition must be an attentive study of the little we know of Mithraism.

2

What was Mithraism?

AN adequate answer to this question is rendered almost impossible by the fact that no records are left to us of the Cult of Mithras. Nothing remains of what was, according to J. M. Robertson, a considerable literature. In his previously mentioned essay on Mithraism we find: "There were in antiquity, we know, from the writings of Porphyry and other authorities, quite a number of elaborate treatises setting forth the religion of Mithras; *and every one of them has been destroyed by the care of the Church.*"[1]

There seems to have been something unnaturally ruthless about the revenge the Christian Church took upon its defeated rival. Not satisfied with destroying his altars, and often slaying and burying his priests in the Mithraic caves in order to desecrate them, the Bishops of the Church destroyed every piece of evidence which might have revealed the true nature of Mithras' cult as practised by men of the Occident. Such information as has been obtained has come mainly from architectural Mithraic remains, from a study of the Mazdean Faith in which its origins are most clearly traced, from writings concerned with other pagan faiths, such as the Eleusinian Mysteries with which it was connected, and from casual references to it discovered in books written by its enemies or the historians and writers

[1] In his *De Abstinentia* (iv, 16) Porphyry refers to Eubulus "who wrote the history of Mithraism in many books", and also to Pallas "in his work on Mithra", calling the latter writer "the best exponent of the mysteries of Mithra". While Jerome in *Adv. Jovinianum* (xi, 14) also speaks of Eubulus as "the author of a history of Mithra in many volumes".

of antiquity. None of which sources can be relied upon to give us the exact and complete information that we seek. Perhaps this can best be obtained by a study of the characters of those known to have been devotees of Mithras, for we shall then understand the nature of the God so slavishly emulated. In every case we shall find them to have been courageous, insensitive, highly disciplined militarists and Kings' men.

It should, however, be understood that this effect comes only from the form of Mithraism known in the West, and not from that of the Asiatic Sun-God who was often beneficent and peaceable in intention, although sun and nature worship are akin, and both lead to an absorption in the outer, physical life. It was to correct this tendency that Zoroaster delegated Mithras to the status of *yazata* in his admirable monotheistic system of which it is necessary to know something if we are to begin to understand the background of Mithraism, and in what way it has affected the consciousness of humanity.

A brief passage in a report of the Emperor Julian's Persian expedition, written by Ammianus, the military chronicler, is worth quoting in this connexion. He writes: (xxii, 6)

> In these tracts are situated the fertile lands of the Magi . . . Plato, that greatest authority upon celebrated doctrines, states that the Magian religion, known by this mystic name of *Machagestia* is the most uncorrupted form of worship in things divine. To the philosophy of this religion, Zoroastres, a Bactrian, in primitive times, made many additions drawn from the mysteries of the Chaldaeans, as did also later Hystaspes (who) . . . when he was boldly penetrating into the unknown regions of upper India, had come upon a certain wooded solitude, the tranquil silence of which is occupied by those incomparable sages, the Brachmans.

In this short citation Ammianus conveys something of the inter-relatedness of Greek, Chaldean, Persian and

Indian thought during the pre-Christian and early Christian eras, which explains the presence in both Old and New Testaments of echoes of pagan myths and teachings that have obviously no place in the strict monotheism of Moses, the major Hebrew prophets and Jesus Christ.

By no Faith was Judaism ever more influenced than by that of the Jews' Persian captors during the Babylonian captivity. All the eschatological teachings, for instance, of heaven and hell, of angels[1] and devils that appeared in Judaism after the Second Captivity, and have been transmitted to Christianity, were no part of the Mosaic legalistic system that, being wholly concerned with regulating the present life, maintained an almost unbroken silence on the subject of the life to come.

Perhaps the best way to convey an idea of the influence exerted by the Iranian religion on both Judaism and orthodox Christianity is to give an outline of the beliefs found in the Zend-Avesta, which was compiled, like the Old Testament, over vast periods of time, the oldest writings having, according to some authorities, been dated as early as 1200–1000 B.C.

The Supreme Being, having no beginning or end, is known as Zarvana Akarana, or Boundless Time. Creation consists of his Emanations, the first being Light who created a perfect world by his Word.

"Next he created in his own image the six Amshaspands, who stand about his throne, and are his agents with the lower spirits, and with mankind, whose prayers they offer up to him, and to whom they serve as models of perfection. . . The next series of emanations were the Izeds, twenty-eight in number, of whom Mithras is the chief. Like the superior order they watch over the purity and happiness of the world of which they are the genii and guardians."[2]

As we have already seen, Mithras was at one time considered to be the seventh Amshaspand, as well as being worshipped as the Sun-God until Zoroaster relegated him

---

[1] The word "Seraphim" is said to mean "the burning ones".
[2] *The Gnostics and Their Remains*. C. W. King.

to a subordinate position to Ahura Mazda; but both before and after the advent of the Prophet, Mithras was regarded as the Sun-God himself, and was worshipped at Pontus as the Supreme God long before the Christian era.

The third series of emanations in the Zoroastrian theory of creation were known as Ferouers, infinite in number, which are the Thoughts or Ideas in the mind of Ormuzd—reminiscent of the Good Form theory of Plato—that preceded their outward manifestation.

We now come to details so closely akin to the Old Testament legends that the influence of Persian thought upon it would seem to be beyond dispute. The figure of Lucifer the fallen angel is, in Zoroastrianism, Ahriman, the second-born of the Supreme Being. Originally created as pure as Ormuzd, he falls into errors of ambition, pride and envy, and is jealous of his brother. He is punished by being banished to the Kingdom of Darkness and is henceforth known as the Prince of Darkness, the Father of Lies; in fact, the Satan, the fallen angel, with which we are so familiar in the Hebrew Scriptures.

In imitation of his brother's creation of Light, he creates an opposing three series of angels of darkness, known as Devs or Devas, that are the authors of all evil; and when Ormuzd creates the good harmless animals, Ahriman replies by making a vicious and venomous variety. Throughout this battle between the powers of Light and Darkness, the devil is the ape of God, the creator of the shadow which is the distortion of the true object.

As a source of universal life, Ormuzd created what is known as the Bull—although the Persian word for both Bull and Life is the same. From the blood of this Bull which is slain by Ahriman the first pair of beings are born, male and female. They are corrupted by Ahriman who tempts the woman with offerings of fruit and milk.

Add to these details the fact that Zoroaster was supposed to have been miraculously conceived by his mother when she was only fifteen, and that a Turanian Prince (the persecuting Herod of the story) attempted to destroy him

when he was a baby; that the spirit of God descended upon
him at the age of thirty, and that he was afterwards tempted
by Angra Mainyu, the Lord of Evil, and the antiquity of
the Zoroastrian Faith compared with that of Christianity
assumes a deep significance.

The Zend-Avesta, with its Babylonian origins, formed
the background of Mithraism, as the Old Testament, with
its Chaldean connexions, formed the background of the
New.

Describing the origins of Mithraism, Cumont writes:

> The basal layer of this religion, its lower and pri-
> mordial stratum, is the faith of ancient Iran from which
> it took its origin. Above this Mazdean substratum was
> deposited in Babylon a thick sediment of Semitic doctrines
> and afterwards the local beliefs of Asia Minor added to
> it their alluvial deposits. Finally, a luxuriant vegetation
> of Hellenic ideas burst from this fertile soil and partly
> concealed from view its true original nature.

Before we go on to examine the little we know of this
composite religion as practised from the time of Darius,
i.e. Mithraism *per se*, it will be as well to examine the
Babylonian influences that undoubtedly account for the
similarity of ideas existing in Mithraism and Christianity
that so puzzled and alarmed the priests of both creeds who
were ignorant of the common parentage of the two Faiths,
and led them to accuse one another of imitation.

Today, when we have access to the results of scientific
research found in modern books on comparative religion,
what was a deep mystery to the uninformed priests of the
early Christian era, is seen as the natural consequence
of the evolution of religious thought through the contact of
one civilization upon another. Something of this was,
of course, recognized by the scholars even in those days.
As we have seen, Ammianus states clearly that Zoroaster
added the Mysteries of the Chaldeans to the Iranian
religion, in approximately the same period that the captive

Israelites were being most influenced by the Babylonian religion.

In his essay on *The Religion of Babylonia,* W. St. Chad Boscawen quotes Emanuel Deutsch as saying "how remarkable was the change wrought in the Hebrew people during the period of the captivity. They entered the land a people ever falling into idolatry, and falling from the service of the national god. In no way were they centralized either in national or religious life, with no great national ambition, with only a law applicable to desert life, and no code suitable to civic life. Yet in the short period of about sixty years they return from their captivity a new people."

Boscawen gives it as his opinion that the captivity was truly the *renaissance* of the Jewish people.

Entering Babylon with an incomplete law, they emerge with a religious and secular code perfect in all its branches. With these facts before us we cannot too highly estimate the influence of Babylonia as a centre of religious development and influence.

He points out that the Babylonian idea of a central Temple fed by other Temples was afterwards imitated by the Jews in the establishment of synagogues; that the great festivals of the Hebrews and Babylonians correspond almost day for day; that Nisan corresponded to the Passover; Tisri to the feast of the tabernacles, and that the festival of Adar strangely resembles that of Purim. Before the days of Abraham circumcision was a Chaldean custom, and the Babylonian Sabbath resembled, and was as strict as that of the Jews:

No food was to be cooked, no fire to be lit, the clothes of the body might not be changed, it was even unlawful to wash. . . . One remarkable restriction was that no medicine should be taken. "Medicine for the sickness of his body he shall not apply," which, no doubt, gave rise to the Pharisaic question to Jesus, "Is it lawful to heal on the Sabbath day?"

Having entered Babylon with primitive laws unsuited to the city and town-dweller, the Jews returned to Judah perfectly legally equipped, and credit for this must certainly be given to their contact with the older civilization. Boscawen writes:

> We now find the captivity producing that wonderful compendium of laws, entering into the minutest details of civic, domestic and social life, the Talmud;

But of far more importance than the similarity of laws, rites and festivals is that of the concept of God, which of course dates much earlier than the time of the Captivity, and must have existed from the days of Abraham who significantly came out of Ur of the Chaldees. When we consider that the first God of Ancient Babylon was the Sea God, we understand the derivation of the strange passage Psalm xlii:

> Deep calleth unto deep at the noise of thy waterspouts: all thy waves and thy billows are gone over me.

But in the course of time, the Golden Being that arose out of the sea at dawn and returned at night to his Father's house, bruising as he arose the head of the serpent of darkness who each evening wounded the heel of the returning son, became, firstly, the mediator between man and the invisible God of the Deeps, and then superseded the Father. Merodach, the Sun-God, took precedence of the Sea-God, as, later, Merodach, under the name of Mithras, usurped the place of Ormuzd.

The age-long controversy as to whether the Pentateuch was written before or after the first captivity has never been resolved. But that these five books bear witness to Sun-God worship is undeniable. The description of the Flood in the Old Testament is practically identical with the Mithraic legend; and the story of Joseph with his Twelve Brethren has strong resemblances to the idea of the grain-producing Sun-God, the Sustainer of Life, and the Twelve Signs of the

Zodiac. There is also the significant passage in Deuteronomy iv, 24.

But if there are indications of Sun-Worship influences in the Pentateuch, there is undeniable evidence of its symbology in the Books of the Prophets.

In Isaiah lxvi, 15 we find:

> ... the Lord will come with fire and with his chariots like a whirlwind, to render his anger with fury, and his rebuke with flames of fire.

Micah also gives a clearly recognizable picture of the Sun-God in the words:

> ... the Lord ... will come down and tread upon the high places of the earth. And the mountains shall be molten unto him, and the valley shall be cleft, as wax before the fire. ... (Micah i, 3, 4.)

And in Habakkuk iii, 3, 4. we read of God:

> His glory covereth the heavens .... and his brightness was as the light ... and burning coals went forth at his feet.

Psalm xcvii, 1–5 gives a similar picture:

> The Lord reigneth ... a fire goeth before him, and burneth up his enemies round about. His lightenings enlightened the world ... the hills melted like wax at the presence of the Lord.

An equally Mazdean concept is found in Psalm civ, 1–4. The burnt sacrifices, and fire falling from heaven, of which we read so much in the Old Testament, are clear indications of the heritage from Sun-worship. And the description of Elijah's ascent to heaven in a chariot of fire (2 Kings ii, 11) is identical with the ascent of Mithras to the Majesty of high. The same fiery chariots on the mountains (2 Kings vi, 17) symbolize the protection of the same radiant God.

But, unaware of this mutual ideological background, it is not surprising that the Mithraic and Christian Fathers were equally startled and alarmed at the discovery of the similarity of their creeds.

In particular must they have been amazed to find that they were both teaching the worship of One who came from the Most High, redeemed the world by the shedding of blood and returned to sit on the right hand of the Father. Small wonder that the Christians could only account for it by imagining the pagan Christ to have been a devil who anticipated the real Christ in order to discredit him; while the Mithraists believed that Christianity was a flagrant plagiarism of their own faith.

Only time and the growth of knowledge could solve the mystery by enabling the historian to discover the primal origin of this and all other disputed theories; and it is these factors which enabled C. W. King to write, at the end of the last century:

> Mithras was the more readily admitted as the type of Christ, Creator and Maintainer of the Universe, inasmuch as the Zend-Avesta declares him to be the First emanation of Ormuzd, the Good Principle, and the Manifestation of himself unto the world. . . . It was from this very creed that the Jews, during their long captivity in the Persian Empire (of which when restored to Palestine they formed but a province), derived all the angelology of their religion, even to its minutest details, such as we find it flourishing in the times of the Second Kingdom. Not until then are they discovered to possess the belief in a future state; of rewards and punishments, the latter carried on in a fiery lake; the existence of a complete hierarchy of good and evil angels, taken almost verbatim from the lists given by the Zend-Avesta; the soul's immortality, and the Last Judgement—all of them essential parts of the Zoroastrian scheme, and recognized by Josephus as the fundamental doctrines of the Judaism of his own times.

The orthodox Jews, have always taught that their creed was a unique revelation to their race by a God who "chose" them for this honour, a theory quite untenable in days when an extensive study of Comparative Religion has been made possible. The Christian, too, has insisted that the circumstances of the historical Jesus's life, as well as his teachings were unique. It is a little puzzling to know why this should be since, as Bernard Shaw reminded us, "the test of a dogma is its universality," and Truth to be true must be universal. Therefore none of these religious similitudes should disturb the educated man, although it is quite easy to see how men in a less informed age would be shaken and horrified at discovering in a rival Faith the stories of Adam and Eve, the Flood, the Ark, and of Moses (or Mithras) causing water to burst from a rock. Small wonder that it seemed as though devils had been at work. In particular, there was that very unpleasant idea that Abraham had brought with him from Ur, of human and animal sacrifice, the idea of the scapegoat, as Frazer puts it in *The Golden Bough*; the necessity for sacrificing the firstborn of the King, or chieftain, in place of the Patriarch who, in still earlier times, was himself sacrificed. And, although in the course of evolution, following Abraham's substitution of a ram for Isaac, an animal was most commonly used as the sacrificial victim, the general idea was very much in evidence both in the cult of the Tauroctonus Mithras (the God often being identified with the sacrificed Bull), and the theology of Pauline Christianity.

Nevertheless, although Mithraism and Christianity had common origins so remote that it is quite impossible to say wherein the plagiarism originally lay, the change in Christian teachings during the first centuries when it was in close contact with the older Faith cannot be ignored and must be ascribed to the diplomatic eclecticism of the Early Church.

We know that a cave figured prominently in the rites of the Mysteries, and, according to Plotinus, one of those writers who, while obviously knowing a great deal about the

cult of the Sun-God, has left us tantalisingly few details, the
cave symbolized the body to which the bewitched Soul
makes its descent (the neo-platonic idea of the 'fall' of man)
and from which it emerges to make the reascent to its Divine
Source, where alone it can find rest, peace and bliss.

In the First Ennead, Tractate VI (Beauty), we find a
short but explicit reference to the highest meaning of the
Mysteries in the words:

> We must ascend again towards the Good, the desired
> of every Soul . . . to attain it is for those who will take the
> upward path, who will set all their forces towards it, who
> will divest themselves of all that we have put on in our
> descent: so, to those who approach the Holy Celebrations
> of the Mysteries, there are appointed purifications and
> the laying aside of the garments worn before, and the entry
> in nakedness—until, passing, on that upward way . . .
> each in the solitude of himself shall behold that solitary-
> dwelling Existence . . . the Source of Life and of Intellec-
> tion and of Being.[1]

This is evidently the philosophical concept lying behind
the process of gradual initiation found not only in the
Mysteries of Mithras, but in other secret societies, ancient
and modern, derived from these. The worthiness of the
Initiate has always to be proved step by step, his interest
being sustained by promises of ever higher attainment of
virtue and occult knowledge. There were degrees in the
Mysteries as there are in Freemasonry and similar cults.
These are described by C. W. King, quoting a treatise
entitled *Le Culte de Mithra*, by M. Lajard, in the words:

> These degrees were divided into four stages, Terrestial,
> Aerial, Igneous, and Divine, each consisting of three.
> The Terrestial comprising the Soldier, the Lion and the
> Bull. The Aerial, the Vulture, the Ostrich and the Raven.
> The Igneous, the Gryphon, the Horse, the Sun. The

[1] *Plotinus. The Enneads.* Translated by Stephen MacKenna. (Faber and
Faber Ltd.)

Divine, the Eagle, the Sparrow-Hawk, the Father of Fathers.

Animal masks and skins were worn to denote the various degrees, and it was these Twelve who were depicted as sharing the Last Supper of the Sun-God before he ascended into Heaven. The worshippers assembled in groups or brotherhoods, addressed each other as 'brother', and were initiated by 'Fathers', the chief of whom, *Pater Patrum*, 'Father of the Fathers' was seated at Rome, and was, according to Tertullian, limited to one wife. He adds that the sectarians of the Persian God, like the Christians, also had their 'virgins and their continents'. Cumont, evidently unaware of the Gnostic teaching on this point, remarks: "the existence of this kind of Mithraic monachism appears to be all the more remarkable as the merit attached to celibacy is antagonistic to the spirit of Zoroastrianism."

It was, however, an integral feature of the system of Plotinus, which, significantly, was based on the idea of emanation and gradation, previously thought peculiar to the ancient Persian religion from which Mithraism was derived. And Porphyry tells us that in order to investigate the Persian methods of philosophy, his Master went so far as to join the army and accompany the Emperor Gordian in his campaign against Persia. Plotinus taught the necessity for the Soul's liberation from all commerce with the body, and upheld the ideal of absolute purity. This was in accordance with the teachings of the great Masters of thought throughout the ages, although it has seldom been taught by the churches and sects supposed to be perpetuating them. But it has always been a feature of esoteric teaching since chastity is well known to be a source of power, whether of the temporal or spiritual variety; and Roman Mithraism was a religion of temporal power.

The number twelve, like that of seven which is Mithras' own number, plays an important part in the Mysteries. The Twelve Signs of the Zodiac were always represented in the Mithraic ceremonies, and undoubtedly numerology and astrology (the Babylonian inheritance), were prominent features of the secret doctrines of the cult. The sacred animal masks, for instance, were considered by pagan theologians to have been allusions to the Signs of the Zodiac, and related also to the teaching of metempsychosis.[1] This is a particularly interesting theory in the light of modern, evolutionary ideas, since it suggests an instinctive feeling of unity with the lesser creatures that may well have obtained in the race-consciousness of humanity long before it was rationalized by Darwin. Metempsychosis is based on the idea that man in his present state is so near to the animal kingdom that he might easily revert to it, which is, in itself, an implication that he has at some time emerged from it. But the Christian Fathers saw nothing in these masked ceremonies but obscene and primitive paganism. Jerome (*circa* 356) wrote (Ep. CVII, *ad Laetam*):

> A few years ago, did not your kinsman Gracchus . . . when holding the office of the prefect of the City, break down and burn the cave of Mithras, with all the monstrous images which pervade the initiatory rites, as Corax, Nephus, the Soldier, the Lion, the Persian, Heliodromus, and Father?

In addition to Mithras' Twelve helpers of bird, animal and human origin, there were twelve consecutive trials known as The Tortures that had to be undergone by the neophytes before they could take part in the Mysteries. These included many painful austerities, and trials by water, fire, cold, hunger, scourging, branding, bleeding, and even the menace of death, in short the sort of hardening up

[1] In the *De Abstinentia* (ii, 56, iv, 16) Porphyry (*circa* A.D. 232) writes:
"The magi were divided into three grades according to the assertion of Eubulus. Of these the highest and most learned neither kill nor eat any living thing, but practise the long established abstinence from animal food. For in all the highest grades the doctrine of metempsychosis is held, which also is apparently signified in the mysteries of Mithra; for these through the living creatures reveal to us symbolically our community of nature with them."
In Adv. Jovinianum i, 7 and ii, 14 Jerome quotes Eubulus as saying that there are three classes of magi among the Persians, the first of which, men pre-eminent in learning and eloquence, confine their food to pulse and vegetables alone.

process that has to be undergone by our modern commandos The ordeal was a long one, lasting, according to the various reports available, from fifteen to forty-eight days, and only after the aspirants had proved their worth by coming forth victorious from these trials could they partake of the Baptism from which they emerged as full-fledged Soldiers of Mithras.

This Baptism differed in nature from that of the Early Christians, however, whose total immersion was originally intended to be the outward and visible sign of a complete and final purification of mind and Spirit, a unique occasion in the life of the initiate. For the Mithraist it was a means in itself of washing away the stains of the soul, and as such had frequently to be undergone, for, as in the case of the absolution bestowed by the Catholic confessional, the stains continually reappeared!

In Mithraism there was more than one Baptismal rite; at least three distinct forms are known to us, that of a sprinkling with water and making what has been described as the mark of the cross on the neophyte's head, but which is far more likely to have been the similar sign of the Sword of Mithras; that of total immersion in living water, and, finally, the regenerative bath in the blood of a Bull, the popular ceremony of the Taurobolium.

Tertullian (A.D. 265) writes on this subject:

> The Devil whose business it is to pervert the truth, mimics the exact circumstances of the Divine Sacraments in the Mysteries of Mithras. He himself baptizes some, that is to say, his believers and followers; he promises forgiveness of sins from the Sacred Fount and thereby initiates them into the religion of Mithras; thus he marks on the forehead of his own soldiers: thus he celebrates the oblation of bread: he brings in the symbol of the Resurrection, and wins the crown with the sword.

The final words relate to a rite which Tertullian describes in more detail in another passage when he refers to

Mithras

the Soldier of Mithras "who when he is undergoing initiation in the cave, in the very Camp of the Powers of Darkness, when the crown (garland rather) is offered to him (a sword being placed between as though in semblance of martyrdom) and about to be set upon his head, is instructed to put forth his hand, and push the crown away . . . saying at the same time. 'My crown is Mithras' . . . He is immediately known to be a "Soldier of Mithras", if he rejects a garland when offered to him, saying that his crown is his god. Let us therefore acknowledge the craftiness of the Devil, who copies certain things of those that be Divine, in order that he may confound and judge us by the faithfulness of his own followers."

The crown, according to the teachings of the Kabbala, is the highest honour that can be bestowed on man, being the first of the ten emanations from Adam-Kadman, the first emanation of the supreme being. Therefore the gesture of the Mithraic initiate meant that henceforth he would put his God before all. On the exoteric level it probably involved the refusal to wear garlands bestowed by the Romans upon their heroes and men of merit, in much the same way as the Quakers refuse worldly honours.

In the matter of the Eucharist, the Devil of whom Tertullian speaks certainly well deserved his title of Ape of God, for Justin Martyr complains:

The Apostles in the Commentaries written by themselves, which we call Gospels, have delivered down to us that Jesus thus commanded them: He having taken bread, after that He had given thanks, said: Do this in commemoration of me; this is my body. Also having taken a cup and returned thanks, He said: This is my blood and delivered it unto them alone. Which things indeed the evil spirits have taught to be done, out of memory, in the Mysteries and Initiations of Mithras. For in these likewise, a cup of water, and bread, are set out with the addition of certain words, in the sacrifice or act of worship of the person about to be initiated: a thing which ye either know by personal experience or may learn by inquiry.

It will be noticed that Justin Martyr of whom the late Bishop of Birmingham observed that by modern standards he was "without the restraint needed for rational inquiry", not only describes the Gospels as being written by the Apostles under whose names they appear, apparently unaware that the date of the earliest, that of Mark, was A.D. 70 or 100, but also attributes to the Mithraic Devil a pre-cognitive "memory" of Christian rites established long after those of the Phrygian God. Which brings us to the important matter of the approximate date when the influence of Mithraism came to be felt on the policies of Rome.

For some reason hard to determine, Professor Franz Cumont tends to put this much later than all the rest of the available evidence suggests, in one instance writing that it began to take root during the time of Trajan (A.D. 98–117) and in another suggesting that it was the initiation of Commodus (A.D. 180–192) into the Mysteries of Mithras which first aroused interest in the cult among the dignitaries of the Empire and high standing officers, who hastened to follow their sovereign's example, implying that until that period, Mithraism had been chiefly the religion of the slaves and common soldiers, quoting the well-known statement of Plutarch that the cult was originally brought to Rome by captive Cilician pirates (66 B.C.). But this theory is rendered completely untenable even by other statements in his own book, notably that Nero (A.D. 54–68) "had already expressed a desire to be initiated into the ceremonies of Mazdaism by the Magi whom King Tiridates of Armenia had brought with him to Rome, and this last-mentioned prince had worshipped in Nero an emanation of Mithra himself."

As we have already seen, the Kings of Armenia and Pontus were both ardent Mithraists long before the time of Christ, the dynasty of Mithridates ending only with the victory of Pompey over Mithridates VII, more than sixty years B.C. Therefore the ceremonies of Mazdaism referred to were, without doubt, those of Mithraism. But a far more convincing argument against Cumont's dating lies in the fact that not only were Castor and Pollux said to have been initiated into the Eleusinian Mysteries, but also the Emperor Augustus who was known as the Son of Apollo, and who, as we shall see in a later chapter, was favoured even before his birth with the patronage of the Sun-God. Cumont would seem to be unaware of the connexion of the cult with the Eleusinian Mysteries. Nor does he take into account the fact that—according to Justin—the King of Pontus, Mithridates VI, who died 123 B.C., had become a friend and ally of the Romans, furnishing them with a fleet in the Third Punic War, and giving them military help against Aristonicus. It is quite unlikely that the soldiers and sailors thus lent to Rome, coming from a land where Mithras was so ardently worshipped, and whose kings believed that his divine afflatus had endowed them with authority, would have omitted to speak of their deity or failed to practise their sacred rites.

There is no doubt whatever as to the popularity of the cult of Mithras among the fighting forces. It was, as Cumont says,"predominantly a religion of soldiers," and "the principal agent of its diffusion was undoubtedly the army". Certainly no intelligent officer or ruler could fail to see what an asset such a cult could be to empire building, arousing as it did an overwhelming enthusiasm for, and allegiance to, the sovereign whom they believed to be an emanation of the God himself.

Furthermore, the Romans had been given some practical proof of the ability of the Sun-God to arouse bravery, discipline and endurance in his followers, not only in the outstanding case of Alexander the Great, but also during the reign of Mithridates VII, when it had taken three of their finest generals, Sulla, Lucullus and Pompey, to conquer the army of one whom Cicero named "the greatest monarch who ever sat on the throne".

This King of Pontus was indeed the perfect soldier of

Mithras, non-attached, passionless, disciplined, inured to hardship, sleeping for whole months during his campaigns on the frozen snow and hard earth; ambitious, cruel and ruthless, but possessed of immense personal courage and genius in the art of war. He was also a skilled physician, a man of letters and a remarkable linguist. It is said that he spoke the languages of the twenty-four nations he conquered as fluently as his own, and he wrote a treatise on botany in Greek. It is impossible that such a prodigy should have gone unnoted by his foes, and that the source of his disciplined courage, his stoical endurance—his religion— should have been unknown to them. Therefore while Plutarch was undoubtedly correct in supposing that the captured Cilician pirates from Tarsus—ardent Mithraists who had defied the power of Rome for so long—were a source of the dissemination of Mithraism in the Western world, they were not the only one or even the first. But putting the date, as Plutarch does as late as 66 B.C., the cult was already long-established in Tarsus, and had been flourishing for many years when Paul was born into that city. His obvious acquaintance with the Mithraic religion and its rites, traceable, as we shall see, in his Epistles, provides self-evident proof that the cult was known and practised long before the date assigned to it by Cumont.

An even more incontestable proof that Mithraism was not only known to, but was already a powerful foe of the Christians in the first century is the book of Revelation whose writer E. W. Barnes describes as suffering from "half-mad resentment" at the persecutions recently endured by himself and his co-religionists. It is an impassioned diatribe not only against Rome itself, which is significantly referred to as Babylon, but more particularly against the religion that was responsible for its policies. The references to the Beast and his Mark, as well as many others, can, as we shall presently show, only be ascribed to the writer's knowledge and detestation of Mithraism.

From New Testament and other evidence, therefore, it would seem that, at least from the time of Paul when the

Early Church was dragged from its obscurity, it found its implacable foe in the Cult of Mithras, the influence of which had long been apparent in the deification of Julius and Augustus, and the worship of Vesta and Apollo.

It was to this deification that Jesus was obviously referring in Mark xii, 15–17. It was recorded that the on-lookers marvelled at his ingenius reply to the Herodians who wished to make him commit himself when they asked whether they should pay tribute to Caesar. Had he answered in the affirmative he would be condemned of approving the detested pagan occupation, and so have lost the sympathy of his hearers. Had his reply been, No, he would stand convicted of enmity against Caesar and liable to be charged with sedition. Instead of which, he raised the whole matter from the political to the spiritual level, indicating that the wrong lay in the deification of the Caesars. His "Render to Caesar the things that are Caesar's, and to God the things that are God's" was a subtle separation of the human ruler from divinity, well understood by his mono-theistic audience, the reverse of the Mithraic identification of the ruler with the Divinity.

Although the Roman legionaries proved successful missionaries of Mithras in all the lands of their occupation in the West, nowhere was their success more evident than in Germany. Cumont speaks of the "marvellous extension" that Mithraism took in the two Germanies from the time that the Eighth Legion, who occupied Upper Germany in A.D. 70, introduced the cult there. He writes:

> Of all countries Germany is that in which the greatest number of Mithraeums, or places of Mithraic worship, have been discovered. Germany has given us the bas-reliefs having the greatest dimensions; and certainly no god of paganism ever found in this nation as many enthusiastic devotees as Mithra.

The Mysteries evidently had a special appeal for those barbarians, making, as it did, a religion and virtue of their favourite inclination—warfare. Studying the subsequent history of Germany we are forced to conclude that the spirit of Mithras survived fully in that area, however much lip-service has since been paid to the newer God of Peace and Love. Significantly Cumont suggests that this country formed the bridge by which Mithraism crossed from the East to Britain. After stating that there was reason to believe that Mithras was being worshipped in York, London, Chester and Caerleon in the middle of the second century, he adds "and that Germany served as the intermediary agent between the far Orient *'et penitus toto divisos orbe Britannos'*."

We were told before the last world war that not only did Mussolini's Fascists have a cult, the symbol of which was the bundle of sacred twigs that figures in the Iranian religion; but that Hitler's Strength Through Joy movement was based on some sort of pagan sun-worship which suggests that even at such a late date, the spirit of Mithras still lingered in the race-consciousness of countries that had from the first been most hospitable to its ideals—Italy and Germany. And certainly by whatever name Hitler's war-gods were known, the chief of them, the invincible leader that sent the German nation to its temporary doom, was the resurrected Mithras. For, as Cumont writes of the Mithraists:

> They did not lose themselves, as did the other sects, in contemplative mysticism; for them the good dwelt in action. They rated strength higher than gentleness, and preferred courage to lenity. From their long association with barbaric religions, there was perhaps a residue of cruelty in their ethics. A religion of soldiers, Mithraism exalted the military virtues above others.

This description, while it vividly reminds us of the Nazis, does not, of course, only apply to them. The first two sentences might well refer to the modern Christian, and to the general viewpoint of Protestant Christendom.

According to Cumont, it was the conquest of Macedonia by Darius I that first brought the cult of Mithras in its final form, and the idea of Emperor worship, to the West. The cult of the Sun-God would have been well established by the time of Alexander the Great (356–323 B.C.) who was a typical Mithraist, not only in his military prowess but in his belief in the divinity of Kings, for we read in Lemprière that, after conquering Darius III he ordered himself to be worshipped as a God, and put Callisthenes to death for refusing to obey. He dressed in the Persian manner, having evidently, as is the custom of natives of subject nations, adopted the ways, manners and Gods of the one-time conqueror of his country.[1] His devotion to the Persian Sun-God would have made it easy for him to understand and accept the similar sun-worshipping cult of Egypt, when he conquered and occupied the Nile Valley. In Egypt the Sun-God was completely identified with the Pharaoh. Horus, Amon-Re—what did the name matter? Here was again the radiant being from on high who gave authority and protection to the Kings of the earth, and fought their battles for them. Therefore Alexander found no difficulty in accepting the Egyptian form of Sun-worship and offering sacrifices to the local gods, in return for being deified as the son of Amon. Let all nations acknowledge his divinity! This eclectic spirit of Alexander united and strengthened the links between the Egyptian, Persian and Greek Sun-cults.[2] The similarity between their beliefs became more and more apparent. The sacred Bull, Apis, of the Egyptians was easily identifiable with the primordial Bull of Mithras.

But, as we have seen, it was Mithras who became the

---

[1] In a work by the Pseudo-Callisthenes, date uncertain, the meeting of Darius and Alexander is described in the words (iii, 34):

"Alexander then seeing the great pomp of Darius was moved almost to worship him as Mithra the divine, as though clothed in barbaric splendour he had come down from heaven—such was his splendid array."

In the Syriac translation the order is reversed, and it runs:

"And when Darius saw Alexander he did obeisance and worshipped Alexander, for he believed that he was Mihr the god, and that he had come down to bring aid to the Persians. For his raiment was like that of the gods, and the crown which rested upon his head shone with rays of light."

[2] *The Nature and Function of Priesthood* by E. O. James. (Thames and Hudson.)

inspiration and chief deity of the four rulers of his quartered empire, and the dynasty of Mithridates undoubtedly started a clearly traceable chain of Mithras-worship from the Kings of Pontus to the Emperors of Rome and so on to the Germanic and French monarchs, Louis XIV even being known as the Sun-King. And it is generally admitted that the mantle of imperialistic Rome eventually fell on Britain in the last century. Nor is it without significance that the British Monarch still wears the Mithraic Radiant Crown.

It is quite certain that we were sufficiently impressed by the Roman administration to adopt the methods of our one-time conquerors. Our buildings, our roads, our legal and colonizing systems are but a few of the signs that bear eloquent witness to this fact. What has not been so generally understood is that we also adopted their most popular God.

We did not do this deliberately or consciously. It was a psychological infiltration conveniently made possible by an eclectic Church that rightly called itself Catholic. While insisting upon winning the race with Mithras for spiritual world-leadership, it was wise enough to see that if it were to become the Universal Church of its aim, the spirit of Mithras could not be allowed to die or be completely replaced by the gentle, non-violent, wholly merciful policy of the original Christian faith, which had nothing in its psychological armoury to enable it to impose itself on reluctant nations. True Christianity sought to win converts by persuasion and love; but that was a long-term policy, useless to power-lovers and "realists" who desired the immediate government of humanity.

To such as these Christianity was a beautiful and advanced ideal that could only survive if upheld by the swords of the Soldiers of Mithras. Therefore there must be compromise. A place must be found in the all-embracing Church of Rome both for the pacific creed of the Teacher of Galilee and for the cult of the bellicose warrior-God. In a word, the hope of the world, according to such thinkers, lay in an attempt to reconcile the irreconcilable. The present state of the world is the result of this age-old tension, this perpetual state of conflict within the Church in which has been vested the moral leadership of Christendom, a conflict naturally reflected in the minds and hearts of its congregations, and so in the world and its policies that these congregations project.

This at least solves the mystery of why the Western world, after nearly two thousand years of nominal acceptance of the Creed of Christ finds itself in an era of violence far exceeding that recorded as being punishable by the near-annihilation of humanity in the days of Noah.

Today it is over America that the Mithraic eagle, Rome's emblem, so ominously hovers. When the first settlers fled in the *Mayflower* from religious tyranny and persecution, they were following a right instinct in attempting to cut themselves off from the pagan heritage. But their descendants, as a nation, became so intoxicated with the thought of liberty that they were blinded to the fact that through their ever-open, hospitable doors might come elements which threatened the existence of that liberty, Mithraic elements from Rome, Germany and Gaul, with the seeds of totalitarianism, militaristic and ecclesiastical, firmly embedded in their psychological make-up. Now the nation's emblem, legalistic and military systems, and familiar words like "veterans", "Senate" and "Senators" may well fill the thoughtful observer with foreboding.

But we have still to discover when and how the Fellow in the Cap was incorporated into the Christian fold; why and how he disappeared as though he had never been, and above all, where he has been living and thriving since the fourth century of our era.

To do this, we may begin with an examination of evidences of the Sun-God in Occidental antiquity, followed by a close study of the New Testament, as well as the dogmas and ceremonies of Christian Orthodoxy, although even then we shall not have exhausted the deity's numerous hiding places. For, as we shall find, the Cult of Mithras, which, in the fourth century, appeared to vanish from the face of the earth, meets us today in the West wherever we turn, not only in the teachings of the Christian Faith, and the churches founded in order to perpetuate these teachings; not only in the secret societies that have preserved elements of the discredited ancient Gnosis, and have faithfully guarded, though sometimes unaware of the fact, certain aspects of Mithraism and its initiation rites, but chiefly and essentially in the spirit of Western man who has been so badly misled and misguided by the faulty education given to him by those who claimed to be training humanity into the worship of the Prince of Peace when, in fact, they were training him into the worship of the invincible warrior-God. The bunting-draped walls and altars of our churches reveal to the awakened eye the worship not of the supposedly victorious Christ but of the apparently vanquished Mithras.

Those earnest Christian Fathers zealously burning and tearing up every scrap of written evidence as to the nature of the cult they wished to exterminate may, in some cases, genuinely have thought that they were saving humanity from the contamination of paganism. But these could only have been the most ignorant of the Bishops. The scholars could not have failed to know of the adulteration of the original creed of Christ by Mithraism, and must surely have foreseen that their action, far from eliminating that cult, would be perpetuating and protecting it in the name of Christianity. Nothing short of this, and the resultant fear of their complicity in such adulteration being discovered, could account for the meticulous care and fanatical fervour with which they destroyed everything relating to their former rival. To allow Mithraism to be seen for what it was: the creed of violence and worldly power, the Gospel of Imperialism, its literature plainly revealing its nature and aims, would mean that they could not back the policies of the State upon whose goodwill the Church depended; could not advocate the taking up of arms even in defence of the Faith, and to wage "holy" wars, lest well-informed congregations should indignantly object:

"But this is not Christianity; it is Mithraism!"

3

The Sun-God in Antiquity

Of arms I sing, and of the man who first
From Trojan shores beneath the ban of fate
To Italy and coasts Lavinian came . . .
    . . . till what time
A city he might found him, and bear safe
His gods to Latium . . .[1]

THESE opening lines to Virgil's *Aeneid* reveal a far earlier
introduction of the Sun-God into Italy than has so far been
suggested, although, in the days of Aeneas, his cult took a
different form from that by which it was known after its
introduction by Darius into Macedonia (*circa* 485 B.C.)
But it is clear that the Trojans established the worship of
the Sun-God in Latium centuries before Augustus, at the
bidding of the Sibylline Oracles, sent for the goddess within
whose cult Mithras, as Atys, was concealed. From Virgil's
and other, evidence it is obvious that the fellow in the Cap
had invaded Italy, as the lover of Cybele, both from
Phrygia and Greece, centuries before he appeared in the
guise of the warrior God, via Macedonia and Pontus.

To the early Christian Fathers, by whom his Persian
ancestry was evidently unsuspected, Mithras was known as
the Phrygian God. It was to his Phrygian cap that St.
Augustine referred so disrespectfully. And it was in Phrygia
more than a millennium before the days of the Caesars that

---

[1] *The Aeneid* from the Poems of Virgil, translated by James Rhoades. (Oxford
University Press.)

54

his Mysteries were celebrated with those of the Goddess, Cybele, in whose cult he appeared bearing a ball in one hand and leaning on a fir tree, the tree into which he was transformed as a punishment for his infidelity to the Goddess, and which was always associated with his cult. It is in all probability the origin of our Christmas tree that was introduced into Britain by the Germans in whose country the cult of Mithras was more popular than in any other land of the West. It was evidently this male God who directed Aeneas, in a night vision, to Italy, and who was referred to in the lines:

> When lo! the sacred emblem of the gods,
> The Phrygian Penates, out of Troy
> Borne with me from amidst the blazing town
> Seemed, as I lay in slumber, to stand forth
> Before mine eyes, clear in a flood of light.

Atys, Apollo, Mithras—the name mattered little; the God was the same, the virile Sun-God who inspired the physically courageous, eye-gouging Trojan "heroes" to their feats of valour, as surely as later he inspired Mithridates VII and the Mithraic Roman Emperors to prowess on the battle-field.

Cybele, having been the chief deity of Phrygia, there can be no doubt that she and her consort were the gods that Aeneas transferred from burning Troy to Italy where she was transformed into the Magna Mater who was admittedly one of the oldest and most respected deities of the early Roman Empire. If Dörpfeld's dating is correct, the fall of Troy, and therefore the first introduction of the Phrygian God into Italy, may be placed somewhere between 1500–1200 B.C.

It was also about this time (1356 B.C.) that Eumolpus, King of Thrace, first introduced the cult of Cybele into Greece, where it was established under the name of the Eleusinian Mysteries of Ceres who had long been worshipped in Attica.

It was believed that Ceres had gone to Greece and taught Triptolemus of Eleusis everything concerning agriculture. Therefore when Eumolpus brought his cult of Cybele from Phrygia, the two earth-goddesses were easily identified as one and the same, and Erechtheus, the King of Athens, was glad to establish the Eleusinian Mysteries in grateful memory of the favours granted to Attica by the Goddess.

Eumolpus was made Hierophantes, or high priest, by Erechtheus. But later they killed each other in battle. The terms of peace made by the opposing parties were that the priesthood should ever remain in the family of Eumolpus, and the regal power in the house of Erechtheus, thus separating Church from State. The priesthood continued in the family of Eumolpus for 1200 years, despite the fact that anyone appointed as Hierophantes was obliged to remain in perpetual celibacy. This might well have been the starting point of the peculiar stress on chastity noted in the later, militaristic cult of Mithras.

Ceres was also said to favour the Island of Sicily as a retreat while she waited for the yearly visit of her daughter, Proserpine. Therefore Sicilians made a yearly sacrifice to her, and her daughter was publicly honoured with an offering of bulls, the blood of the victims being shed on the waters of the fountains of Cyane. This would explain the later sharing of the Taurobolium by the priests of Cybele and Mithras.

Suetonius tells us that, among the Emperor Tiberius's female ancestors was the famous vestal virgin, Claudia, who had been accused of incontinence. When the ship bearing the image of Vesta, or Cybele, to Rome became stuck on the shoals of the Tiber, and no man could move it, Claudia prayed that the gods would enable her to perform this task in proof of her innocence, and was immediately enabled to guide the ship to port with her girdle.

In a footnote to this incident, referring to Vesta as the Idaean Mother of the Gods, J. C. Rolfe, PH.D. writes:

Cybele, a Phrygian Goddess worshipped near Mount Ida. In the year 204 B.C. her cult was introduced into Rome, where she was worshipped as the Magna Mater.[1]

But, as we have already seen, this date is far too late. We have Virgil's evidence, and Lemprière definitely states that it was Aeneas who introduced the mysteries of the Goddess Vesta (Cybele) into Italy. And since the mother of Romulus who died in 714 B.C. was a vestal virgin, and the twin brothers, Castor and Pollux, to whom a temple was erected in the Forum and who were worshipped as the constellation, Gemini, were both said to have been initiated into the Eleusinian Mysteries, Lemprière's date is obviously the correct one.

But although Mithras, as Atys, reached Rome at such an early date, Mithras, the Sun-God, and special protector of Kings and Emperors, or Mithraism in the definitive form it assumed in the West after the conquest of Macedonia by Darius, reached Rome more directly from that country. For it is obvious that Alexander the Great was the hero, example and inspiration of both the first Caesars, and that it was his form of Mithraism that took root in Rome.

Suetonius relates that when Julius was serving in Farther Spain, he noticed a statue of Alexander the Great in the Temple of Hercules, and "heaved a sigh as if out of patience with his own incapacity, having as yet done nothing noteworthy at a time of life when Alexander had already brought the world to his feet". This was evidently a turning point in his life, as he asked for his discharge and returned to Rome.

There is no evidence to show that he was ever initiated into the Mysteries, but that his titular divinity was the Sun-God is evident from his ancestry. For he was supposed, according to Virgil, to be a descendant of *IULUS*, the son of Aeneas who, when he was an infant, at the time of his

1 *Suetonius,* with an English translation, by J. C. Rolfe, PH.D. (William Heinemann Ltd.)

parents' flight from Troy, was observed to have tongues of fire playing about his head.

Julius referred to this ancestry in his oration, when quaestor, to his Aunt Julia of whom he said that her family on her father's side were the Julii who went back to Venus, finishing with the Mithraic utterance:

> Our stock, therefore, has at once the sanctity of kings, whose power is supreme among mortals, and the claim to reverence which attaches to the gods, who hold sway over kings themselves.

It was evidently in view of these claims that he was eventually deified by the Hierophantes who brought the doctrine of the divinity of Rulers and the Divine Right of Kings to the West.

Augustus, on the other hand, *was*, like Alexander, initiated into the Mysteries.

Suetonius writes that, during his invasion of Alexandria, "he had the body of Alexander the Great brought forth from its shrine, and after gazing on it, showed his respect by placing upon it a golden crown and strewing it with flowers." He also tells us that, at one time, Augustus's official seal was engraved with the image of Alexander. And it was evidently into the form of the Mysteries introduced by Darius and understood by Alexander that the Emperor was initiated. For although the rites of Cybele and Mithras were always sufficiently alike to enable some of them to be celebrated together, the initiation by the Twelve Tortures was exclusively male, and, of still greater importance, while Cybele symbolized the Moon, Mithras was her antithesis, the Sun, and it was the Sun-God who particularly favoured Augustus and with whom he was identified even before his birth.

It was said that his mother, Atia, sleeping in the Temple of Apollo, yielded to the embraces of a serpent which left its indelible mark upon her body, and that ten months after this incident, Augustus was born, and thereafter regarded

as the son of Apollo.[1] Among other signs and portents,
Octavius, Atia's husband, dreamed that the sun rose from
his wife's womb; and when he came late to the House,
having been detained by her confinement, Publius Nigidius
prophesied that the ruler of the world had been born. The
priests of Thrace, from which country Cybele had originally
journeyed to her Eleusinian home, when consulted by
Octavius, also made the same prediction since such a
pillar of fire arose from the oblation of wine poured on the
altar that it mounted to the very sky, an omen that had
only happened once before, and that to Alexander the
Great when he sacrificed at the same altar.

Octavius also dreamed that his son appeared to him
wearing the radiant crown of the Mithraic rites, in a
chariot drawn by twelve white horses. As an infant, too,
Augustus was said to have disappeared from his cradle,
eventually being found at the top of a high tower, his face
turned to the rising sun.

In his youth there appeared many omens, including
the arrival of twelve vultures, as he was taking the auspices
in his first consulship, the number twelve and the vulture
being prominent features in the Mysteries of Mithras.

From the evidence before us we must suppose that,
since the days of Darius, Atys had become more closely
identifiable with Mithras, and that his cult had become an
exclusively masculine branch of the Mysteries. Atys had,
in some sense, separated himself from the mother-Goddess,
like a child grown to manhood who insists upon standing
on his own feet. He was no longer subservient to her but
to his Father, the Sun, with whom he was so closely identified
that the son could say of the Father, 'I and my Father are
one.' The earth-Goddess had brought forth a God of power
dedicated to subduing and conquering both the earth and

---

[1] P. Papinius Statius (first century A.D.) declared in his epic poem, the
Thebais, that different nations give to Apollo different names. . . . The Achae-
menians call him Titan, the Egyptians Osiris, the Persians Mithra. And the
writer of the *Homilies*, erroneously ascribed to Clement of Rome, writes in the
6th Book ix–x: "Apollo is to be regarded as the sun in his course, the offspring of Zeus, named also Mithra, as he completes the cycle of the year."

the world. Their rites might be celebrated together since they were inseparably linked, but only as night is linked with day in the cosmic order, for Cybele represented the Moon and Mithras the Sun. The Eleusinian Mysteries were the synthesis that embraced both deities, but in practical politics, the Goddess of peace and agriculture had been, for centuries, increasingly superseded by the God of War.

The original Eleusinian Mysteries had been for both sexes but with the Goddess and her vestal virgins playing the leading roles. That they afterwards became, in great part, the militaristic, all-male Mysteries of the Mithraism known during the later part of the Roman Empire is obvious from the fact that they produced not only the intrepid Alexander the Great but also the perfect soldier of Mithras, Mithridates VII, so very much the type of the Emperor Julian who was such a credit to their mutual Faith during the last days of the cult.

Suetonius tells us that when Augustus became Pontifex Maximus after the death of Lepidus, he destroyed more than two thousand prophetic books of Greek or Latin origin, retaining "only the Sibylline books and making a choice even among those; and he deposited them in two gilded cases under the pedestal of the Palatine Apollo." Augustus was evidently a sectarian who may have had some idea, like Constantine and Julian after him, of establishing a form of solar monotheism, uniting all the cults of Rome under the supreme Sun-God, since Apollo was chosen as custodian of the sacred books. From the voluntary gifts of the populace he bought and dedicated costly statues of Apollo and other gods, and it is interesting to note that he had the silver statues originally set up in his own honour melted down, and with the money made from them dedicated "golden tripods to Apollo of the Palatine". It is clearly one of those tripods that is depicted in the unearthed bas-relief of Mithras' Last Supper, referred to by Cumont and illustrated in his book, *The Mysteries Of Mithra.*

Another passage from Suetonius suggests an even fuller connexion with the rites of this Last Supper. He says of Augustus:

There was besides a private dinner of his, commonly called that of the "Twelve Gods", which was the subject of gossip. At this the guests appeared in the guise of gods and goddesses, while he himself was made up to represent Apollo.

In describing Augustus's appearance, Suetonius writes, "He had bright, clear eyes, in which he liked to have it thought that there was a kind of divine power, and it greatly pleased him, whenever he looked keenly at anyone, if he let his face fall as if before the radiance of the sun." He also reports that, scattered over the Emperor's body were birthmarks, "corresponding in form, order and number with the stars of the Bear in the Heavens".

The secrecy of the Eleusinian Mysteries, which was also so evident in the Cult of Mithras, and even in the modern secret societies that, as we shall see, have descended from it, was so solemnly observed that, as Lemprière tells us, "if anyone appeared at the celebration . . . without proper introduction, he was immediately punished with death", as, also, was anyone who spoke of the mysteries revealed to him, which was supposed to bring down divine vengeance upon him.

After telling us that Augustus was initiated into the Mysteries, Suetonius adds that when he was trying to judge a case in Rome that involved the privileges of the priests of Attic Ceres in which secret matters were brought up, "he dismissed his councillors and the throng of by-standers and heard the disputants in private."

Of the twelve Caesars, although all paid homage to the Gods, Augustus alone was an initiate into the Mysteries. And it is not without significance that he was by far the best of these rulers. Undoubtedly Mithraism, inferior though it was to Christianity as a religion, and primitive in most of its rites, produced a very superior quality of follower compared with the other pagan religions. This was in part due to the fact that the initiatory rites called for such self-discipline, austerity and courage that only the finest type of devotee could hope to reach the goal of "Soldier of Mithras". None of the other Emperors had characters that would have entitled them to this honour. Nero, it is said, wished to be initiated, but Suetonius tells us that "in his journey through Greece he did not venture to take part in the Eleusinian Mysteries, since at the beginning the godless and wicked are warned by the herald's proclamation to go hence". This may well have accounted for the diffidence of the previous Roman Emperors.

Unlike his fellow-Caesars, Augustus died peacefully and painlessly as he had always expressed a wish to do, and an ex-praetor swore on oath that, after the Emperor's cremation, he had seen his form ascending to heaven.

The Mystery of Mithras is a very real one, and impossible to solve without the clue of Mithras' relationship to the cult of Cybele. For even taking into account the assiduity with which the Catholic Church sought to expunge the remembrance of his name from human consciousness, we are still confronted, if we wish to prove our assertion of the antiquity of the warrior-making aspect of the Mysteries, with the question of why his name is never found among the ancient writings of Greece and Rome.

Because of this lacuna, it has so far proved easier to concentrate, as Cumont has done, on the Persian ancestry of Mithras, and to date his appearance in Rome from the days when he was openly worshipped throughout the Empire by the legionaries and their local converts. Yet those who maintain, as some do, that the Mysteries of Mithras were introduced into the West as late as the age of Trajan, must account for the existence of Alexander, Artaxerxes Mnemon, Mithridates VII and Augustus Caesar.

But once we have established the connexion between the Sun-God and the Eleusinian Mysteries, we can understand the reticence of such writers as Virgil, Ovid and Suetonius, for the penalty of disclosing the true nature of those Mysteries was death.

In the circumstances, we can only wonder that Virgil and Ovid made as many references to the Phrygian God

and his cult as they did, even though his Mysteries were
never mentioned by name and would only have been
recognizable to initiates. No Mithraist could fail to detect
the identity of the God referred to by all three of these
writers as Apollo.

As we have seen, Virgil's *Aeneid* is actually a history of
the cult, and Aeneas and the other heroes are obviously
of the type aimed at by the Soldiers of Mithras. Virgil hails
Augustus as the son of Apollo, and traces his ancestry from
the Phrygian heroes who brought their gods to Rome.
He recounts the mating of Phrygia and Italy in the persons
of Aeneas and Lavinia, and so establishes the date of the
entry of the cult into the latter country. But he does more
than this. In describing the perilous descent of Aeneas to
the Land of Dis in search of the shade of his dead father,
there is a strong probability that he is referring to the
initiation rites of the Mysteries.

The Rev. Lucas Collins, in his book on Virgil, tells us
that "Bishop Warburton, in his well-known 'Divine
Legation', expended a great amount of learning and
research to prove that in the descent to the shades in the
sixth book (of the Aeneid) we have a sketch, scarcely
veiled, of the great Eleusinian Mysteries."[1]

What we have since learned of the Mithraic initiation
rites and their horrors makes this theory seem highly probable
and it may account for the fact that Virgil made such
strong efforts just before he died, to get hold of the incomplete manuscript in order to burn it, and, failing,
begged his friends to destroy it. He may well have felt that
he had revealed too much for the good of his soul!

If Bishop Warburton was right, and the experiences of
Aeneas in the Land of Dis do indeed constitute an account
of the teachings as to life after death contained in the
Eleusinian and Mithraic Mysteries, the Catholic Church is
seen to be indebted to Mithras both for its doctrines of
heaven and the fiery lake which come so obviously and
directly from his Zoroastrian connexions, and for those of

[1] *Virgil* by the Rev. Lucas Collins M.A. (William Blackwood and Sons.)

limbo, purgatory and hell as found in the *Aeneid*. And with these pagan concepts Christian congregations have been plagued, threatened and bullied for centuries, in spite of the fact that no such theories can anywhere be discerned in the teachings of Jesus Christ.

Again, if this supposition is correct, it would seem that Ovid, in his *Metamorphoses*, was alluding even more explicitly to the beliefs of the cult of Mithras, for not only does he relate, like Virgil, the descent of Aeneas to the underworld, but his whole theme is related to the theory of metempsychosis that is strongly suggested by the bird and animal masks and degrees that were so prominent a feature of the Mysteries of Mithras, whose followers could hardly fail to recognize the connexion.

Moreover, his *Fasti* appears to have been arranged in a definitely Mithraic design. Lemprière informs us that "the *Fasti* were divided into twelve books, the same number as the constellations in the Zodiac", a significant statement when we remember the importance of astrology and the number twelve in the cult of Mithras. Yet surely there should have been some clearly traceable evidence of this cult in a work which described the various religious rites and ceremonies of Ovid's times, especially as he was actually exiled to Pontus, that stronghold of Mithraism, from which he wrote his Epistles? Perhaps the explanation of the absence of any recognizable reference to the cult lies in Lemprière's further statement that, of the twelve books of the *Fasti*, "six have perished, and the learned world have reason to lament the loss of a poem which must have thrown so much light upon the religious rites and ceremonies, festivals and sacrifices of the ancient Romans as we may judge from the six that have survived the ravages of time and barbarity."

It is quite possible that it threw all too *much* light on a subject which came under such strict censorship from the pontiffs of a later date.

The secrecy that surrounded the cult of Mithras from its inception must obviously have been a powerful aid to those who wished to exterminate it. Both friends and foes were united from first to last in keeping it hidden from the world. Only when it became popularized by the legionaries did it come to the surface with its Temples and sculpturings, the discovered ruins of which have, after all these centuries, led to inquiry into this forbidden subject.

An additional explanation as to why the name of Mithras was heard so late in the history of the Roman Empire may possibly be provided by a further paragraph in Lucas Collins's book where he writes:

> The Romans had a regular formula for the evocation of the gods from the enemy's city, and inviting them, with promises of all due honours and sacrifices, to transfer their seat to Rome; and to attack any city without these solemn preliminaries was held to bring a curse on the besiegers.

To this passage he adds the significant footnote: "For this reason, says Macrobius, the real name of Rome and of its guardian deity was always kept a secret."

This custom would certainly explain the continual references made to Apollo by Virgil, Ovid and Suetonius, since we know that this is one of the many aliases of Mithras who was evidently only allowed to emerge from his disguise when his cult had spread to all parts of the Roman Empire through the missionary zeal of the legionaries who constantly swore by his name.

4

Mithras in the Epistles

As the writer of the article on Mithras in *The Standard Dictionary of Folklore and Mythology* (Funk and Wagnalls) points out, if a follower of Mithras were to enter the Catholic Church today, he would find most of the essentials of his religion taught and practised: "Baptism for the remission of sins, the symbolic meal of communion including consecrated wine, the sign on the brow, redemption, salvation sacramentary grace, rebirth in the spirit and the promise of eternal life."

He would also recognize in the robes of the priests the sumptuous garments of the Magi; the name of the Bishop's tall cap would echo the name of his god, the derivation of the word *Mitre* being the Greek *Mitra*, which was also one of the spellings of the name of the Fellow in the Cap. He would note that the *Pater Patrum*, or Pope, wore the Persian tiara, and that the sword of Mithras, although now called a cross, was still worshipped as a symbol of sacrifice, and that He who hung upon that cross wore either a halo or crown of thorns both denoting the true nature of the regnant deity, symbolizing the Light or rays of the sun or the Radiant Crown which always adorned the brow of the Sun-God. He would certainly feel that his God had proved invincible since, even in apparent defeat, he was thus being worshipped in the very stronghold of his rival's temple.

But how different would be the feelings of any one of those God-seekers who had followed the Master and heard him preach on the hills of Galilee if he could gaze on such a scene! He would stare aghast and bewildered at the Roman ceremonialism, the glitter of jewels, the incense, the Latin incantations and fantastically garbed priests. He would be horrified to find the walls of the Church dedicated to the worship of one who came not to destroy but to fulfil the Mosaic law, adorned with forbidden pictures and images and, even more shamefully, in a church supposed to be propagating the Gospel of peace and goodwill to all men, hung with the emblems of Mithraic militarism. He might well exclaim with Erasmus:

> How come the bishop's staff and sword to agree? . . . that theologians preach war with the self-same lips with which they proclaim Jesus Christ, the Peacemaker? . . . Oh you cruel shameless lips; how dare you call Him your Father whilst you rob your brother of life?

As a follower of the strictly monotheistic Teacher who, in refusing personal worship, declared: There is none good but one, that is God, he would be shocked beyond measure to find the man, Jesus, hailed as "very God", and to learn that man's salvation was supposed to be ensured by the fact that the Teacher had been hung on the Cross, instead of depending on the individual's personal search for the Kingdom of God, his obedience to the demands of the Sermon on the Mount and the Decalogue.

Looking about him and listening to the perversions of the original doctrines, he would ask: How has all this happened? From whence has all this come? What have these oriental robes, these jewels, this incense to do with the simple Teacher of Galilee who had no place to lay his head?

The answer is a complex one but must undoubtedly include a description of the part played in this metamorphosis by the ingenuity of Saul of Tarsus.

His birthplace provides us with the first clue. Tarsus was a great centre of Mithraism. From its mountain fastnesses the Cilician pirates, disciplined Mithraists, had for many years defied the power of Rome. It is unthinkable that the highly educated Saul should have remained in ignorance of this long-established cult flourishing in his native town.

In *The Shadow of the Third Century*, Dr. A. B. Kuhn goes so far as to write: "Internal evidence points to the fact that Paul himself had been a member of the Eleusinian, Dionysean or Bacchic Mystery schools." This cannot be ruled out as a possibility especially in view of the place of his birth, but it is unlikely as he seems to have been every inch a Jew and a staunch upholder of orthodox Judaism until his conversion. What is far more probable is that he had imbibed the teachings and phraseology of the Sun-worshippers from his own Scriptures, especially from the Apocalyptic writings such as those of Ezekiel, Daniel and the Book of Enoch, all of which bear strong evidence of Persian inspiration. In his recently published *The Authentic New Testament*, Dr Hugh Schonfield says of such writings: "This literature drew much of its imagery from Babylonian and Persian religious concepts." Therefore it is quite certain that Paul who, as he declared, was "a Jew born in Tarsus . . . yet brought up in this city at the feet of Gamaliel and taught according to the perfect manner of the law of the fathers" would have been well versed in such writings and accustomed to thinking in terms of their imagery. The more likely possibility seems to be that the Mithraic influence reached him from both sources: possibly unconsciously from that of his own Babylonian-Persian inspired Scriptures and directly from such knowledge as he must have acquired of the cult so popular in his birthplace. It would certainly have been the latter that accounted for his militaristic terminology that so often seems to refer to the training of a soldier of Mithras. Moreover, he and his father were both Roman citizens, as he reminded his captors in Acts xxii, 25–28. For this privilege they would have been obliged to swear allegiance to the Emperor, and at least to pay lip-service to the state religion, bowing the knee to the gods of the Empire of which Mithras—under the name of Apollo— was already an outstanding one.

Paul was a theologian, cultured, intelligent and

ambitious, his ambitions, after the incident on the road to Damascus, being centred on the creed of his adoption that he wished to save from the condition in which he found it—a small, persecuted Jewish sect—and to establish it as a universal religion. For which purpose, as far as in him lay, he went "into all the world and preached the Gospel". As he preached he assimilated. His Epistles reveal him as a great eclectic; and what he assimilated was undoubtedly used to make Christianity, or what he believed to be Christianity, acceptable over the widest possible area, and especially to the climate of opinion in Rome prevailing in the first century of our era.

It is interesting in this connexion to note that, according to Acts xviii, 1–3, he lodged for some time with a fellow tent-maker, Aquila, born in Pontus, and it is permissible to assume that these two deeply religious men would have discussed from time to time the pagan religion which had permeated both their birth-places, Pontus, being the chief centre from which Mithraism had radiated to the Western world.

As we know, Paul's Epistles constitute the first canonical writings of the Christian Church, and from them it is evident that he was familiar with the beliefs and practices of the cult which even in his day we must presume both from his and John the Divine's references to it, as having been recognizable as the most formidable foe of Christianity. There can hardly be any doubt, for instance, that he was referring to the Mithraists when, in the first chapter of Romans, he spoke of those who "changed the glory of the incorruptible God into an image like to corruptible man, and to birds, and four footed beasts, and creeping things". What were these if they were not the animal masks that indicated the Mithraic degrees, later so scornfully enumerated by Jerome? And if this assumption is correct it constitutes a further proof that Mithraism was being openly practised in Rome at the time of the Pauline ministry, for he was writing to Romans and obviously presuming that they understood to what he was alluding, and therefore to what was going on in their midst.

It must be remembered that Paul had no personal knowledge of Jesus; all that he knew was from hearsay, except for his psychic experience on the Road to Damascus But the vision he then had of the Master took place in consciousness, not in the external world, and what he saw was his own idea of the Teacher of Galilee, an idea which might well have been influenced by his former religious beliefs and experiences, one of which was evidently an extensive knowledge of Mithras and the rites of his cult. He had more direct access to the concepts and practices of Mithraism than he ever had to the actual words and teachings of Jesus Christ, for in his time none of the four Gospels had been written, and he had to rely on information given to him by Christian converts or by an occasional eye-witness, such as Peter.

But in fact, he continually and explicitly states that he did not gain his knowledge in this way. In Gal. xi, 6, for instance, he writes: "Those who were of repute imparted nothing to me." And in Gal. i, 11, he says, "For I make known to you, brethren, as touching the gospel which was preached by me, that it is not after man. For neither did I receive it from man, nor was I taught it, but it came to me through the revelation of Jesus Christ."

It should be noted here that Paul's own account of his experiences after his conversion given in the first chapter of Galatians, completely contradicts that of the writer of Acts who, in chapter nine, says that, after he was struck with blindness, Paul first went to Damascus where, having been healed by Ananias, he began preaching; then escaping from the antagonistic Jews, went to Jerusalem where "he assayed to join himself to the disciples; but they were all afraid of him, and believed not that he was a disciple". In another account Acts xxii, 17, 18, it is definitely stated that Paul went to Jerusalem. But Paul himself writes to the Galatians:

When it pleased God who . . . called me by his grace, to reveal his son in me, that I might preach him among the heathen; immediately I conferred not with flesh and blood: *neither went I up to Jerusalem* to them which were Apostles before me; but I went into Arabia, and returned again to Damascus. Then *after three years* I went up to Jerusalem to see Peter, and abode with him fifteen days. But other of the Apostles saw I none, save James the Lord's brother.

From this we must conclude that, for three years, Paul only knew Jesus Christ through "revelation", his own spiritual concept, which seems to have been that of the universal, eternal, cosmic Christ rather than that of the personal and historic Jesus of Nazareth; and that he learnt all he knew of the Teacher of Galilee during a fifteen-day visit with Peter, from his host and from James. But by then his own revelationary concept had crystallized and he was fully convinced that God had reposed in him the special task of taking the Gospel to the Gentiles and so universalizing the Truth. But from first to last it is obvious that he believed, and was eventually successful in persuading others to believe, that his information as well as his instructions and appointment to ministry came direct from Jesus Christ and through no earthly intermediary. Acts xxvi, 12–18, also 1 Tim. i, 1 and 1 Cor. xi, 23–26 make this perfectly clear. Therefore, while not questioning for a moment his undoubted understanding of, and spiritual affinity with the Mystic of Galilee, clearly shown in such passages as his exhortation to the Athenians, Acts xvii, 24–28; his beautiful description of the method of spiritual evolution, 2 Cor. iii, 18; and, above all, his famous dissertation on the nature of Love, 1 Corinthians xiii, we must remember that he had other knowledge of the Gnostic variety, and—although perhaps unrecognized by himself—other affinities.

One of the latter seems to have been for the discipline, loyalty, courage, austerities and devotion involved in militarism. The passages in his Epistles expressing this point of view leave us feeling that, in different circumstances, he might have been a very creditable Soldier of

Mithras. In Ephesians vi, 10–17, for instance, he exhorts the followers of Christ to exhibit the same alertness, zeal and preparedness as that manifested by the Roman conquerors:

> Put on the whole armour of God, that ye may be able to stand against the wiles of the devil. For we wrestle not against flesh and blood, but against principalities, against powers, against the rulers of the darkness of this world, against spiritual wickedness in high places. Wherefore take unto you the whole armour of God, that ye may be able to withstand in the evil day, and having done all, to stand. Stand therefore having your loins girt about with truth, and having on the breastplate of righteousness; and your feet shod with the preparation of the gospel of peace; above all, taking the shield of faith, wherewith ye shall be able to quench all the fiery darts of the wicked. And take the helmet of salvation, and the sword of the Spirit, which is the word of God.

It is true that this distinctly Mithraic utterance, and others like it, referred only to spiritual warfare, but it suggests that Paul was fully appreciative of the quality of many of Mithras' followers and felt that those of Jesus Christ might well emulate the congregations of the rival Faith. In which he was in agreement with Tertullian who, when pointing out the rejection of worldly honours by the Mithraists and their capacity for martyrdom, said, "Blush, my fellow Roman soldiers, even though ye be not to be judged by Christ, but by any soldier of Mithras'." But this emphasis on militaristic qualities was a mistake in tactics if Paul's thought had been to maintain the non-violent outlook of the Founder of the Creed of his adoption. We have only to consider the above words and to imagine them issuing from the lips of Jesus to perceive their incongruity. And there is no doubt whatever that they and similar exhortations provided the precedent for the composition of such hymns as;

> Onward Christian soldiers
> Marching as to war,
> With the cross of Jesus
> Going on before

with all the martial spirit they evoked, enabling muscular Christians like General Gordon to go to battle with the Bible in one hand and a death-dealing implement in the other.

Even with the comparatively slight knowledge we have of Mithraism and its liturgy, it is clear that many of Paul's phrases savour much more of the terminology of the Persian cult than that of the Gospels. For instance, Tertullian and other writers have made much of the symbology of Sword and Crown used in the Mithraic initiation rites, and in 2, Tim, iv, 7, 8, we read:

> I have fought a good fight, I have finished my course, I have kept the faith. Henceforth there is laid up for me a crown of righteousness which the Lord, the righteous judge, shall give me at that day.

Such words might well have been spoken by a newly initiated Soldier of Mithras, but one cannot imagine them being uttered by Jesus or his immediate followers. Philippians iv; and 1 Thess. ii, 19, both refer to what at the time of writing have been thought of as the Mithraic rather than the Christian crown, the Radiant Crown of the Sun-God. Paul was introducing a new terminology into the original Faith; and there is no doubt that, in many cases, that terminology was Mithraic.

That peculiar passage in 2 Thess. ii, in which the writer foretells the appearance and destruction of the anti-Christ might well refer to Mithras. Paul sees that the day of Christ cannot be established until men cease to worship the false god.

> That day shall not come, except there come a falling away first, and that man of sin be revealed, the son of perdition; who opposeth and exalteth himself above all

that is called God, or that is worshipped; so that he as God sitteth in the temple of God, showing himself that he is God.

This description might conceivably apply to a Roman Emperor demanding deification, but Paul, the Roman, who still prided himself on being freeborn, would hardly court death by such an arraignment of the highest earthly authority, and it seems far more likely that it applied to the Fellow in the Cap who was, as we know, the greatest rival and most persistent persecutor of the Christian Faith at this time. Such a theory seems confirmed by the further passage: "For the mystery of iniquity doth already work: only he who now letteth *will let*, until he be taken out of the way." The last words may refer to the state authorities who favoured Mithras and permitted the continuance of his cult. And then come the lines which, like others in the Epistles, suggest that Paul did not wholly disapprove of the more metaphysical aspects of Sun-God philosophy, but that he was determined that Jesus Christ and not Mithras should be identified with that glorious and beneficent Being:

And then shall that wicked be revealed whom the Lord shall consume with the spirit of his mouth, and shall destroy with the brightness of his coming.

This coming having already been described in the previous chapter, in the words; "The Lord Jesus shall be revealed from heaven with his mighty angels in flaming fire," a prophecy that might have come straight from the Zend-Avesta!

As a monotheist Paul, like Zoroaster, would have been careful to separate the concept of That which the Sun symbolizes from the burning orb itself, but he was not averse to using the symbology of Sun worship in describing the Supreme Being, as we see in 2 Cor. iv, where he writes:

For God . . . hath shined in our hearts, to give the light of the knowledge of the glory of God in the face of Jesus Christ.

Paul's one concern was that, in the eyes of humanity, this Light should be transmitted from the face of his Master and not from that of Mithras. And since, as we have seen, from the writings of Tertullian and Justin Martyr, the god of the rival Faith was considered to be the devil, we can hardly doubt that the passage in 2 Cor. xi, 14,15, relates to the Sun-God, the 7th Amshaspand or Angel of Light known as Mithras. It reads:

Satan himself is transformed into an angel of light. Therefore it is no great thing if his ministers also be transformed as the ministers of righteousness.

There can be no question of the detestation in which the rival cult was held, and yet, for Paul the shining armour of militarism, symbolizing conquest and triumph, obviously had a glamorous appeal. His metaphors constantly betray this:

Let us cast off the works of darkness and let us put on the armour of Light.

And again, in 2 Timothy ii, 3–5, when he might have been issuing orders to a Soldier of Mithras, he was certainly enjoining his "son Timothy" to adopt the qualities worshipped in the warrior God rather than those of the compassionate and merciful Jesus.

Thou therefore endure hardness, as a good soldier of Jesus Christ. . . .

(Since when had the Teacher of Galilee an army under him?)

No man that warreth entangleth himself with the affairs of this life; that he may please him who hath chosen him to be a soldier, and if a man also strive for masteries, yet is he not crowned, except he strive lawfully.

Strife! Austerity! Non-attachment! Mastery! Power! all these masculine virtues have obviously a great attraction for Paul. But to those familiar with the teachings of the

Gospels, the exhortations to meekness, humility, long-suffering, the compassion and tenderness evidenced in the healing works, the gentle persuasion that sought to win the hearers to a love of, and so to a surrendered obedience to, the Father, these militaristic allusions come with something of a psychological shock, as being unnaturally out of keeping with the spirit of the Gospels.

When Jesus declared that he was the Light of the world, he was obviously implying that for the world his Gospel constituted enlightenment, and, in that sense, the metaphor of Light is legitimately used in the Epistles, as in 2 Cor. iv, 4, and 1 Thess, v, 5. But in 1 Timothy vi, we once more find the phraseology of the sun-worshippers:

> The blessed and only Potentate, the King of kings, and Lord of lords: who only hath immortality, dwelling in the light which no man can approach unto; whom no man hath seen, nor can see.

This surely depicts the unapproachable Ormuzd far more surely than the ever available Spirit of Love of whom Jesus said: "I and my Father are one," and prayed that his followers might experience a similar at-one-ment.

But if Paul's Epistles have Mithraic echoes, and contain, as in the next chapter we shall see that they do, even closer affinities with the rites of Mithraism than anything yet quoted, the writer of the Epistle to the Hebrews who is now authoritatively stated not to have been Paul, actually gives the Mithraic account of creation derived from Mazdaism, in the words:

> God . . . hath in these last days spoken unto us by his Son, whom he hath appointed heir of all things, by whom also he made the worlds. . . .

Where, throughout the Gospels, does Jesus make any claim to have made the worlds? Yet Timeless Being sends forth Ormuzd, and later Mithras for just this purpose. The passage continues:

Who being the brightness of his glory, and the express image of his person . . . when he had by himself purged our sins, sat down at the right hand of the majesty on high . . . and again when he bringeth . . . the first-begotten into the world, he saith, and let all the angels of God worship him. And of the angels he saith, who maketh his angels spirits, and his ministers a flame of fire . . .

Here we have the Avesta account of the Emanations, primarily of the Firstbegotten, then the hierarchy of angels, the Amshaspands, the *Izeds* or *yazatas*, "flames" of the original bright-burning fire. If we compare this account of creation with that found in the first chapter of Genesis, there can remain no doubt of the Persian influence on the writer of the Epistle to the Hebrews.

In this Epistle, too, occur three allusions to Jesus Christ as Mediator (Heb. viii, 6; ix, 15; xii, 24), which was, as we know, the special function of Mithras, the word never being mentioned in the Gospels. Jesus did not regard himself as one standing between man and his God, but as the Example, showing how each man may himself become one with the Father, by following, or emulating him; or, as Paul more explicitly described it, by putting on the Mind of Christ, and so thinking the thoughts that directly led to the acts of Jesus of Nazareth. The concept of Mediator, on the other hand, widens the distance between God and man, repudiates the mystic experience of direct communion with God, and opens up the whole field of priestcraft, with its interceding saints, its guardian angels, and absolutions. It is, in fact, ritualism and ceremonialism as distinct from immediate spiritual experience, and with the latter only was Jesus Christ concerned.

Whether Paul is responsible for the Epistle to the Hebrews or not, the idea of Jesus as Mediator is undoubtedly a Pauline conception, as we see from 1 Timothy ii, 5. The theory comes strangely from one who wrote of the way of direct at-one-ment by contemplation:

We all with open face beholding as in a glass the glory of the Lord are changed into the same image from glory to glory even as by the Spirit of the Lord.

But in Paul, as in so many religious teachers, the mystic conflicted with the priest. From the foregoing he obviously knew the true method of direct communion, as practised by the Founder of his Faith and the true mystics of all time, but as priest he was drawn to the idea of mediation and of the Christ as mediator, which, as a function, had so endeared his followers to Mithras.

The writer of Hebrews, also, whoever it may have been, had fully accepted the Mithraic role for the Teacher of Galilee, and with it, that cult's concept of the Supreme Being; for the twelfth chapter of the Epistle ends with that forthright and surprising statement: "For our God is a consuming fire."

How strange a concept for a self-described follower of one who taught that God was the loving Father of all, hearing us always, and healing all our sicknesses and sins!

A transforming spirit had certainly been at work between the time of the crucifixion and the publication of the Epistles.

As a mystic Paul could perfectly well understand Jesus's declaration of his unity with the Source of all when he declared, "I and my Father are one"; and as a Gnostic, he clearly comprehended the reference to the pre-existence of the eternal Christ-nature, or son of God, in the words, "Before Abraham was, I am"; but the personal teacher, Jesus of Nazareth he never seems to have understood, nor even to have attempted to understand. Rather he boasted: "Henceforth know we no man after the flesh: yes, though we have known Christ after the flesh, yet now henceforth know we him no more." But he was mistaken in thinking he had ever known *Jesus* Christ "after the flesh", in the sense of comprehending the special individual contribution that this great Teacher made to the spiritual life of mankind, and to the age-old Divine Science that both he and Paul had learned from the esoteric teachings of their mutual Faith. Paul, the Roman, failed to comprehend the implications of the non-violence manifested in the life of the Mystic of Galilee. He visualized him in his eternal aspect in the imagery of the triumphant, all-conquering Sun-God. He had no clear picture of him as the living expression of compassionate love and non-violence who chose to bear the cruelty of his fellows rather than combat it with similar force and so lose his hold on his sense of at-one-ment with that all-beneficent God that he understood most clearly as Love.

The chief reason for Paul's lack of comprehension of the nature and outlook of Jesus was that there was so little of the woman in the apostle to the Gentiles. Like most Jews, he despised "woman" and "womanliness", outwardly and inwardly. Whereas Jesus, as the perfect man, the manifestation of the divine Father-Mother, possessed, like the archetype, cosmic man of so many religious systems, an exact balance of male-female attributes, compassionate Love being as much in evidence in his life as power.

In Paul one looks vainly for the gentler, feminine qualities. We have, of course, his famous and much quoted exhortation on charity in 1 Corinthians xiii, which is probably one of the most perfect pieces of rhetoric achieved by any member of the human race. But it remains just that: something chiefly of the intellect, an entirely different attitude to that of Jesus of Nazareth, who did not talk so brilliantly about Love, but *was* Love personified, the image and likeness of this divine attribute, continually expressing it in his compassion for his fellow men as he walked among them, healing them of their woes, infirmities and physical ills, letting deeds rather than words prove the omnipresence of a God of compassionate Love. In Jesus men saw the divine, tenderly ministering mother-love, entirely lacking in Paul. It is impossible to imagine the Apostle to the Gentiles sorrowing over Jerusalem, in the words: "O Jerusalem, Jerusalem . . . how often would I have gathered thy children together, even as a hen gathereth her chickens under her wings, and ye would not!" As impossible as to imagine Jesus standing by unmoved, as Saul did, when the gentle Stephen was being stoned to death.

It is usually maintained that Saul's conversion entirely changed his character; that after the episode on the Road to Damascus, he was a completely different man. But there are hints in the Epistles that the change may not have been so radical as is generally supposed, especially when one notes his fury at the undoubtedly unpleasant sexual sin that he condemns in 1 Corinthians v, 1–5. Moffatt's version of his words is more revealing than the rather involved King James's version, and runs: "I have consigned that individual to Satan for the destruction of his flesh, in order that his spirit may be saved on the Day of the Lord Jesus."

Such a non-Christian pronouncement not only perpetuates the entirely false idea that a man may be regenerated by tormenting his flesh, or indeed by any form of punishment, but obviously and directly paved the way for the appalling martyrdoms and iniquities of the Inquisition of which the Church was later guilty. They had Pauline authority for departing from the very essence and nature of the creed of Christ, and for an unashamed display of pagan cruelty and violence. The man, demented with pain as he lay tortured on the rack, the screaming woman burning at the stake, were, according to the perverted minds of their tormentors, having their "souls" saved. And the devilish Inquisitors could quote the words of the apostle to the Gentiles in justification of their monstrous acts. Such fatal misleadership was the direct result of Paul's lack of the tender, protective, mother-love so conspicuous in the life of Jesus. And this lack rendered him constitutionally incapable of recognizing the true nature and outlook of the Mystic of Galilee, which accounts for the startling difference between the picture of Jesus of Nazareth as found in the Gospels and that of the transcendent, universal Christ— by no means confined to the Christian Faith—visualized in the Epistles of Paul and those of his school of thought.

5

Mithras in the Gospels

The Nativity.

> Paul, a servant of Jesus Christ, called to be an apostle, separated unto the gospel of God . . . concerning his son Jesus Christ our Lord, which was made of the seed of David according to the flesh; and declared to be the son of God with power, according to the spirit of holiness, by the resurrection from the dead.
>
> (Romans i, 1–4.)

In these words Paul is evidently stating the current belief of the Christian Church on the subject of Jesus's birth and parentage, and he explicitly states that Jesus was of the House of David, an ancestry traceable through the line of Joseph but not through that of Mary (Matt. i, 1–16). There is no suggestion here of a virgin birth. On the contrary, it is obvious from his words that the Apostle to the Gentiles believed that Jesus was the son of Joseph according to the flesh, but that his high spiritual attainment, culminating in the resurrection, entitled him to be thought of as the son of God: a whole and perfect man.

In the first gospel to be written, that of Mark (*circa* A.D. 70–100), who was supposed to have had his information direct from Peter, the intimate of the Master, there is no mention whatever of the Nativity which, had it happened as Matthew and Luke afterwards recorded it, would have been among the most miraculous events of the life of Jesus Christ,

81

and therefore of infinite importance to his devoted disciple. Nor is there any reference to it in the gospel of John (*circa* 90–110) which, although it was almost certainly not actually written by the beloved disciple, may be supposed to be based upon information provided by him. And he who knew both Jesus and his mother so intimately would hardly have failed to mention an event of such moment and significance that would obviously have been frequently referred to by Mary whom, at the request of her dying son, John had taken to live with him.

It is only in Matthew (*circa* 100–110), and Luke (*circa* 100), written after the eclectic thought of the missionizing Church had added its garnerings to the original Gospel teachings, that we find the Nativity stories, which not only differ and savour strongly of pagan myths, but are also somewhat puzzlingly discredited by the addition of the genealogical table in Matthew which seeks to prove historically that Jesus was the son of Joseph, and therefore a remote descendant of David. This in itself constitutes a very good reason to suppose that the Nativity stories were later additions to the original data, made by zealots who, as a result of missionary endeavours among the heathen, may have felt that the God-man of what was hoped would one day be the universal religion, must not be allowed to appear less divine than the gods and heroes he would be superseding.

As we know, the idea of a God mating with a mortal woman was a very familiar one with both Greeks and Romans. The ancient warrior-heroes and men of outstanding genius or achievement, as well as Emperors such as Julius and Augustus, were almost invariably said to have been the offspring of one of the deities. Dionysos, Perseus, Ra, Atys, Zoroaster were all supposed to have been born of a god and a virgin. Zoroaster, according to the later Avesta, had also prophesied that a saviour was to arise born of his seed and that of a virgin.

This prophecy, perpetuated in Mithraism, must early have caught the attention of the rival Church whose scribes seem to have drawn heavily on Mithraic sources in the compilation of their Nativity stories. For Mithras, the rock-born, had, also, as we have seen, been worshipped by shepherds, and the Magi were the wise men of Persia![1] The legend of the Massacre of the Innocents, as recorded in the New Testament, must be historically suspect, for Herod died in the year 4 B.C., and no mention of what would have been his supreme crime is made by Josephus who had so carefully compiled a list of all his others. It would there-fore seem to be a resuscitation either of the Zoroastrian story, or of Pharoah's attempt to kill all the first-born of the Israelites at the time of the infancy of Moses—a recurrent horror story, like those that are put about concerning the enemy in modern wars. No secret is made of the fact that the date of Jesus's birth has never been known to the Church; but it is curious that Mithras' official natal day should have been deliberately chosen as the date on which to celebrate the birth of his rival, especially when we consider at how late a period, according to Chrysostom who died in A.D. 407, it was added to the Christian Calendar. In Hom. XXXI he states that the reason for the choice of this date of Christ's birthday, that had *lately* been fixed at Rome, was that "while the heathen were busied with their own profane ceremonies, the Christians might perform their holy rites without molestation".[2]

Incidentally one of the "profane" ceremonies with which the heathen busied themselves to celebrate the Birthday of the Invincible One was that of the perennially popular circus, described as *The Great Games of the Circus*. On one occasion it was recorded that twenty-four con-secutive races of chariots were exhibited in the Circus Maximus.

[1] Indeed, the story of the Magi would appear to have been taken bodily from a passage in the Zend-Avesta which reads:

"You, my children, shall be the first honoured by the manifestation of that divine person who is to appear in the world: a Star shall go before you to conduct you to the place of his nativity; and when you shall find him present to him your oblations and sacrifices; for he is indeed your lord and an everlasting king."

[2] *The Gnostics and Their Remains* by C. W. King.

It is deeply ironical that the profane ceremonies of the heathen have been so eagerly and whole-heartedly adopted by a once pious and austere Christendom which despised such revellings; although the modern Boxing Day Circus is but a mild climax to the orgy of commercialism and whole-sale massacre of birds and beasts, followed by the gluttony and self-indulgence by means of which our present-day "Christendom" appears to imagine it is fitly celebrating the Christ-mass, the appearance on earth of the Perfect Man.

The Baptism.

Two of the most important rites both for the Mithraists and the Early Christians were Baptism and a communal meal, but whereas the Mithraic Baptism appears to have been one of the Twelve Trials through which the initiate had to pass to gain a place in the Cave of Mithras, for the Christian, it was the one essential condition for membership in the Early Church, and for being admitted to the fellow-ship meal which was intended to be a sort of communion of saints partaken only by those finally purged of the sins of the flesh.

In the Gospel of Mark, the first to be written, the ministry of Jesus Christ is pictured as having started with this all-important rite:

> And it came to pass . . . that . . . Jesus was baptized of John in Jordan. And straightway coming up out of the water . . . there came a voice from heaven, saying, Thou art my beloved son in whom I am well pleased. And immediately the spirit driveth him into the wilderness. And he was there in the wilderness forty days, tempted of Satan . . .

This account implies that the Baptism of Jesus Christ was much more than a ritualistic immersion in water. It is indeed a universal and essential spiritual experience, and was recognized as such by the early Christians, many of whom believed that the Master's spiritual life commenced at the time of his baptism and not at his nativity. In his Eighteenth Epistle to the Bishops of Sicily, Pope Leo, in the middle of the fifth century A.D., was having to rebuke members of the Church for believing that Jesus was "born of the Holy Ghost" at the time of his Baptism, a theory which would have conflicted embarrassingly with the later so laboriously built up Nativity stories and all the ceremony that went with them. But the earlier belief must have been generally held, for Chrysostom writes firmly: "It was not when he was born that He became manifest to all, but when he was baptized," and this was undoubtedly true in the sense that it was at this moment that Jesus appears to have had his faith confirmed that he was in very truth the son of the Highest; this being the result of having achieved the state of total purification essential to such realization.

Thus Jesus transcended and transformed the earlier concept of Baptism. John is said to have preached "the baptism of repentance for the remission of sins". This was the ritualistic idea of doing penance and being cleansed of current sins; but he said of Jesus: "I indeed have baptized you with water; but he shall baptize you with the Holy Ghost," with the whole Spirit of Goodness which, suffusing the being, would remove all sense of sin and entirely regenerate the man. It was this inward total purification by Spirit that was the true Christian Baptism. Jesus submitted to the symbolic purification by water only after the inward purification was complete. John the Baptist evidently aimed at this ideal sense of Baptism, but lacked the Whole Spirit, the perfect knowledge that would ensure the inward transformation. Although it would seem that he afterwards advocated this higher concept, for in *Jewish Antiquities* xviii, v.2. Josephus quotes John the Baptist as teaching: "that Baptism would be acceptable to him (God) only in those who used it, not to escape from sins, but for purification of the body, if the soul also *had previously been thoroughly cleansed by righteousness.*" In other words it was not meant to be a mere ritualistic act but the outward and visible sign of an attained inward and spiritual grace.

It was to this true concept of baptism that Jesus was evidently referring when he said to a puzzled Nicodemus: "Except a man be born again he cannot see the Kingdom of God." Undoubtedly the reference was to his own rebirth which his early followers so rightly dated from the time of his baptism; for the total purification to which he attained gave him the inner assurance (the voice from the heaven within) that he was indeed the son of God in whom the Father was well pleased; and that recognition alone had made his ministry possible.

Except a man be born of water and of the Spirit, he cannot enter into the Kingdom of God.

The purification springing from the knowledge of his divine Selfhood, had enabled him to become aware of the Kingdom of God: of living in a spiritual atmosphere in which the law of harmony ruled supreme. Without this realization, this assurance, there could have been no ministry; and what was true for him was true for all men. Therefore he taught that it was essential for his followers to share this experience if they, too, would enter the Kingdom of God, abiding in the consciousness of the presence and power of Good.

For Jesus, the entire experience was a spiritual one, as is evident from the interview with Nicodemus. It was spiritual regeneration that was necessary; man being reborn, as the butterfly is reborn from the chrysalis, and no amount of physical immersion in water could ensure this.

It is explicitly stated in John iv, 2, that "Jesus himself baptized not, but his disciples." This was evidently an early example of the Church materializing a spiritual teaching and so eventually losing the meaning of it. The disciples would have known that John, the Essene, baptized with water—the outward symbol which must give place to the inward rebirth ("He must increase, but I must decrease," John iii, 30)—and that Jesus had once submitted to this outward expression of the all-important inward cleansing of the soul. Therefore, this symbolical ceremony that had been done once for the example of all men was retained as the initiatory ceremony into the Early Church. At first it was clearly understood, as we see from Chrysostom's comment, that the outward rite only symbolized the all-important inward cleansing, the complete surrender of the life and will to God, the putting on of the Mind of Christ; therefore, to sin after Baptism was inexcusable, as it denied the thoroughness of the purification. Nevertheless temptation was inevitable. It is noticeable from Mark's account that immediately Jesus had experienced his rebirth and assurance of his divine sonship, he was tempted of the devil, the Father of Lies, the spirit of negation, to believe that he was something less than the Perfect Man. But every temptation was firmly resisted, thus proving the Master to be without sin. These tests were inevitable, even for the reborn; but they had the Master's example as to how they could be overcome. As E. W. Barnes tells us in *The Rise of Christianity*:

> The baptized convert was "in Christ" . . . As we read the Pauline letters and the Epistle to the Hebrews, we are left with the impression that the writers believed that he who was in Christ could not fall into sin.

Certainly those who had actually put on the Mind of Christ could not do so, but obviously such spiritual evolution was rare, and many that were baptized were later proved to have been too optimistic about their own spiritual state. The penalties for lapsing seem to have been rather severe, and eventually so many became doubtful of their capacity to resist temptation after Baptism that they put off this ceremony until their death-beds, thus showing the degeneration of the original concept of Baptism, the rite having become a magical means whereby sins were remitted by external pardon instead of being the outward and visible sign that those sins had been purposefully and finally abandoned by the baptized person. This perversion of the original meaning must have come from priests who had in

the course of time allied their concepts of baptism with
those of other and less pure creeds, especially that of Mithraism which, as we have seen in an earlier chapter, did have
a form of baptism *for the remission of sins.*

It is a great deal easier to have one's sins remitted by
a sacramental rite than by a thorough, self-imposed cleansing
of the inner man; and the easier method of their ideological
rivals would have weighed heavily in the Mithraists'
favour in the struggle for capturing the allegiance of the
multitude. There can be no doubt whatever that compromise
eventually led to complete perversion and misunderstanding
of the orginal idea of baptism, for, in the course of time, even
the dead could be baptized by proxy with the blessings of
the church (1 Cor. xv, 29, 30), and infant baptism was
instituted, both practices being wholly incompatible with
the demand for self-purification and rebirth. Neither has
the sprinkling of water and the mark of the cross on the
forehead of modern usage any connexion with the total
immersion practised and advocated in the Gospels. But in
Mithraism there was such a rite, and the mark on the
forehead of initiates was, as we see from the citation on
page 43, commented upon by Tertullian whose description
of the Mithraic baptism is that of the Catholic Church of
the present day and not that of John or Jesus, a fact which
indicates that the mimicry ascribed to the devil was equally
active in the Early Church.

But the baptism of the Mithraists that was a feature of
their Twelve Trials was the baptism of blood, whereby the
initiates identified themselves with their God who was at
once the slayer of the Bull and the Bull that was slain.
Bearing this in mind, it is not difficult to see how the original
teaching of Jesus which, like that of all the greatest world-
teachers, was of salvation through self-purification and
God-realization, became superseded by the demoralizing
doctrine of vicarious atonement, or salvation through the
saviour's blood. This deviation is most noticeably traceable
in the Epistle to the Hebrews to whose audience the arguments would be familiar from the primitive past of this

race, with its hideous habits of animal sacrifice so detestable to the higher sense of God entertained by Jesus and the major prophets. It is discernible also in the Epistles of Paul, and 1 John i, 7; v, 6, 8, all leading thought back to the pagan and primitive belief in salvation through vicarious atonement instead of through the total purification of consciousness symbolized by the baptism of water and of spirit, explicitly taught by the Master. For this was found to be too difficult. There must be a simpler and less painful route if Christianity were to be the universal Faith visualized by such zealots as Paul. Even if in the process it ceased to be Christianity. The situation could hardly be better stated than it was by Sir James George Frazer when in *The Golden Bough*, he spoke of "Shrewd ecclesiastics who clearly perceived that if Christianity was to conquer the world it could do so only by relaxing the too rigid principles of its Founder, by widening a little the narrow gate which leads to salvation." And then went on to draw a parallel between the history of Christianity and that of Buddhism, saying:

Both systems were in their origin essentially ethical reforms born of the generous ardour, the lofty aspirations, the tender compassion of their noble Founders, two of those beautiful spirits who appear at rare intervals on earth like beings come from a better world to support and guide our weak and erring nature. Both preached moral virtue as the means of accomplishing what they regarded as the supreme object of life, the eternal salvation of the individual soul. . . . But the austere ideals of sanctity which they inculcated were too deeply opposed, not only to the frailties but to the natural instincts of humanity ever to be carried out in practice by more than a small number of disciples. . . . If such faiths were to be nominally accepted by whole nations or even by the world, it was essential that they should first be modified or transformed so as to accord in some measure with the prejudices, the passions, the superstitions of the vulgar. This process of accommodation was carried out in after ages by followers who, made of less ethereal stuff than their masters, were for that reason the better fitted to mediate between them and the common herd. Thus, as time went on, the two religions, in exact proportion to their growing popularity, absorbed more and more of those baser elements *which they had been instituted for the very purpose of suppressing.*[1]

But the "absorption" started early in the history of Christianity. In Paul's Epistle to the Romans vi, 3–5, we are confronted with the conception of baptism which was to become the canonical version. For Jesus it had meant just one thing, the total purification essential to a higher concept of life; the rebirth whereby man recognized himself as the son of God; the process of spiritual evolution. But Paul was now linking it up with the death of Jesus on the cross. The followers of the Perfect Man must now identify themselves with his death in order that they might have hope in the resurrection from the dead and live with him. This may have been merely another way of saying that they must put off the old man (slough the earthly chrysalis) and put on the new man (emerge as the butterfly) "which after God is made in righteousness and true holiness" (Ephesians iv, 22–24), but it was very unfortunate that he should have used that particular symbolism, for Mithras, in his *role* of Bull, or Life, was slain, pierced in his side with a sword, and his followers were enthusiastically baptized in the regenerative life-blood. Here we see clearly enough the absorption of the pagan idea, which while it might have been good for the purpose of attracting converts from the pagan ranks, was fatal to the maintenance of the original Christian concept of Baptism in its purity. Throughout the Pauline Epistles we find this harping on the death aspect of the baptismal rite, which led directly to the morbid identification of the initiate with the suffering Christ (instead of with the risen, purified, triumphant son of God), that has always been so stressed by the Catholic Church. And Paul's viewpoint appears to have been eagerly adopted, as perhaps was

[1] *The Golden Bough,* vol 5.

inevitable when he was dealing with pagans and with Jews whose past history was so continually involved with primitive blood-sacrifices. We also find the same idea in the First Epistle General of Peter.

Reading this scholarly message with the figure of the simple, impetuous fisherman described in the four Gospels in mind, and remembering the explicit statement in Acts iv, 13, that both Peter and John were *unlearned* men, it is unthinkable that it could have been written by the Apostle himself. Its style is not unlike that of Paul, and it was almost certainly written by an intellectual dignitary of the Early Church.

No one pretends that the Second Epistle was written by Peter. It has been dated much later, about A.D. 150, and nothing is officially known about its authorship; but the opening paragraph, coupled with an illuminating sentence in George Lamsa's Introduction to Mark's Gospel, provides us with a clue. The Second Epistle opens with the words:

> Simon Peter, a servant and an apostle of Jesus Christ, to them that have obtained like precious faith with us through the righteousness of God and our Saviour Jesus Christ.

And Lamsa, after reminding us that the author of the First Epistle wrote from "the church that is in Babylon", went on to say: "It is interesting to note that the Patriarch of the Church in the East whose See was at Seleucia, Persia, assumed the title Shimon Peter (Simon Peter), and this title has been carried to the present day."[1]

It is therefore possible that the writer of the First Epistle also merely assumed the name of Peter. If this was not the case, either the second paragraph was edited by one who had been infected by Paul's later interpretation of the rite of Baptism, or the Apostle's concept of the creed of Christ must have been strangely changed since the days when his Master walked the earth. It is noticeable, too,

[1] *Gospel Light* by George M. Lamsa. (A. J. Holman Company.)

that he is writing to Pontus, the headquarters of Mithraism from whence it permeated the Western world. The opening paragraph runs:

> Peter, an apostle of Jesus Christ, to the strangers scattered through Pontus, Galatia, Cappadocia, Asia and Bithynia, elect according to the foreknowledge of God, the Father, through sanctification of the Spirit unto obedience and sprinkling of the blood of Jesus Christ.

As we know, there was no suggestion whatever of the sprinkling of blood in the concept of Baptism as taught by Jesus Christ, such a rite, which belonged to primitive Judaism, being one of the things that the new religion had undoubtedly "been instituted for the very purpose of suppressing" (to quote Fraser), to judge by Isaiah's condemnation of animal sacrifices hundreds of years previously, and Jesus's own purging of the Temple. On the other hand, the Baptism of Blood was one of the most distinctive features of Mithraism, and was still being practised at the time when the Epistle of Peter was written, this horrible custom being described by C. W. King, in the words:

> The Taurobolium, or Baptism of Blood, during the later years of the Western Empire, held the foremost place as the means of purification from sin, however atrocious. Prudentius has left a minute description of this horrible rite in which the person to be regenerated, being stripped of his clothing, descended into a pit which was covered with planks pierced full of holes; a bull was slaughtered upon them, whose hot blood, streaming down through these apertures (after the fashion of a shower bath) thoroughly drenched the recipient below. The selection of the particular victim proves this ceremony to be in connexion with the Mithraica, which latter, as Justin says, had a "Baptism for the remission of sins"; and the Bull being in that religion the recognizable

emblem of life, his blood necessarily constituted the most effectual laver of regeneration.[1]

This, then, may be presumed to have been the genesis of the idea found both in the Pauline Letters and the First Epistle of Peter, as it is undoubtedly the antecedent of the modern bull-ring so curiously permitted in Roman Catholic countries where the Pope has supreme influence over the policies of the people. And clearly it has no connexion whatever with the Creed of Christ. It is ironical to reflect that reference to the redeeming blood of Jesus Christ still met with in the teachings of orthodox Christianity, and the repellent references to rivers of blood found in the hymnals of the Salvation Army, stem not from the teachings of Jesus but from the Mithraic Taurobolium.

The Miracle of the Marriage in Cana.

In Matthew ii, 23, we read that Jesus "came and dwelt in a city called Nazareth that it might be fulfilled which was spoken by the prophets, He shall be called a Nazarene."

This is an odd and most unsatisfactory statement for we shall search the Old Testament in vain for any prophecy referring to the Messiah as a Nazarene. In addition, there seems to be a definite doubt as to whether a place called Nazareth existed at the time of Jesus Christ's birth. George Lamsa remarks in his book, *Gospel Light* that no town of that name was mentioned in the Old Testament; while Arthur Weigall writes:

> Many critics have argued that there was no such place as Nazareth, for, outside the Bible, there is no reference to it as a village either before the Christian era or in the first three centuries A.D.[2]

He goes on to suggest that the name was invented at a later date, and attached to an appropriate village, in an

[1] *The Gnostics and Their Remains.*
[2] *The Paganism in Our Christianity* by Arthur Weigall. (Hutchinson & Co. Ltd.)

attempt to explain the fact that Jesus was often called, "The Nazarite".

But the actual and far simpler reason for this designation would appear to have been that Jesus was, in fact, a member of the sect of Jewish holy men known as Nazarites or Nazarenes.

These saintly and separated men, of whom Samson was one until Delilah persuaded him to break his vow of continence, were dedicated to God before they were born; and it is quite possible that Mary, the mother of Jesus, a member of a priestly house, and, like the rest of her people, eagerly awaiting the promised Messiah, may have so dedicated the child that was to be born to her, in her prayers. It would explain the passages in Luke ii, 19, 51, where she is said to have pondered the incidents of the Nativity, and kept all the sayings of Jesus in her heart. Such words do not suggest the confident assurance of a woman who knows that she has given birth to a Messiah, but a watchful woman alert to any signs that her prayers had been answered. Had she afterwards mentioned to any of the disciples that before his birth she had dedicated her child to God, this might easily have provided the nucleus for the eventually authorized Nativity stories, when the simple fact had been recounted from mouth to mouth, worked upon and elaborated as is the custom with stories in the East, until it reached the point where it could be identified with the prophecy of Zoroaster.

And there is indeed plenty of evidence to suggest that Jesus was a Nazarene. By other Jews his first followers were always referred to as Nazarenes, as in Acts xxiv, 5. It was only by the Gentiles that they were called Christians.

In his *The Authentic New Testament*, translated from the Greek, Dr. Hugh J. Schonfield renders the passage that in the King James's version runs: "I am Jesus of Nazareth whom thou persecutest" (Acts xxii, 8) as, "I am Jesus the Nazarene whom you are hunting". And, again, in Mark i, 23 he translates: "What have we to do with thee, thou Jesus of Nazareth?" as "What do you want with us, Jesus the

Nazarene?" Finally, and most conclusively he tells us that the teachings of the Sermon on the Mount were those of the sect of Nazarenes.

Yet the statement from Matthew ii, 23, would appear to be trying to cover up the fact of his connexion with this sect, as though, for some reason, it were better not known. And, as we shall see, there might well have been a very good reason, certain teachings and actions of the Sun-God not being in the least compatible with the conduct of a Nazarite.

The behaviour and beliefs of the Nazarenes and the Essenes[1] were said to be similar. They were the ascetics of Judaism, and neither shaved, married, nor used strong drink. Writing of the Essenes Philo tells us that they "give innumerable demonstrations by their constant and un-alterable holiness throughout the whole of their life, their avoidance of oaths and falsehoods, and by their firm belief that God is the source of all good but of nothing evil. Of their love of virtue they give proofs in their contempt for money, fame, and pleasure; their continence and endurance; in their satisfying their wants easily; in their simplicity, cheerfulness of temper, modesty, order, firmness, etc. As instances of their love to man are to be mentioned their benevolence, equality and their having all things in common."[2]

"Their constant and unalterable holiness" certainly describes the conduct of the chief Character of the Gospels. "Their avoidance of oaths" calls to mind the injunction in the Sermon on the Mount "to swear not at all . . . but let your communication be yea, yea, nay, nay; for whatsoever is more than these cometh of evil;" while the firm belief

---

[1] After comparing the beliefs and practices of the Essenes with those of the primitive Christians, in an essay on the Essenes, published in 1864, Dr. Christian Ginsburg wrote: "It will therefore hardly be doubted that our Saviour himself belonged to the holy brotherhood." The similarity of the two sects could easily lead to this mistake. But to accept Dr. Ginsburg's statement, it would be necessary to ignore all the pointed references to Jesus as a Nazarene. John the Baptist was almost certainly an Essene, but it is obvious that the two men did not belong to the same sect.

[2] Quoted from *Dictionary of Christian Biography*, by Smith and Wace.

that God is the source of all good, but of nothing evil was implicit in every act of Jesus Christ and explicit in the statement (James i, 17):

> Every good gift and every perfect gift is from above, and cometh down from the Father of Lights, with whom is no variableness, neither shadow of turning.

A further interesting piece of information on the subject of the Nazarites comes from the essay on Ancient Judaism by the Rev. H. W. Oxford in *Religious Systems of the World*, where he writes:

> From the story of Samson, and Amos xi, 11, 12, we see that they abstained from drinking wine and cutting their hair, i.e. they avoided all connexion with the cult of ancestors.

From Numbers vi, 2, to which the last words refer, we find that the Nazarites "separate themselves unto the Lord" which seems to imply that they relinquish their fleshly parentage and cleave to their spiritual origin, devoting themselves wholly to the things of the Spirit. This would explain what have always seemed to be hard sayings of the Master:

> Call no man your father upon the earth: for one is your Father which is in heaven (Matthew xxiii, 9)

(a peculiar teaching by one whose race had always made so much of human parentage and procreation, and which set such a store on obedience to the fifth Clause of the Mosaic Decalogue); and the reply when one of the disciples asked the Master to allow him to go and bury his father: "Follow me; and let the dead bury the dead" (Matthew viii, 22); such apparent callousness becoming understandable if Jesus was calling his disciples to be Nazarites, in accordance with the instructions found in Numbers vi, 2–7.

All these factors, combined with Jesus's celibacy—in itself a very strong argument, for except in the case of holy and separated men, members of some ascetic sect, it was considered a sacred duty by orthodox Jews to beget children, and according to the Mosaic Law one of the greatest curses was leaving no offspring to carry on the family name—point to the conclusion that Jesus was, in fact, what in Acts xxiv, 5, was so clearly implied, a Nazarite. And if this was the case, the story of the Miracle at Cana cannot possibly be true of the Galilean Teacher. As it appears only in one Gospel, the probability is that it was written in by one accustomed to the worship of the Sun-God who would see nothing wrong in the Perfect Man of his faith indulging in or providing intoxicants.

But this was far from being the Judaic concept of sanctity. And in commenting on this incident, George Lamsa, the Assyrian writer and lecturer who has convinced ethnologists that the customs and language of the tribe into which he was born have not changed since the times of Jesus Christ, tells us that Holy Men were, and still are, bidden to marriage feasts that they may restrain the conduct of the guests who, on such occasions, have access to an unaccustomed amount of strong drink. He writes:

Religious men who attended banquets not only decline to purchase wine for the guests but also urge the guests to stop drinking because they fear drunkenness which, as often happens, results in quarrels and perhaps murder. Generally religious men do not drink. They try to pacify guests who insist on more wine. . . . Jesus had divine power but would he use it to supply more wine to guests who had already been drinking too much? The scriptures condemn drunkenness. (I Cor. vi, 10.)[1]

Yet the New Testament account reads:

The third day there was a marriage in Cana of Galilee; and the mother of Jesus was there; and both

[1] *Gospel Light*, George M. Lamsa. (A. J. Holman Company.)

Jesus was called, and his disciples, to the marriage. And
when they wanted wine, the mother of Jesus saith unto
him, They have no wine. Jesus saith unto her, Woman
what have I to do with thee? Mine hour is not yet come.
His mother saith unto the servants, Whatsoever he saith
unto you, do it. And there were set there six waterpots
of stone. Jesus saith unto them, Fill the waterpots with
water, and they filled them up to the brim. And he saith
unto them, Draw out now, and bear unto the governor
of the feast. And they bare it. When the ruler of the feast
had tasted the water that was made wine . . . the governor
of the feast called the bridegroom, and saith unto him,
Every man at the beginning doth set forth good wine;
and when men have well drunk, then that which is
worse: but thou hast kept the good wine until now.
(John ii, 1–11.)

The last sentence makes it obvious that the guests had
already reached the fuddled state which blurred their
discrimination as to the quality of the wine. Is it conceivable
that the Perfect Man of the Christian Faith would deliberately encourage intoxication? Such an act belongs to the
worshippers of Soma or Bacchus. And even if the water
turned wine was rendered non-intoxicant by some magical
power resembling a conjuring trick, this miracle, in that it
encouraged a wrong habit and the belief that intoxication
was permissible, would still be unworthy of one who stood
for the model of perfection, and used his divine power for
the far more worthy and noble purposes of healing the sick,
sinful, blind and maimed, and raising the dead. It is noteworthy, as Lamsa points out, that when Jesus answered
John the Baptist's query as to whether he was the Messiah
by relating his works, he did not include the wine-miracle.
The other exhibitions of Divine Power were consistent with
the teaching of an all-beneficent God of Love whose will
for man was unchanging good, and whose over-ruling law
was that of harmony. But to pander to a carnal appetite
and worldly custom was in an entirely different and inferior

category, savouring more of the miracle man of the primitive Faiths than of a Teacher in the highest state of evolutionary consciousness.

On the other hand, wine-drinking has always been a feature of the worship and ritual of sun and nature gods. Oblations are drunk to the deity whose warmth and light turns the juice of the grape into wine; and this would appear to be the act symbolized in the story of the Miracle at Cana. In the form that it has come down to us it reads like a compromise between the Jewish conscience and Mithraic custom; for Jesus is first recorded as rebuking his mother for making the suggestion that he should transform the water, saying, Woman, my hour has not yet come, inferring that such an act was not worthy of the evocation of Divine Power. But finally the nature of the Sun-God triumphed. It was inevitable that his very presence should have transformed water into wine, and his disciples, with the reaction not of ascetic holy men but of followers of Mithras-Dionysos, were reported to have been impressed and convinced of the nature of their Lord by this miracle.

The Roman Catholic Church, whose prelates have apparently never seen anything inconsistent in this miracle with the highest ethical conduct, has a special day on its calendar for its celebration; and curiously enough, has chosen the same date as that on which the pagans celebrated the Miracle of Andros in their worship of Bacchus— 6 January. In this month a fountain in the island of Andros was said to yield wine during the yearly festival in honour of the god.

The miracle of Cana, and the partaking of wine in the Eucharist have naturally confused the thought of Christians on the subject of intoxicants, and probably account to a great extent for the alcoholism of what was once geographically Christendom. A Church which uses wine in its rites, and whose monks and supposedly holy men actually fabricate strong *liqueurs*, such as Chartreuse and Benedictine, can hardly hope to lead their congregations to abstinence.

There is, however, as we see, a strong case for supposing that this laxity is not due to the teachings and example of Jesus Christ, but to the cult of Mithras that adulterated and supplemented his teachings.

The Cursing of the Fig Tree.

And when he saw a fig tree in the way, he came to it, and found nothing thereon, but leaves only, and said unto it, Let no fruit grow on thee henceforth for ever. And presently the fig tree withered away. (Matthew xxi,19.)

Here is another incident that must have proved puzzling to many whose concept of the Christ was that of an invariably compassionate Saviour. Such a ruthless, impatient act is so completely unlike the impression we get from the Gospels, of a patient, loving healer of men, even though we dismiss the statement in one of the Gospels that it was not the season for figs, since, as George Lamsa reminds us, the leaves and fruit of a fig tree appear at the same time.

It may just be that as the tree bore leaves and no fruit, it had become barren, and Jesus was attempting to show, as in the Parable of the Talents, that those who did not contribute to life, did not properly perform their appointed task, or who professed to be what they were not, like the Pharisees of his time, had no place on the earth. In which case it has been imperfectly recorded and remains an untypical act of the Master, for, as Lamsa points out, it was the custom of travellers to take the fruit from the trees as they passed, and this tree might already have given its fruit.

On the other hand, the story is perfectly understandable as a Sun-God myth. For what is it that withers the fig or any other tree but the sun? And if a tree fails to obey, fails to respond to the sun, it is already dead or dying. As an illustration for the necessity of obedience to the Sun-God such an incident might well belong to the Cult of Mithras. As it stands, it makes no sense as part of the original Creed of Christ, the Creed of Compassion.

The Sabbath Day.

The Sabbath was made for man, and not man for the Sabbath. (Mark ii, 27.)

When Jesus said: "Think not that I am come to destroy the law, or the prophets: I am not come to destroy, but to fulfil," he meant, if we are to judge by his conduct, that he came to show men how to exceed the letter of the law, to give a more perfect obedience to the commandments; to obey them more fully. But, sometimes, especially in the case of the fourth and fifth clauses, this fuller obedience appeared to the superficial observer to be a flouting of the law. This is particularly true of the fourth commandment relating to the keeping of the Sabbath Day.

At the time when it was conceived it was thought to be an inspired teaching. The seventh day was to be one of rest with and in the Eternal, who also, it was believed, had ceased from work on that day. It was to be a day when the released slave-workers from Egypt were to have the privilege not only of ceasing from toil and experiencing the freedom of rest, but also of "turning in the will to God", and "thinking only the thoughts of God". This exalted concept was evidently in the mind of the writer in the Talmud who wrote: "If all of Israel observed the Sabbath day fully only once, the Messiah would be here."

But this high ideal had certainly not been maintained, and in Jesus's day the observance of the Sabbath had deteriorated into a fantastic number of material prohibitions, and far from thinking the thoughts of God, there were constant wranglings about such niceties of the law as whether one should be permitted to carry a handkerchief on the holy day. In that state it came into the category of "the superstititious observance of days", which in itself made it completely irreconcilable with the Gospel of Jesus who came to teach that every thought on every day of every week must be of God, and that man should entirely surrender to His Will and be perfect as the Father was perfect.

To such a perfectionist the setting aside of one day in the

week for such purposes was to defraud God and abandon the way of salvation. He felt so strongly on this point that twice in the Gospels he is shown to have flouted the letter of this particular Mosaic Law, though well knowing what the penalty might be. According to Matthew xii, both incidents took place on the same day, first, as Jesus and his disciples walked in a cornfield plucking the grain, and then in the synagogue where he healed a man with a withered hand; and it was recorded that this behaviour on the Sabbath was so heinous in the eyes of the beholders that "they went out and held a council against him, how they might destroy him".

But until Jesus had broken down this pagan idea of dedicating certain days to God, he could not hope to get the people to accept the necessity of every day being a holy day, wholly and completely surrendered to God. Yet nothing less than this could lead to the evolution, or salvation, of mankind.

It would appear that the Early Church Fathers understood and accepted this point of view; for Origen observes in *Against Celsus* viii 22: "to the perfect Christian all his days are the Lord's"; and Irenaeus, in the second century writes in *Against Heresies* that Jesus cancelled observance of the Sabbath, while Tertullian in his *Answer to Jews* states that "to Christians Sabbaths are unknown".

But when Christianity became the official religion of the Roman Empire it had to conform to the customs of the Imperial city and, as in many other cases, to do in Rome as Romans do. And the Mithraic Roman always celebrated the Lord's day, or Sun-day. Before his conversion, indeed, Constantine made the keeping of Sunday as a day of rest compulsory, and spoke of it as "the venerable day of the Sun". His subjects were used to this weekly festival and would resent its absence; therefore it had to be included in the worship of the new God.

In addition to this fact, the Christians, according to the Didache, had from the start, taken to meeting together on the first day of the week in memory of their Lord's resurrection, and to partake of a communal meal. So gradually Sunday came to be generally accepted as a special, or holy day, which was the very idea Jesus had tried to replace with a higher.

In the first centuries Christian worship was mingled with holiday making on the Lord's Day, as it is in the Roman Catholic Church today. But the Protestants have gone right back to the Sabbatarian concept of Moses and the Pharisees in their observance of the Sabbath; and the practice of Mithraism is once more preferred to the example of Jesus Christ. It is certainly far easier to be pious for one day than to strive to put on the Mind of Christ for seven; but only the harder path can lead to the overcoming of this world and the attainment of the Kingdom of Heaven.

What God Hath Joined . . .

What God hath joined together, let not man put asunder.

Upon this instruction, with the accompanying teachings in Mark x and Matthew xix the Catholic Church has founded its divorce laws and what it has named the *sacrament* of marriage, or holy wedlock—in the majority of cases, as much a misnomer as "holy" wars. On this authority the institution of Christian marriage came into being, in spite of the fact that the New Testament instructions, if they were given by Jesus at all, were given to a polygamous audience.

It must often have been puzzling to students of religious history to find the celibate Teacher who was intended to be the Example in all things, legislating for the propagation of a world whose end he had predicted and confidently expected, teaching that it would be replaced by the Kingdom of Reality in which there would be no marrying:

People in this world marry and are married, but those who are considered worthy to attain yonder world and the resurrection from the dead neither marry nor are married . . . and by sharing in the resurrection they are sons of God. (Luke xx, 34–37.)

Here is an explicit statement that son-of-Godhood cannot
be achieved by those who are still marrying and giving in
marriage, nor could the "world yonder" that he had come
to reveal to them be attained by those in this carnal state
of consciousness, but only by those who are resurrected
from the chrysalis of their earthliness and animalism, so
obtaining a higher concept of life.

But from whence came this emphatic conviction that in
heaven, the perfect state, there could be no marriage?

Illumination was recently cast on the subject in the
course of a Third Programme Talk on the BBC by Professor
David Daube, an authority on Judaism, entitled *The
Gospels and the Rabbis*, when he pointed out that the command
"What God hath joined together, let not man put asunder",
referred to the statement in the first chapter of Genesis:
"male and female created he them", which was taken by
the ancient Rabbis to mean that the original and perfect
man, the Adam-Kadman of the Kabbala, made in the
image and likeness of the Whole male-female God, was
androgynous, and that "in the ideal creation, man and
woman had constituted one being".

It is obvious that in a perfect being male and female
attributes would be perfectly balanced, and this equipoise,
the blending of compassion with power, the constraining of
will by Love, and of Justice by mercy, is very noticeable in
the chief figure of the New Testament. Jesus was a celibate,
not as a discipline or as the result of taking the vows of a
Nazarite but because he was in a state of perfect equipoise,
whole, or holy, lacking nothing, and so not craving either
for male or female in order to experience completeness. He
was a citizen of what Professor Daube described as "the
ideal world, when male and female had been united", and
it was to this state of inner sufficiency, this wholeness, this
worthiness to enter into "yonder world", this evidence of
son-of-Godhood that he was calling mankind. He had
factually evolved to that state of completion and perfection
that had been held as an ideal in the consciousness of his
race since the first chapter of Genesis had been written.

But it was far from being confined to Jewish thought. The Yang and the Yin of Taoism expressed the same concept. There are other instances one could cite. In Plato's Symposium, Aristophanes speaks of androgynous beings that a cruel fate had cut in two and who ever after had frenziedly sought for their other half, in order to experience completion and fulfilment. In the Ophite text-book, we find: "The Man that is above is of both sexes," or, more explicitly, he "is neither male nor female, but a new creature"—a precognitive vision of evolutionary man. This is evidently the implication of the bisexual nature of the pagan Gods; especially stressed as we have already seen in the case of Mithras as the Persian Sun-God, before he forsook the "Woman" and degenerated into an all-masculine war-God under Imperialistic influences.

These concepts may be considered evolutionary anticipations of the character of the Perfect Man, seen in the gentle and wise Buddha 500 years before it was manifested by the compassionate and dynamic Jesus Christ. They were, and are, the signs of those who are taking, or have taken, the next step in spiritual evolution, and have arrived at a state of integration and equipoise, the result of completely outgrowing their animalism, craving and lust. It was to this perfect state that Jesus of Nazareth called humankind. And if Professor Daube was right in assuming that he had in mind the doctrine of the Ancient Rabbis when he quoted "male and female created he them", and "what . . . God hath joined together, let not man put asunder," he was surely reminding his listeners—the Pharisees, who would be certain to understand the allusion—of the true marriage, or welding of the male and female aspects in one being, which must never be severed, since such severance must result in both man and his universe becoming unbalanced—as they so obviously have. In this case, his words could not be taken to approve human marriage which entails an acknowledgement from both parties that they have severed the inward male and female, otherwise they would not be seeking the missing half externally.

Whether he gave the lesser teachings for the regulation of marriage and divorce as stated in Mark x and Matthew xix, or whether these were written in by embarrassed Christian Fathers who, since the end of the world had not come in an external form as had been so confidently expected, found themselves faced with the difficult task of legislating for the animalism of those who were still very much of this world, and occupied with perpetuating it, cannot now be known. But even if, by his words, Jesus catered for the unevolved elements in humanity, in his personal life he steadfastly manifested the true ideal. If men were to accept him as an example, and follow him, they must deny the fleshly concept of themselves, forsake their animalism and generate within consciousness that divine equipoise that would eliminate all craving, balancing the male power, strength, knowledge and will, with the female love, compassion, intuition and gentleness. And they must do this, as Paul afterwards explained, by putting off the carnal mind and putting on the Mind of Christ; in other words, by ceasing to identify themselves with the animal creation and thinking of themselves instead as the spiritual sons of God. Jesus Christ was the living proof that this method worked, and that this transformation could be made in the present life, and that now, as Paul put it, was the day of salvation, the day when man could consciously co-operate with the evolutionary urge and become a new and finer species, so being "saved" by the teaching and example of Jesus Christ from the distressing situation of the Centaur, the symbol of unevolved humanity's plight—the torso of *homo sapiens* striving to free itself from the animalism of its lower limbs.

This liberation has always been the aim and way of the higher religions, those which Dr. Albert Schweitzer has so uncomprehendingly designated as the world-negating systems, as distinct from the world-affirming variety found in different forms of sun and nature worship and in all forms of materialism. Dr. Schweitzer's designation is itself negative. Had he really understood the aims of the great Liberators, he would have used the term "world-transcendence", the substitution of a higher state for a lower. In the same sense, to speak of self-denial as part of the Christian way is a negative presentation of the positive aim of God-Realization of which self-noughting is a natural and inevitable effect. The attempt to achieve the effect without the cause, which has been the habit of Churchianity, accounts very largely for the failure of religion.

The world-affirming sun-worshippers, however, have always had a positive need of some sort of sexual regulation if that world were to be perpetuated in an orderly way. In addition, the Roman Mithraists needed what has since been called cannon-fodder, more and more well-disciplined Soldiers of Mithras, while the prospering Roman Church desired ever larger congregations. In neither case could the implications of Jesus's personal chastity and equipoise be profitably faced. Let those dedicated followers of the Galilean who understood the original teachings of their Master, and who aimed at achieving the divine balance, go into monasteries and nunneries and get on with their self-perfectioning. But the masses could only be held on a looser rein. Their animalism was too strong. It must be curbed but not completely outgrown. The Church would compassionately mediate between them and an Example too high for them to follow. It would soften the path of the weaker brethren—at a price; the price of thought-control. The Church would "interpret" the teachings of Jesus Christ, and the masses would accept that interpretation instead of going direct to the original source; and if that interpretation included some of the more earthbound beliefs of Mithraism, it was a merciful condescension of the Church to their unevolved condition.

Jesus Christ spoke to the Son of God in man; Mithraism spoke to the remains of the animal within him, to that part of him that was at home in this world, a world made beautiful and productive by the Sun, a world to which the animal within man clung even while the divinity within him sought desperately for something higher and more perfect than what, when the Sun no longer dazzled the eyes, could be plainly seen as a dark and fearsome jungle where on all sides life was sacrificed on the altar of life; the world that belonged to the animals but in which evolving man was a pilgrim and stranger, whose home was "yonder world" of which the Master had spoken and in the consciousness of which he lived; a world whose inhabitants constituted one perfect being, male and female, joined in full God-Realization, and which no whole, or holy man, would ever wish to put asunder.

The Purging of the Temple.

There are two different accounts of this incident, those of Matthew and Mark are similar but that of John differs in that it introduces the detail of the scourge.

Mark's record (Moffatt's version) is as follows:

> Then they came to Jerusalem and entering the Temple he (Jesus) proceeded to drive out those who were buying and selling inside the temple; he upset the tables of the money-changers and the stalls of those who sold doves, and would not allow anyone to carry a vessel through the temple; also he taught them, "Is it not written," he asked, "my house should be called a house of prayer for all nations? You have made it a den of robbers."

While John's version reads:

> Now the Jewish passover was near, so Jesus went up to Jerusalem. There he found, seated inside the temple, dealers in cattle, sheep and pigeons, also money-changers. Making a scourge of cords, he drove them all, sheep and cattle together out of the temple, scattered the coins of the brokers and upset their tables, and told the pigeon dealers, "Away with these! My Father's house is not to be turned into a shop." (John ii, 13–17.)

Whether this is an historical incident in the life of Jesus of Nazareth or not, the difference in the two accounts strongly suggests that they were written from hearsay, and

were not the reports of eye-witnesses. It will be noted that
in each case it is said that *Jesus* entered the temple, no reference being made to his followers, and the probability is
that whoever recorded the incident pieced different bits of
information together. What emerges from all the accounts
is that Jesus naturally and highly disapproved of the
trading in sacrificial birds and beasts in the house of his
loving Father. How could he, a spiritual heir of the compassionate prophet Isaiah, do otherwise? For the ritual
based on the primitive and horrible theory of vicarious
atonement, the scapegoat theory, which supposes that man
can atone for his wrong-doing by spilling the blood of
living creatures—a ritual still practised in Hindu temples
today—is a terrible and inhumane sight. It is said that such
temples reek like slaughter-houses and that the butcher-
priests' hands and arms are red with the blood of the
slaughtered birds and beasts. Small wonder that the compassionate Jesus "would not allow anyone to carry a vessel
through the temple," for those vessels contained the blood-
offering which the ignorant congregations were taught to
believe would ensure the remission of their sins. Truly the
priests who encouraged that belief and waxed rich on
the money obtained from such butchery, were robbers of the
worst kind, robbing the helpless birds and beasts of their
harmless lives, robbing their congregations of their salvation,
for there is nothing so deadening to the soul and conscience
of man as the theory of vicarious atonement, or the belief
that sin can be forgiven by any means other than by
ceasing to indulge it; and, finally, robbing the credulous of
their hard-earned money by promising them what it was
impossible to give by such means—forgiveness of their sins.

Possibly a synthesis of the two accounts gives a clearer
picture of what really happened than either taken alone,
but the account in John reads more simply and convincingly.
It is necessary to study this incident closely as it has been
constantly quoted by militarists and muscular Christians to
justify the use of violence in certain circumstances, a theory
which has resulted in a series of unchristian atrocities

perpetuated by so-called Christendom throughout the ages, from the Crusades and "holy" wars to the dropping of the atom bomb on Hiroshima.

Yet it was surely natural and inevitable when, seeing the vile traffic still going on in the temple after it had been explicitly forbidden by Isaiah's God-consciousness in the words:

> To what purpose is the multitude of thy sacrifices unto me? I delight not in the blood of bullocks, or of lambs or of he-goats. . . . When ye spread forth your hands I will hide mine eyes from you: your hands are full of blood. Wash you, make you clean . . . cease to do evil, learn to do well,

that Jesus, whose idea of salvation was precisely that of the older prophet, and whose compassionate heart always cast out suffering, should wish at once to put a stop to the butchery. In order to remove the animals it was necessary to use a scourge of small cords since this was the way beasts were herded at the time, but it was no more an act of violence than the use of a crook for the guiding of sheep in the right path. There is no hint that he used the scourge on his fellow men in a punitive manner. Obviously the herded animals in their emergence from the temple would have over-turned anything that impeded them, tables and money-bags and the chairs of the money-changers.

If John's version of the story is true, this is evidently what happened. The story, passing from lip to lip, might well have become embroidered, as such tales in the East invariably do, the impression being gained that Jesus himself overturned the tables. In this connexion it is interesting to note that George Lamsa, in his description of this scene, writes:

> He upset the *trays* of the money-changers. *There were no tables* and they are still unknown in the Orient. Money-changers sit on the ground, close to the walls of the houses.

The italics are mine. This evidence of faulty reportage strongly suggests that these accounts were written in or at least edited at a later date, by a non-Oriental, possibly a Roman theologian, at a time when it was recognized by the Church that a little of the Mithraic spirit was needed in the followers of Christ if Christianity were to conquer the world.

What is quite evident is that the use of physical violence in an endeavour to bring order out of chaos is utterly out of character with all the Master's teachings, and his acts both before and after the incident in the temple. Whereas the God with a scourge was a well-known pre-Christian figure.

It was perfectly in keeping with his creed of compassion that the Master should endeavour to put an end to the cruelty of animal sacrifices; but that he used violence in his attempt to do so is neither indicated in John's version of the incident, nor is it credible in view of what we know of his outlook and customary behaviour.

On the other hand, an exhibition of righteous wrath was very consistent with the character of Mithras; and it is certainly the modern followers of Mithras, and not those of Jesus Christ, who insist that this incident, and what we now find is the incorrect reporting of overturning a few tables and chairs, harming no one, condones the habit of mass homicide and the invention of H-bombs by those who take the name of Christ in vain, and at the same time demand his authority for, and approval of, their unspeakable atrocities.

The Miracles of Healing.

Then he called his twelve disciples together, and gave them power and authority over all devils, and to cure diseases. And he sent them to preach the kingdom of God, and to heal the sick.

These were the orders for the Christians, given to them by the Founder of their Faith. The orders given to the Soldiers of Mithras were to wound in the cause of their nation, and endure; to preach their Gospel by their example of endurance, hardiness and bravery, thus glorifying their insensitive warrior-God in their lives, and teaching others to become similarly indifferent to their own feelings and those of others.

The Mithraic discipline was not easy and seems to have involved the exercise of many virtues, yet they were far less thorough and difficult than those required of them whose duty it was to heal the sick by spiritual means. For that demanded not merely self-discipline but the complete self-noughting which enabled the Master-Healer to say: "I can of mine own self do nothing" (1 John v, 30) and: "the Father that dwelleth in me He doeth the works"; the divine humility involved in the practice of the presence of God, which surrenders the concept of a separate, limited human self for the realization of the one Divine Self, the source of all spiritual power.

This type of selflessness is inconceivable to those who aim, like the Mithraists, at perfecting the human self by mortifications of the flesh and other austerities rather than in wholly putting off "the old man, which is corrupt according to the deceitful lusts", and in putting on "the new man, which after God is created in righteousness and true holiness"—the wholeness which ensues when compassionate Love becomes inseparable from Power, mercy tempers justice, and intuition added to knowledge attains to Divine Wisdom.

Those who believe with the Modernists that the miracles of healing in the Gospels should be discarded as superstitious inventions of a credulous age, have not really perceived the nature of Christianity which is compassionate Love made practical in the affairs of men, the rule of the Kingdom of the God of Love established.

Jesus Christ was far from being of the opinion of the late Bishop Ernest William Barnes who considered that a miracle proved nothing but itself. On the contrary, the Man of Galilee believed that his healing works were the proof of the validity of his ministry and Messiahship:

If I do not the works of my Father, believe me not.
But if I do, though ye believe not me, believe the works:
that ye may know and believe that the Father is in me,
and I in Him. (John x, 37, 38.)

And when the disciples of John the Baptist asked him:
"Art thou he that should come?" he neither affirmed nor
denied but pointed to his works, allowing them to give a
conclusive answer for him:

Go and shew John again those things which ye do
hear and see: the blind receive their sight and the lame
walk, the lepers are cleansed and the deaf hear, the dead
are raised up . . .

He also cited the physical healings as providing evidence
of the actual presence of the Kingdom of God, the existence
of which it was his mission to teach:

If I cast out devils by the Spirit of God, then the
kingdom of God is come unto you.

Mithras and his followers completely lacked the Spirit
of God that heals the inharmonies of the natural world.
They could give no such proof of being actually in contact
with the Divine Power they worshipped. They planned to
conquer the world by force, and could have claimed that
their God induced in them animal courage, bravery,
insensitivity and ensured them the companionship and
brotherhood of the militarist, but his worship inspired in
them no tender, healing love, no compassion which alone
can save the inhabitants of the natural world from the
stark brutality of the animal kingdom in which they find
themselves. The Mithraists slaughtered the outward animal
to do honour to the blood-thirsty God whose tastes were so
similar to those of the Jewish Jehovah, but they did not
seek to overcome, as Jesus so triumphantly had, the animal
within, which permitted their callous, wholesale slaughter

of animals, and, in times of war, of men. We have only to imagine Jesus of Nazareth slaughtering a bull or a fellow creature to understand the immense, impassable gulf existing between Mithraism and true Christianity, and the folly and peril of ignoring that gulf and trying to reconcile the irreconcilable.

Not only did Jesus offer his healing power as tangible evidence of his own authority, but it was the test he set for all time of true discipleship: "He that believeth on me, the works that I do shall he do also."

Mithras' tests were the initiation rites, known as the "Twelve Tortures", endurance tests, to ensure the all-important "toughening" of the initiate.

The Creed of Christ sought to create the man of compassion; the cult of Mithras sought to induce the man of steel.

We have only to look about us today at the increasingly robot nature of those considered to be ideal citizens for the totalitarian state termitary to know which spirit animates the modern world that, while it is on the whole unwilling to call itself Christian, has not perceived that it is innately Mithraic.

Upon This Rock

I say unto you, that thou art Peter, and upon this rock I will build my church; and the gates of hell shall not prevail against it. And I will give unto thee the keys of the Kingdom of Heaven; and whatsoever thou shalt bind on earth shall be bound in heaven; and whatsoever thou shalt loose on earth shall be loosed in heaven.

It is upon these two short and most untypical paragraphs from the Gospel of Matthew (xvi, 18, 19) that the basis of that immense system, the Roman Catholic Church, has always rested. Yet a little thought must show them to provide an extremely flimsy foundation for an organization that depends for its authority upon the Christ-ordained rulership of Peter and his descendants.

The first most obvious objection to the historicity of this episode is that only in Matthew is it reported. As Professor E. O. James points out in *The Nature and Function of Priesthood*, its omission in Mark's Gospel is all the more extraordinary as, according to the Fathers, Peter was supposed to have dictated the Gospel to the writer and to have been with him in Rome. And surely if, during his ministry, Jesus had taken the momentous step of founding a Church, all the Gospel writers would have been aware of the fact and have recorded it at length, giving the greatest possible prominence to what would have been one of the most significant events in the life of their Master. Instead of which, we are left with this most casual of references in but one Gospel.

But a further, even graver, doubt as to the authenticity of this incident must be aroused by the reflection that had it actually taken place, had the Master really affirmed his intention of founding a Church, there would have been no reason for the almost unanimously held belief among the Christians of the first century that the end of the world would take place during their own lifetime. For the founding of a Church obviously implies the idea of permanency, and what purpose could be served by founding a Church in the brief space that, according to what was believed to be the Master's firm prophecy, remained before the end of all temporal things?

History as well as common sense makes it apparent that the Christian Church organization only became necessary when the prophecy showed no signs of being fulfilled, and ecclesiasticism, of which the reported words of Jesus so strongly savour, was just coming into its own, between A.D. 100 to 110 when the Gospel of Matthew is believed to have been written.

The moment must clearly have arrived when the more metaphysically-minded followers of Jesus Christ realized that their Lord's prophecy was meant to be taken in a spiritual sense, and that the end of the world, like the establishment of the Realm of God (actually a simultaneous process) must take place in the individual consciousness, and that the Master's words had merely implied that certain men, such as John the Divine, for instance, would have a vision of "a new heaven and a new earth" before they suffered physical death. Therefore an outward Church organization to spread, and if possible universalize, the new Faith was seen to be necessary.

But by the time the Gospel of Matthew came to be written Christianity had already come into contact with the ideas of its rival as can be seen by a careful study of the Epistles of Paul; and if there is one statement more than another in the Gospels that may be said to be an echo of Mithraism, it is that placed in the mouth of Jesus Christ when he is reported to have said:

"Thou art Peter, and upon this rock will I build my Church."

Mithras and the Rock might have been said to be synonymous. Rock-born, the Sun-God was always worshipped in caves carved from the Rock, and in such a *Specus Mithraeum* took place the rites of initiation including the sacrifice of the Bull, and the sacrament of Bread and Water, known as the Eucharist.

It was natural that Mithras should have his temples. He was the God of this world, and his followers believed that his Kingdom was for ever. Whereas the Teacher who had no place whereon to lay his head, who saw the world as transient and passing away, and whose Gospel was a way of life to be lived by those who wished to attain to the Realm of God instead of identifying themselves with the illusory life of the senses, would have seen no necessity for founding an organization to perpetuate his teachings which must be lived in the thought and lives of men, or be nowhere.

While he did not in any way connect this episode with Mithraic influence, Ernest William Barnes wrote: "It is probably a late addition of no historical value. . . . The theme of his (Jesus's) preaching was the Kingdom of God. His mission, as he conceived it, was to call men to join this kingdom: he had not set out to found a church. . . . He either expected that the kingdom would come with visible splendour in the near future, or else that its manifestation would be inward and spiritual."[1]

Since the Master explicitly stated that the kingdom of heaven was within man, the latter supposition is more likely to be the correct one.

Furthermore, the pun on the name of Peter could not have been made by Jesus if he spoke, as he is commonly believed to have done, in Aramaic; for the play on the words is only possible by the use of the Greek word Petros.

But this is a trivial inconsistency compared with the obviously unhistoric utterance attributed to Jesus, and, ironically enough, found upon the interior base of the dome of the great Christian temple of Rome:

> THOU ART PETROS, AND UPON THIS
> ROCK WILL I BUILD MY CHURCH.

For that is precisely what Mithras succeeded in doing. He who had always been worshipped in rock-based caverns, made his new and permanent home in the temples believed to be founded on the Rock, Peter, and his descendants, who, from the time the lintel was inscribed, have permitted and perpetuated the worship and emulation of the warrior-God. The Early Fathers were undoubtedly correct when they spoke of the "devilish wiles" of Mithraism!

In this connexion, the Mithraic remains found on Vatican Hill and believed to have been part of a former Mithraic temple, become deeply symbolical.

The Eucharist.

When Paul first joined the followers of Jesus he found them a small, Jewish sect, answering to the description by Pliny quoted in the first chapter of this book. At that

[1] *The Rise of Christianity* by E. W. Barnes. (Longmans, Green & Co.)

time they were so conscious of their spiritual unity, and brotherhood under God, so keenly expectant of the imminent end of the world that, like the Essenes, they shared all things in common. And one of their habits was to assemble at a communal Thanksgiving meal to which all had contributed in order to remind themselves and each other of the Master whose followers they were, by thinking and speaking of him and his words and works; for in those days they had no written record of either, the first of the Gospels not having been written.

This meal is described in the *Didache,* believed to have been written about sixty years after the crucifixion and containing descriptions of the church life of the Christians at that date. It was lost for centuries and only discovered in 1873—although its existence had always been surmised—in a monastery in Constantinople. It was in manuscript form, a small manual bound up with some other non-canonical writings and was first printed ten years later.

From it we learn that the communal meal, although ordinary food and drink was served at it as well as sacramental bread and water, was no ordinary repast, but the most important feature in the rites of the Early Church. No one could partake of it who had not been baptized, i.e. wholly purified. Therefore it was evidently intended to be an outward communion of saints, as well as being a thanksgiving meal. The instructions for the ceremony preceding it (*Didache IX*) ran as follows:

In the service of thanksgiving, called the eucharist, give thanks thus. First, for the cup: "We thank thee, our Father, for the holy vine of David thy Servant which thou hast revealed to us through Jesus thy child. Thine is the glory for ever." Then, for the broken bread: "We thank thee, our Father, for the life and knowledge which thou hast revealed to us through Jesus thy child. Thine is the glory for ever. Even as this broken bread was scattered over the mountains and was brought together and made one, so may thy church be brought together from the ends of the earth into thy kingdom. For thine is the glory and the power through Jesus Christ for ever." But let no one eat or drink of your eucharist save those who are baptized into the name of the Lord. For the Lord spoke, in fact, of this food, saying, "Give not what is holy to the dogs."

It will be noticed that all the glory was accorded, and the prayer addressed, to God the Father, Jesus being firmly relegated to the subsidiary place of the son, precisely as the Master himself would have wished. The last line, sectarian, harsh and untypical as it sounds, does make sense in the light of the theory of spiritual evolution; for it implies that those who have not achieved the true sense of purification symbolized by the Baptism are not sufficiently evolved to be able to take the higher spiritual teachings. They are still ensnared and blinded by their animalism and therefore not able to lead the life of the evolved man. Being still carnal, such persons would come to the holy feast, as the communal meal was regarded, solely for the food and human companionship. They would not be able to receive or digest the spiritual food and might misinterpret it and become a danger to the community. As, in the event, many did.

Although both bread and a cup were used sacramentally at this meal, they had no connexion whatever with the body and blood of Christ, as they came to have after Paul's influence had been felt on the eucharist, and as they have continued to have until the present day. It was for this reason that the *Didache*, or ancient teaching, is believed to have been suppressed for so long, as well as being largely ignored since its comparatively recent discovery. For the embarrassing fact had to be faced that if the account in the *Didache* were correct, as there is every reason to suppose that it is, the eucharist as at present performed in the Church and supposed from the account in the Gospels to have been established by Jesus Christ himself, was not so established, and was a later addition to the ceremonial of the Early

Church "written in", like so much else, to the Gospels. It
was, in fact, a Pauline innovation, as indeed, he quite
openly admits in I Cor. xi, 23.

The ceremonial that took place at the end of the holy
feast was described in *Didache X* as follows:

After eating your fill, thus give thanks: "We thank
thee, holy Father, for thy holy name which thou hast
sheltered in our hearts as in a tent; we thank thee for
the knowledge, for the faith and for the immortality
which thou hast revealed to us through Jesus thy child.
Thine is the glory for ever. Thou, Lord and ruler of all,
hast created all things for thy name's sake, and hast
given food and drink to men for their enjoyment, that
they might thank thee. To us thou hast vouchsafed spiritual
food and drink and everlasting life through thy child.
Above all things we thank thee that thou art mighty.
Thine is the glory for ever. Remember, Lord, thy church,
to ward off from it all evil and to make it perfect in thy
love; bring it together from the four winds, made ready
in holiness, into thy kingdom which thou hast prepared
for it: for thine is the power and the glory for ever. Let
grace come and let this world pass away. Hosanna to the
God of David. Whoever is holy, let him come: whoever
is not, let him repent. Maranatha, Amen."

Once again it is emphasized that the eucharist was
intended only for those who were holy, or whole; the
regenerated; those who had actually put on the Mind of
Christ. Otherwise the above was purely a prayer of thanksgiving for the truth Jesus had taught, the spiritual food and
drink of which the material variety was but a symbol, yet
also a cause for gratitude and thanksgiving; and finally an
expressed desire for this world to go and God's kingdom to
come.

All this perfectly conformed to the teachings of Jesus
Christ as we have them in the Gospels. There was no
suggestion that this custom had been ordained by the

Master nor that his flesh and blood should be partaken as having a transforming effect on the eaters. The spiritual transformation had already been achieved by the Baptism which was established for that purpose. The idea of transubstantiation has most obviously pagan origins—demi-gods or men elected as Gods by their fellows were ceremonially eaten throughout the ancient world in the attempt to absorb their goodness by cannibalistic means—and was entirely alien to the thought either of the Master or of his early Jewish followers. But not to the eclectic minded Paul who had long had contact with the pagans and their beliefs. According to 1 Cor. xi, 20–26, the Apostle to the Gentiles, upon closer acquaintance with the communal meal of his fellow Christians, found that it had degenerated from its original pure conception, which is certainly the way with all ritual. Quite obviously the condition laid down for maintaining this purity, the factual regeneration of the participants, had not in all cases been fulfilled. Baptism was undoubtedly becoming in certain instances a mere ritualistic act, such as it is at the present day, without the all-essential spiritual content, so that falsely initiated members came to the feast with a physical and not spiritual hunger. Paul writes:

> When ye come together therefore into one place, this is not to eat the Lord's supper. For in eating everyone taketh before other his own supper: and one is hungry, and another is drunken. What? have ye not houses to eat and to drink in? What shall I say to you? shall I praise you in this? I praise you not. (1 Cor. xi, 20–22.)

There has evidently been an unseemly scramble for food and drink and already it is obvious that it is Paul's intention to alter all this and turn the communal meal into a dignified ceremony worthy of his Master. He was acquainted with the solemn eucharist which had been so effectual in arousing the loyalty and devotion of the followers of Mithras. The sense of brotherhood, closer than any ties of the flesh, which it engendered was not lost on the observant Paul. It was this sense of brotherhood which was so needed if there were ever to be a universal church. If the Mithraic ceremonial which identified the initiates with the body and blood of their Lord could produce such spiritual fervour, what might it not do in the case of the persecuted and crucified Jesus Christ, holding his suffering and sacrifice perpetually in remembrance? This was the rallying point, the idea upon which to focus. The broken bread should no longer be merely the symbol of a church assembled from all parts of the world into one loaf, but the very body of the Saviour. Like the Mithraists, the Christians must have a ceremonial mystery to capture the mind and imagination and arouse in them the same fanatical devotion to their Lord as it had done in the followers of the Sun-God. Paul evidently persuaded himself that this was the will of the Master for in 1 Cor, xi, 23–26, we find:

> For I have received of the Lord that which also I delivered unto you. That the Lord Jesus the same night in which he was betrayed took bread: and when he had given thanks, he brake it, and said: Take eat: this is my body, which is broken for you: this do in remembrance of me. After the same manner also he took the cup, when he had supped saying, This cup is the new testament in my blood: this do ye, as oft as ye drink it, in remembrance of me. For as often as ye do eat this bread, and drink this cup of the Lord, ye do show the Lord's death till he come.

It is evident from the opening sentence that Paul wished to convey to his hearers that this piece of information about the Last Supper had come directly to him from the long-since crucified Jesus Christ. Therefore it must have come through the same clairaudience that he had experienced on the road to Damascus, or he had merely received it intuitively and inspirationally. None of which would have been received as conclusive evidence in a court of law. It remained either what an individual believed, or what he believed had been imparted to him by spiritual means. Had he been told of this ritualistic incident in the ordinary way by one of Jesus's immediate followers, any of those who had actually been present at the Supper, he would most certainly have said so. "I have it on the authority of Mark," he might have written, or, even more convincingly, "of John." But John who lay upon Jesus's breast, the most beloved of the disciples, who presumably knew and understood the Master and his teachings better than all the rest since he loved him most, did not even mention this incident in his Gospel, although had he known of its occurence, he would inevitably have done so, as it constituted a direct and serious demand of his beloved Master.

But Paul does not pretend that the rite was instituted by the Master when he was "in the flesh". Quite plainly and explicitly he states: "I passed on to you what I received from the Lord himself."

Paul was evidently a very eloquent and plausible speaker. He had already convinced the Early Church about the appearance and words of Jesus on the road to Damascus, and so had established a precedent for the belief that he was in some sort of psychic rapport with the Master; therefore it was not difficult to persuade it of the authenticity of these later instructions for altering the nature of their communal meal; and once these were accepted the description of the Last Supper would have been inserted in the Gospels on Pauline authority.

If this is what happened, and there seems no other possible explanation of the passages quoted, the eucharist, as it is solemnized today was not established by Jesus Christ, but by Paul, under the influence of his own concept of the mystical Christ, determined that his Master should not be robbed of the potency of the rites of the Sun-God. Certainly, if a Mithraist had been converted to the newer Faith, he would by this addition to the Christian ritual, find once again his former God surrounded by the twelve signs of the Zodiac, while his worshippers gave thanks for the gifts of their God manifested in grape and grain. He would recognize the ceremony of the oath of allegiance sworn over their cups by the militaristic Mithraists both to Caesar and to their warrior-God. But nowhere in this ceremony would he find any trace of the teachings of the simple prophet of Israel who insisted that God must be worshipped in Spirit and in truth, and not through materialistic symbols since 'the flesh profiteth nothing"—even the flesh and blood of a man-God; and only his Spirit, the inspired Word of Truth, quickeneth.

According to Bingham (*Christian Antiquities,* 1855 ed.) the early Christian sect, the Ebionites, celebrated the communion rite with bread and water. Wine mixed with water appeared in later usage. Paul was not an Essene, or holy man. He was an orthodox Jew who had no scruples about wine drinking, suggesting to his disciple, Timothy, that he should take a little wine for the good of his health (1 Timothy v, 23), so there is no reason to suppose that he did not initiate the adding of wine to the ritual. The fact that the Early Church, under the tutelage of Peter who had known the Master personally, partook of bread and water at their eucharist would seem to confirm that this was the practice of the Master and his disciples, as it must have been if he was, in fact, a Nazarene.

In fairness to Paul it must be noted that his view of the eucharist was that of a commemorative rite, as it is today in the Protestant churches. The cup and the bread were to be used only to remind his followers of his testimony and of his dying to and in the flesh. The idea of transubstantiation was nowhere in Paul's consciousness; it would have been utterly alien to his racial thought and would have appeared to him, as it was, a custom of the ignorant heathen. It was a later addition, when the Catholic church was almost wholly given over to Gentiles, a devolutionary development of the Pauline rite by theologians who saw nothing repellent in the pagan idea of eating the flesh and blood of a God.

The Crucifixion.

Shall I give my firstborn for my transgression, the fruit of my body for the sin of my soul? (Micah vi, 7)

The question posed by the great prophet, Micah, refers to a concept that seems to have dwelt persistently in the thought of pagan and Jew alike in primitive times—that of human and animal sacrifice in an endeavour to propitiate the gods.

In the earliest times, notably in the religion of the Mexicans, it was the King-God himself who was sacrificed and afterwards eaten in order that his qualities should be absorbed by those who came after him. Later, and at least until the days of Abraham, the firstborn son of the King, or Chieftain, was substituted for the Father, as in the case of Isaac. But in more civilized states and times a condemned criminal was used as the victim, and this practice was the basis both of the Persian festival of Sacaea and the Babylonian Saturnalia which, in the day of Jesus, was still practised throughout the Roman Empire.

The idea, as perpetuated in these later masquerades was, as Frazer tells us, one of a false King usurping the place of the real king for a period extending from five days to a year, and then being slaughtered. Dio Chrysostom has described the treatment of the Mock King of the Sacaea, in the words:

> They take one of the prisoners condemned to death and seat him upon the King's throne, and let him lord it, and drink, and run riot and use the King's concubines during these days, and no man prevents him from doing just what he likes. But afterwards they strip, and scourge and crucify him.

Frazer suggests that a watered down version of this custom, practised all over the ancient world from Italy to Babylon, might well account for the otherwise inexplicable behaviour described in Matthew xxvii, 27–31, which has led many scholars to doubt the historicity of the crucifixion story; and points out that the name of Barabbas, which was not a real name but simply meant Son of the Father, may indicate that this was the designation of the criminal annually chosen for the sacrifice at the Saturnalia, or for the Jewish version of that custom, connected with the feast of Purim and the hanging of Haman, and for whom, in this case, Jesus was substituted. Without being historically verifiable, this theory is at least plausible, and would certainly account for the crowning, the royal robes, the mockery, the scourging, and, above all, for the scornful accusation nailed to the cross: THIS IS JESUS THE KING OF THE JEWS, which as Frazer reminds us, no one would have dared to inscribe in earnest with a jealous Caesar, ever wary of such pretensions, on the throne. And it is at least established that the scene recorded by Matthew was a regular part of the Saturnalian festivities that not only took place at that period but still persisted in the days of the Emperor Julian who, in the year 362 wrote his famous satire *The Caesars* for the Saturnalia. Philo Judaeus, in his treatise *Against Flaccus*, written about 40 A.D. describes a mob in Alexandria dressing up an old man in a purple robe and crown, putting a sceptre in his hand, and hailing him as King.

It is certain, therefore, that both the Jews and the Roman soldiers attending the execution of Jesus Christ, were aware of this custom. And here was the "natural" victim—a man facing the accusation that he claimed to be a King. To his accusers, he was filling the role of the false King of antiquity threatening the throne of the true King, or Caesar, and it would have seemed right to them that he should pay the extreme penalty rather than the Barabbas of the year who was no more than a rebel and agitator. Hence the zest with which the loyal Roman soldiers are recorded as having entered into the spirit of the thing. In fact the situation looked so precisely like that of the one commemorated in their yearly festivals that the rough soldiers could hardly have foreborne to call attention to the fact by their mockery.

Matthew, Mark and John provide a convincing una-nimity in reporting the details of the pre-crucifixion events, and, if Frazer's surmise is right, the whole story becomes explicable through its linkage with pagan rites, in particular the Mithraic animal sacrifice, although for the Bull with the side pierced by the sword is substituted the Lamb on the Cross. A strange detail about this substitution is that the place of the Bull in the Signs of the Zodiac was, in ancient times, taken by the Sign of the Ram. Whether this had any astrological significance for the writers of the Gospels, we cannot know; but as we have seen, the signs of the Zodiac played a large part in Mithraism.

As Arthur Weigall pointed out in his book, *The Paganism in Our Christianity*, if Frazer's explanation is true, Jesus was not crucified by the Romans as blasphemer and heretic (the legal punishment for which was stoning or decapitation) but quite literally, as a human sacrifice, as a result of the unredeemed violence in the hearts of men. And he was offered up on that symbol of violence, the Roman and Mithraic Sword, of which the cross is but a crude, wooden counterpart.

In that moment of ignominy and agony—hung on a sword, pierced by a sword, the victim of the cruelty and violence of unevolved, or unredeemed humanity—the world of nature red in tooth and claw indeed seemed to have triumphed over one who had attempted by so persuasively preaching the gospel of Love, peace and goodwill to all mankind, to save men from their own imperfections and from the suffering that these must inevitably bring. Perhaps this climax of violence, this apotheosis of cruelty, and hatred of purity and goodness, served to make the compassionate love of which Jesus was the embodiment more evident. Perhaps the contrast of mob violence with the gentle, patient, harmless figure on the cross was necessary at that time if humanity were to recognize not only what it was in its unregenerate state, but also what it could become by means of spiritual evolution. The picture has remained with us down the centuries. Like the more recent revelations at Belsen, it silently says: This is humanity at its present point of development. And reminds all who regard it of the inhumanity of man to man.

On Calvary the hanged figure of a man pointed to the

alternative. His assassins had the power to repent and become like the harmless, non-violent Lamb of God. At Belsen there was no visible alternative, but the revulsion of feeling, the horror, the remorse, which, in one case at least, led to the almost immediate death of a viewer, proved that the Christly compassion, scorned and slain on Calvary, still lives in the human heart.

In the sense that Jesus demonstrated the evil of violence, symbolized by the Roman sword which sought to destroy the Hope of the World, the hope that man could go higher, evolve to a new and harmless species, by destroying the one man who had succeeded in doing so, he triumphed over his enemies. The fact that this implication has not been gener-ally realized may be explained by the veneration in which the sword of Mithras has been held in the so-called Christian Church. Not only in the effigies of the Crusaders, the warring Michael and his angels, St. George and the Dragon, the flag-draped walls, but the cross of suffering itself which has become the central theme in the worship of one who came, not to hang throughout the centuries on a cross of suffering, but to rise triumphant above both cross and suffering in evidence of his son-of-Godhood. It is the risen Christ, not the suffering martyr, or witness to the evil of the world, that is the saviour of that world. But humanity, not willing to part with the concept of man "after the flesh", reluctant to rise higher in the evolutionary scale, clings to the evidence of its own sins and sufferings, and refuses to look beyond.

Had the Church which was founded to commemorate the Saviour of mankind taught its congregations to focus their attention and desire on the thought of the triumphant, risen, evolved man that each man has it in him to be, and to emulate the Perfect Man instead of worshipping him, the world would already be saved. But this would have meant abandoning both the thought and the use of the Mithraic sword, the triumph of which is revealed not in the empty tomb but on Calvary, that vision of human woe and defeat which appeals to all that is sadistic and apathetic in the human consciousness, concentrating on the Saviour's moment of apparent failure rather than on his actual and eternal victory.

Even the Sun-God rose from the tomb; but Jesus Christ who explicitly said: "My joy no man can take from me" is continually equated by Orthodoxy with sorrow and suffering, with defeat rather than with victory.

No man can deprive the true Christ of his joy, but by concentrating on violence and suffering, both in their lives and in their religion, men of the Western world have very evidently robbed themselves of that joy, which the man of compassion offered, and still offers them—on one condition; that they put on his Mind, renounce their violence, beat the Mithraic sword into a ploughshare, and so become the new man, the risen man seen in the Gospels, but not in the Romish Church, where he remains allegorically and actually nailed to the Mithraic sword in the name of expediency, the sword by which man, whom he sought to save from such a fate, still lives and dies.

The Resurrection.

It can do the cause of Christianity no good to ignore the similarity between the Mithraic legend and the many other nature and sun-god myths relating to the death and rebirth of the deity, and its own Easter celebrations,[1] or to endeavour to explain such similarity away. Such attitudes reveal a spiritual uneasiness, or the fact that more faith is placed in the historical Jesus than in the truth of the teachings of the universal Christ; and this lack of conviction in the religionist does more damage to the spiritual hypothesis than all the ignorant gibes of materialism. Finally, the Truth of the teachings of both the Buddha and the Christ would stand if all the events ascribed to the lives of those Teachers were found to be inventions, but as Sir James George Frazer writes in a footnote to *The Golden Bough*:

> The historical reality both of the Buddha and of Christ, has sometimes been doubted or denied. It would

[1] The date of which was settled at the Council of Nicaea (A.D. 325).

be just as reasonable to question the historical existence of Alexander the Great and Charlemagne on account of the legends which have gathered round them. The great religious movements which have stirred humanity to its depths and altered the beliefs of nations spring ultimately from the conscious and deliberate efforts of extraordinary minds, not from the blind unconscious co-operation of the multitudes. The attempt to explain history without the influence of great men may flatter the vanity of the vulgar but it will find no favour with the philosophic historian.

But if we accept the evolutionary theory, we have less reason to doubt the historicity of the miracles and the Resurrection than most people appear to believe. Another and more plausible explanation of them and the similarity of religious teachings stems logically from that hypothesis.

As we have seen, confronted with the fact that the ceremony known as the Eucharist in the Catholic Church, and the celebrations of the Lord's death and resurrection, had, centuries before, been rites of the pagan religion of Mithraism, the shocked Early Fathers produced the explanation that far-seeing demons had anticipated these teachings in order to discredit them.

Phrased in such terms this theory appears to be wholly ridiculous, but when taken in conjunction with the hypothesis of spiritual evolution, it comes very near to the truth. For in the process of evolution everything must necessarily be anticipated. The wings of Icarus, the stories of flying carpets, the primitive contraption in which the Wright brothers first flew were all "evolutionary anticipations" of the modern air liner or jet plane. And, in the same way, we can trace in the evolution of religious thought primitive beginnings of divine concepts persisting in the creeds of all ages. The simple symbolism of the death and rebirth of the year celebrated by the most primitive tribes was mankind's first, groping attempt to express his stirring urge for immortality, always latent in the soul of humankind. Then, as the urge became more clearly formulated in consciousness, it was natural to visualize a demi-God who had, in fact, overcome death, and, finally, a man like unto themselves, who could triumph over what the evolved thinker, Paul, termed the last enemy. The fact that the recorded crucifixion, resurrection and ascension of Jesus Christ seem so similar to the myths of pagan gods and demi-gods that "anticipated" the event in the New Testament, therefore by no means invalidates these records. The thought of, and desire for immortality in the consciousness of mankind may well have reached the point of demonstration in the person of the most evolved man of the Jewish race. Future ages will not deny the Wright brothers their practical achievement because this was preceded by fanciful legends about flying carpets.

And even if this were not so, even if the human appearance known as Jesus of Nazareth had not visibly triumphed over death and the grave, the fact that his Gospel still remains intact today, still discernible by those with eyes to see as the salvation of the world, is a living proof of the immortality of his redeeming spirit.

But there is one argument that would seem to prove without shadow of doubt that Jesus did appear in some convincing and tangible form to his followers after his crucifixion and entombment, and that is the fact that, at the time of his trial all his followers abandoned him except John. And it was not a momentary panic, but a deep disillusionment and failure of faith, since they returned to their nets, deliberately returned to their old way of life from which Jesus had called them, taking up the threads of existence as though there had never been this divine interruption. For them it was all over; the dream-fantasy was at an end; they felt they had been chasing a spiritual will-o'-the-wisp, and were ashamed of their credulity. And then, in a matter of a few weeks, this craven, disillusioned band of men were somehow electrified into action, banding themselves together once more to preach the Gospel of the teacher they had failed, openly, well aware of the danger, and with the utmost enthusiasm and conviction.

Something very convincing, very concrete, must have happened to effect this sudden and dramatic change of attitude, and it seems both difficult to believe and unnecessary to suppose that this was anything less than the confirmation of their Master's prophecy that he should conquer death. What else could have induced them all to risk imprisonment and physical death as they did by going out into the Roman world and preaching the gospel, and doing the works that had sent their Master to Calvary? They must have had proof (blind faith cannot account for it since that had failed them at the hour of crucifixion) that their Redeemer lived and was factually with them always "even to the end of the world". Fearful men must be given practical assurance if they are suddenly to become brave, and this is what evidently happened to the followers of Jesus of Nazareth. Could the transforming power have been less than the fulfilment by their Master of a hope that had been evolving in the consciousness of man throughout the ages—that of the continuity of individual life?

The fact that the resurrection stories differ in the various gospels does not invalidate them. They were written long after the events described took place, and the human mind is fallible. But several details in the records when pieced together make very good sense in the light of the findings of modern investigators of ESP.

Perhaps the most arresting statement is that found in the record of John:

> The first day of the week cometh Mary Magdalene early, when it was yet dark . . . and seeth the stone taken away from the sepulchre . . . and . . . she turned herself back and saw Jesus standing and knew not that it was Jesus. Jesus saith unto her, Woman, why weepest thou? She, supposing him to be the gardener, saith unto him, Sir, if thou have borne him hence, tell me where thou hast laid him, and I will take him away. Jesus saith unto her, Mary. She turned herself and said unto him, Rabboni; which is to say, Master. Jesus saith unto her, Touch me

not; for I am not yet ascended to my Father and your
Father; to my God and your God.

There has always been a divergence of opinion as to
whether the resurrected body of Jesus was actually of the
same substance as that which was crucified, or was composed
of a less gross form of matter, akin to the "materializations"
of psychic phenomena or the astral body of the Theosophists.
The bulk of evidence in the New Testament suggests that
the latter theory may be the correct one.

In John's account, Mary reached the sepulchre "when
it was yet dark". This and the fact that she was weeping
would account rationally for her non-recognition of Jesus
until he spoke to her, so that this in itself does not necessarily
imply a change in his appearance. But his words are very
significant:

"Touch me not; for I am not yet ascended. . . ."

It was as though the touch of gross matter from which
he was evolving might draw him back to the state of consciousness that he was striving to outgrow.

But if this were the case, it is difficult to understand why
he afterwards invited the disciples (Luke xxiv, 39) to handle
him and see, asking Thomas to thrust his hand into his
side, in both cases strongly suggesting that the resurrection
body was of the same gross material as that which had been
crucified. Had Jesus become so convinced of the illusory
nature of matter and of the substance of Spirit that the
human touch had lost its power to affect him? or were the
above accounts later elaborations of the story by writers
who did not understand the evolutionary necessity for
transcending matter? The latter supposition fits all the rest
of the facts much better. It explains how Jesus could appear
to the disciples in a room where the doors were closed
(John xx, 19). It would also account for the Master's
various post-mortem appearances, on the sea-shore and
the Road to Emmaeus, and the fact that the two apostles
walking that road did not recognize him even when he
talked with them. Not until he blessed the bread in his

customary way did they recognize him (Luke xxiv, 30, 31). Nor could he immediately have vanished out of their sight had his body been of the ordinary, physical kind.

Only the evolutionary theory, too, could explain his final severance from his followers:

> And he led them out as far as Bethany, and he lifted up his hands and blessed them. And it came to pass while he blessed them, he was parted from them.

The final line "and carried up into heaven" is said not to belong to the original version. The implication is that the concept of the body as gross matter was finally dissolved. Jesus Christ had "ascended to the Father"—Pure Consciousness, in which there can be no evidence of limitation or materiality. And the disciples now aware of this fact, since it had been demonstrated before their eyes, "returned to Jerusalem with great joy"—and also with great and extraordinary courage. For they who had hidden themselves for fear of being identified with the Master and his teachings were now "continually in the temple, praising and blessing God"; a state of mind which brought upon them the experience and power of the Pentecostal anointing, after which they fearlessly and persistently went out into all the world and preached the Gospel as they had been bidden.

Scientifically, we cannot admit of an effect without a cause. The effect of sudden and absolute courage appearing in men who had so recently been ready to desert one whom they had previously believed to be the Messiah and Son of God, could not have "just happened", especially as it necessitated once again, and this time finally, leaving their ordinary means of livelihood. It is necessary to postulate a cause, and a very strong cause for such a *volte face*; and what stronger or more likely cause, in the circumstances, could there have been than that recorded in all four Gospels: the confirmation of their original faith by tangible and undeniable evidence that Jesus Christ was indeed the Son of God, or spiritually evolved man, that he had claimed to be?

The Atonement.

My sheep hear my voice, and I know them and they follow me: and I give unto them eternal life: and they shall never perish. . . . I and my Father are One. (John x, 27, 30.)

Holy Father, keep through thine own name those whom thou hast given me, that they may be one, as we are . . . that they all may be one; as thou, Father, art in me, and I in thee, that they also may be one in us: . . . and the glory which thou gavest me I have given them; that they may be one, even as we are one: I in them, and thou in me, that they may be made perfect in one. (John xvii, 11, 21–23.)

Be ye therefore perfect, even as your Father which is in heaven is perfect. (Matthew v, 48.)

The above passages reveal clearly the idea of the at-one-ment of God and man which Jesus, in company with the greatest seers and mystics of all ages, came to teach mankind. And by his own conduct he taught others how to achieve this at-one-ment: by divine living; living divinely in the thought of God, and by practising His presence, until God becomes for each man that which in fact He must ever be—the one reality.

Paul while retaining this universal mystic conception of the divine Unity, taught quite a different concept of atonement. In place of the truly Christian doctrine of at-one-ment through the regenerate life, he substituted the pagan concept of atonement through death.

In Roman iii, 23–25, he writes:

For all have sinned, and come short of the glory of God; being justified freely through his grace through the redemption that is in Christ Jesus: whom God hath set forth to be a propitiation through faith in his blood, to declare his righteousness for the remission of sins that are past, through the forbearance of God.

And in Romans v, 8, 9:

> But God commendeth his love towards us, in that, while we were yet sinners, Christ died for us. Much more then, being now justified by his blood, we shall be saved from wrath through him.

What has this dark and primitive doctrine to do with the simple teaching of Jesus who was never guilty of evolving the doctrine of vicarious atonement that so shocked the honest, modern Gandhi that he refused to call himself a Christian, for all his Christ-likeness, saying that he wished to be saved not from the consequences of his sins but from sin itself. In this he was at one with Jesus but not with Paul, for the Master taught, as all the major world-teachers have done, that sin is forgiven only when it is forsaken. Each man must, therefore "forgive" himself; no one can do this for him. Nor did Jesus ever present a picture of a wrathful God from whom man must be saved but always of an eternally loving, wholly beneficent Father who desired only good for His children.

But the pagans had always believed in redemption through sacrifice and vicarious atonement. As Weigall points out:

> Adonis, Attis, Dionysos, Herakles, Mithra, Osiris, and other deities, were all saviour-gods whose deaths were regarded as sacrifices made on behalf of mankind; and it is to be noticed that in almost every case there is clear evidence that the god sacrificed himself to himself.[1]

Therefore when a Mithraist was confronted with the story of a great prophet who called himself a son of God, and who had been crucified and had risen again, he would at once have seen the hero of the story as "the bull of Mithra killed by the God who was himself". (*Ibid.*) And it is not difficult to understand how the zealous Judaic-Christian

[1] *The Paganism in Our Christianity* by Arthur Weigall. (Hutchinson & Co.

missionaries would have seized upon this mystical explanation of what had once seemed to them to have been the
shameful death of their Master on a cross like a common
criminal.

From the time of Abraham their race had known of the
belief in the efficacy of human and animal sacrifice as a means
of propitiating the deity. Searching the Scriptures in the
light of this popular belief, they may well have imagined
that they had found the correct explanation of their Master's
tragic experience, an explanation that would conclusively
prove his Messiahship since if it were true he had indeed
saved mankind from the burden of sin.

It will be seen from a close scrutiny of Paul's Epistles
that he accepted this point of view with caution and reserva-
tions but he undoubtedly supplied the authority for the
hardening into dogma of the doctrine of vicarious atonement
which has always been so prominent a feature of the
Christian church. The writer of the Epistle to the Hebrews
on the other hand shows full acceptance of the pagan
theory, saying forthrightly (Hebrews ix, 12): that Christ
by his own blood "entered in once into the holy place
having obtained eternal redemption for us. For if the blood
of bulls . . . sprinkling the unclean, sanctifieth to the purify-
ing of the flesh; how much more shall the blood of Christ,
who through the eternal Spirit offered himself without
spot to God, purge your conscience from dead works to
serve the living God."

All this is recognizably pure Mithraism, no hint of
which can be found in the teachings of Jesus Christ as
recorded in the Gospels.

But the idea evidently spread during the first century
like a forest fire, not only among the pagans but the Christians.
In the First Epistle of Peter i, 18, 19, we find:

Forasmuch as ye know that ye were not redeemed
with corruptible things . . . but with the precious blood
of Christ, as of a lamb without blemish and without
spot . . .

And in the First Epistle of John i, 7.

> . . . the blood of Jesus Christ his son cleanseth us
> from all sin.

In fact, it is impossible to avoid the conclusion that
from the time when the Epistles were written, the Christian
Church had accepted the pagan "rationalization" of the
crucified and risen Saviour, the God, or son of God, who
had not merely been crucified like a criminal at the instigation of Orthodoxy and the occupying Power but had
himself elected to die as a living sacrifice for the trans-
gressions of mankind. As Weigall writes, in the light of
this theory:

> Jesus not only fulfilled the Judaic scriptures, but he
> also fulfilled those of the pagan world; and therein lay
> the great appeal of early Christianity. In Him a dozen
> shadowy gods were condensed into a proximate reality;
> and in His crucifixion the old stories of their ghastly
> sufferings and sacrificial deaths were made actual, and
> were given a direct meaning.

There can be no doubt that this familiar idea had much
to do with the popularizing of the New Faith. But it is
bitterly ironical that in order to popularize the Creed of
Christ it had to be perverted; for not only did this primitive
belief entirely reverse Jesus's vision of a perfect all-loving
Father, who asked for nothing more and nothing less than
the love of His children and their obedience to the beneficent laws made for their protection, presenting instead the
picture of an inhuman monster who could only be appeased
by the shedding of innocent blood, but it was in direct
conflict with the main theme of Jesus's gospel.

The explicit teaching that man is saved, or redeemed
only by following the Perfect Man in his experiences of
total purification and rebirth, i.e. of spiritual evolution to a
higher species, must automatically annul any theory of

at-one-ment by any other means. No one can atone for another's sins, or prevent the result of those sins. Each man must do this for himself, by ceasing to sin, by becoming at one with his sense of perfection, or, in theological terms, becoming Christ-like. He does this by means of his own spiritual evolution, not through the death and resurrection of another.

Jesus's immense contribution to the universal evolutionary process was his example; he was the transitional man, showing not only that the transition could be made, but *how* it could be made. Without such proof humanity would have no sense of direction, would not know in what its salvation consisted and could have no assurance that the thing could be done.

Therefore the debt we have been supposed to owe the Founder of our Faith for his vicarious atonement, still remains in all its immensity; for what he did was to establish the all-essential precedent, the living proof, that at-one-ment with God could be obtained in the present life, and in this sense he became for ever the hope of the world.

But when this doctrine is perverted to imply that man is freed from the consequences of his own behaviour by the sacrifice of another the spiritual law contained in the words: "Whatsoever a man soweth, that shall he reap," known in the East as the Law of Karma, is violated and the law of Justice annulled.

It is true that by at-one-ment with the Perfect Man we may put off our sins and, with them, their effects, and so find ourselves freed from "the law of sin and death"; but that cannot be achieved by the death of any man but only by the living of a regenerate life. And the biggest stumbling-block to the living of that life throughout the ages has been the disastrously misleading doctrine of vicarious atonement.

The Kingdom of God.

For the Mithraist, the heavenly kingdom was that to which their God ascended in his fiery chariot after partaking of the Last Supper with his Twelve followers. It was a spatial heaven localized in the skies, in the centre of which was the shining mansion where Mithras would be standing ready to welcome the Faithful into its golden gates as a Father welcomes his children home.

For the Christian, listening to the words of Jesus Christ himself, the kingdom of God was an inner condition, a perfect state of consciousness to be realized, as the Master had realized it, even while he was still an inhabitant of the earth, for "The Kingdom of God is within you."

A similar idea had, centuries before, been held by Plato when he wrote of the Ideal State, "it is laid up in heaven as a pattern for him who wills to see, and seeing to found a city in himself. Whether it exists anywhere or ever will exist is no matter. His conduct will be an expression of the laws of that city alone, and of no other."[1]

It was indeed as an expression of the perfect laws obtaining in his Father's kingdom that Jesus Christ existed. He was governed within by higher rules than those operating in the world about him, and this fact gave him access to the higher law of harmony, which, as Paul of Tarsus afterwards explained, freed a man from the lower laws of sin and death, even as a knowledge of the laws of electricity enables a man to substitute light for darkness which would seem a miracle to a man unaware of such laws.

Inasmuch as they can be explained, this would account for the much-debated physical healings found on almost every page of the four Gospels. To deny that these healings took place, and therefore to deny their implications which, as we have seen, Jesus so specifically pointed out, is not only to denude his Gospel of its meaning, but to deny the existence, or possibility of realizing, the Kingdom of God. For it was by consciously living in that Kingdom, by the perpetual consciousness of God's government of his every action: "The Son can do nothing of himself, but what he seeth the Father do: for what things soever he doeth also these doeth the Son likewise" (John v, 19)—that these healings were possible to Jesus and those who lived near enough to

[1] *The Republic of Plato*, Everyman's Library. (J. M. Dent & Sons Ltd.)

his vision also to realize the kingdom of harmony "at hand", or within.

Jesus, like Plato, saw that government must precede the founding of the external State; that the truly God-governed man, the regenerate or evolved man, would necessarily objectify a better world than that which was the externalized state of the animalistic man of present experience. Even to obtain Mithras' space-time heaven a man must have earned his right to enter into the heavenly places by continual tests of endurance which made of him a more self-disciplined, and therefore a *better* man (according to the Mithraic ideal). The difference lay in the conceptions of the Perfect Man, the model towards which men must strive. On the one hand, the invincible Mithras, on the other, the compassionate Christ; two concepts of quite diverse excellence, appealing to men of completely opposite characters. For the extrovert, the world and its glory, conquest and victory, with, at the end of it, an equally tangible and still more glorious kingdom in the heavens above. For the introvert, the rejection of this world, the flesh and all evil, and a surrendered at-one-ment with the highest good in consciousness, which has been for all time the heaven within of the great mystics of every creed.

In reading the New Testament accounts of the life of Jesus Christ, it is impossible to avoid the impression that he was obsessed by the thought of the Father and His kingdom. His Gospel might be called that of the Kingdom. His works proved that the laws of that Kingdom were accessible to him; his teachings were all of how to attain to that Kingdom, and his parables, describing it, all related to states of mind.

The Kingdom of Heaven is like unto . . . these simple stories began, and then went on to describe a man who found a pearl of great price and sold all that he had to obtain it, showing the need of the renunciation of all lesser values in order to obtain that which was of supreme worth, the inward realization of the presence of God.

The necessity of separating the good, or God-derived

thoughts from the bad in order to establish the Kingdom within was pointed out in the parables of the Wheat and Tares, of the net cast into the sea, of the householder "who produces what is new and what is old from his stores". The parable of the Wedding Feast depicted the Kingdom of Heaven at hand awaiting the coming of the guests but showing how lethargy, apathy, the mesmeric quality of worldly cares and attractions keep them from the feast. The necessity for true forgiveness, for seeing our brother man rightly as equally a citizen of the ideal state, is stressed in the parable of the King and the Unjust Servants who lacked the compassionate desire to share the good available with others, and who therefore were incapable of realizing the Kingdom of compassionate Love within. The necessity for mental alertness if one is to cast off the apathy which so often prevents entry to the ideal state is clearly shown in the parable of the Wise and Foolish Virgins. The guest who arrived at the Wedding Feast and was rejected for his unsuitable garment, was the man who is unprepared for the spiritual feast, lacking the essential purification of thought and life needed before the joys of the Kingdom can be experienced. The parable of the Talents emphasized the importance of using all we have of spiritual knowledge in order to increase it until, like the grain of mustard seed in the earlier parable, it fills the horizon, revealing the infinity of the Kingdom of God; for unless it is used, fanned into flame by constant desire for the good, the divine spark in man will remain hidden or barely suspected, and there will be no consciousness of the heavenly Kingdom.

In all these stories Jesus was telling his hearers on what lines they must think in order to become worthy of the Kingdom of God. And it is obvious that their thoughts would be very different from those of the Mithraists who strove for mastery over themselves and the world, the mastery achieved by will-power, repression, oppression and force instead of by complete surrender to and the embodiment of Divine Love.

The ultimate goal, the heavenly kingdom for the

Mithraist was to reign in spendour with Mithras in his golden mansion, having achieved immortality by the help of their God. The ultimate goal for the Christian was that spiritual at-one-ment with God which was eternal life; the Kingdom of God within.

Both these concepts are traceable in the New Testament, and in orthodox Christianity, but since they conflict and are irreconcilable it is surely reasonable to assume that the teaching of an exoteric heaven was either a later addition to the Gospel records after the Early Church had come into contact with Mithraism and its beliefs, or that it was a personal representation added to the sayings of Jesus Christ by a Jewish writer whose concept of the hereafter had already been influenced by the Mazdean teachings of a spatial heaven and hell.

The Parousia.

And he said to them all, if any man will come after me, let him deny himself, and take up his cross daily, and follow me. For whosoever will save his life shall lose it; but whosoever will lose his life for my sake, the same shall save it. For what is a man advantaged if he gain the whole world, and lose himself, or be cast away? . . . But I tell you of a truth, there be some standing here, which shall not taste of death, till they see the kingdom of God.

The last sentence which has been the cause of so much misunderstanding throughout the centuries, is simple and understandable enough if taken in its context and interpreted in the light of the Master's other teachings about the Kingdom of God, in particular his explicit statement that this kingdom was *within* men.

With this definition in mind, the above teachings are clearly seen as directives as to how to achieve spiritual evolution in the present life. If a man wishes to be where the Master was in the evolutionary scale, he must deny his finite, limited, personal *chrysalis* state of life, take up the cross, the distinctly difficult task of daily and hourly

abandoning this lower concept of man, and live in the
Christ-consciousness, visualizing his son-of-Godhood, and
living up to this vision. He who would save, or cling to his
temporal sense of life, identifying himself continually with
the physical man, will inevitably lose this sense of life
since it is mortal and finite; but he who denies it, abandons
it, for the higher life manifested by Jesus Christ, will enter
into the consciousness of immortality. And what is a man
advantaged if he gain the whole visible world which, for all
its riches, is temporal, transient and illusory, and loses his
consciousness of life eternal, the Realm of the Real?

Then, after giving the instructions, the Master holds out
hope of the immediacy of the prize: some of those listening
to him will attain the divine consciousness in which he
himself dwells, the Kingdom of God *within*, even as he has
done, in this present life, before passing through the experience of physical death. And doubtless some of his true
followers did see the "new heaven and the new earth" so
evident to their Teacher. Indeed, no other interpretation
can be put on Paul's words: "We *have* the Mind of Christ."
Heaven, like Nirvana, can and should be experienced by
men even while they still walk the earth. Jesus was constantly impressing this fact upon his hearers in his teachings
of the Kingdom of God. We find him emphatically stating
that those about him were already experiencing that
Kingdom when he said:

> If I with the finger of God cast out devils, no doubt
> the kingdom of God is *come upon you*. (Luke xi, 20.)

This implies that everyone who experienced his spiritual
healing had seen the kingdom of God, or, as Moffatt
illuminatingly translates it, the Reign of God, the Rule or
Law of Harmony. Therefore, undoubtedly, his prophecy
that some of his hearers should not die before they had seen
this kingdom was fulfilled.

Why, then, was there all this confusion about the second
advent? Why did the majority of Christians in the first

century confidently expect a physical return of their Master?

The explanation seems to lie in the Eastern propensity for elaborating a statement as it passes from mouth to mouth, and by the time Jesus's original words had reached the scribe who wrote Mark's Gospel, they had been expanded into most untypical rhetoric strongly reminiscent of Sun-God worship. This is how the account appears in Matthew xxiv, 27–31, and it differs very little in Mark:

> . . . As the lightening cometh out of the East, and shineth even unto the West; so shall also the coming of the son of man be . . . immediately after the tribulation of those days shall the sun be darkened, and the moon shall not give her light, and the stars shall fall from heaven, and the powers of the heavens shall be shaken: and then shall appear the sign of the son of man in heaven.

Here we have a totally different concept of heaven to that already ascribed to the Master. This is the localized heaven in the sky, of Mithraism, instead of a spiritual state within the consciousness of man.

> And then shall all the tribes of the earth mourn, and they shall see the son of man coming in the clouds of heaven with power and great glory.

What is the glorious light that appears in the heavens, dispersing the clouds but the sun itself? Here without doubt is reference to the sun-god, and not to the simple Teacher of the spiritual way of inner purification.

> And he shall send his angels with a great sound of a trumpet, and they shall gather together his elect from the four winds, from one end of heaven to the other.

Here we have the imported Zoroastrian angels, and the whole account written in the style of the Revelation of John or of the Book of Daniel, but utterly unlike that of the preacher of the Sermon on the Mount. It seems obvious that the original account has been written up and dramatized by someone acquainted with descriptions of the Sun-God, possibly some over-zealous follower who could not bear to paint a less glorious picture of his Master than that which would have been portrayed by a Mithraist in describing his God. Jesus Christ must not only enlighten the world, be the spiritual Light shining in the darkness of materialism, he must also embody light on the physical level and be represented as the true Sun-God.

Unfortunately the writer does not seem to have realized that by turning the Master's simple and clear statement into an elaborate and impossible prophecy, he would be endangering his reputation as a Prophet. For undoubtedly the words were widely accepted as an explicit prophecy; and until this day it does not seem to be realized that if Jesus did use the words credited to him by both Matthew and Mark, and really believed that he would be returning within a few years in clouds of glory, he was not only mistaken but stands convicted as a false prophet. Since this is unthinkable in the Perfect Man, the only alternative is that he did not make any such prophecy, and that the simple account in Luke records his actual words. In the light of these it is seen that the Second Advent, like the Kingdom of God, is an inward experience which comes to a man when the Mind of Christ which has first appeared outwardly to him in the teachings of a great Master, beckoning him as an evolutionary goal, becomes his own mind, "judging" his every thought and deed, and he realizes the presence of the Christ within.

This is not merely an intellectual rationalization of a misinterpreted statement of the Master; it can, and has, been proved in the experience of all who have truly followed him, and who therefore no longer argue about the nature of the Parousia since they have already experienced it in the inner life. The son of God has truly been revealed to them in clouds of glory, and in a far more practical and transforming manner than could be achieved by the spectacular appearance of a human form in the clouds, whether this was identified as that of Jesus Christ or Mithras.

The Last Judgement.

The Orthodox teaching of The Last Judgement that has terrified many simple souls throughout the ages is based on a single passage in the Gospel of Matthew xxv, 31–34, which reads:

> When the Son of man shall come in his glory, and all the holy angels with him, then shall he sit upon the throne of his glory: and before him shall be gathered all nations: and he shall separate them one from another, as a shepherd divideth his sheep from the goats: and he shall set the sheep on his right hand, but the goats on the left.

Apart from the fact that, according to this statement, the Judgement is to be of *nations*, presumably as to whether they are Christian or pagan, the Judge from that point onward is referred to as a King. On no other occasion in the Gospels is Jesus represented as a judging King, and although from the passage in Luke xix, 38–40, it is evident that Jesus regarded himself as a King in the sense of being the Christos, or God-anointed, it is equally evident from John vi, 15, that he did not wish this to be understood in a literal sense. This is brought out strongly in John xviii, 36, 37, when, after he has been accused of calling himself a King, an accusation almost certainly based on the incident already referred to in Luke xix, when the materialistic Pharisees would have taken his answer to their rebuke literally, he explicitly tells Pilate: "My kingdom is not of this world: if my kingdom were of this world, then would my servants fight, that I should not be delivered to the Jews: but now is my kingdom not from hence."

This was interpreted by Pilate to mean that he was in *some* sense a King, for he asked "Art thou a King, then?" and Jesus replied "Thou sayest that I am a king," evidently meaning that this was the charge brought against him; but immediately went on to explain in what sense he was a king. "To this end was I born, and for this cause came I into the world, that I should bear witness unto the Truth." This would be understood by Jew and Pagan alike to refer to the Messiah, or Christos, the Anointed One.

The rest of the twenty-seventh chapter of Matthew is utterly unlike the picture we are given throughout the Gospels of a compassionate Saviour.

> Then shall he (the King) say also unto them on the left hand, Depart from me, ye cursed, into everlasting fire, prepared for the devil and his angels . . . and these shall go away into everlasting punishment: but the righteous into life eternal.

Now, as we have already seen, the lake of everlasting fire was that fate prepared for Ahriman, the Mazdean Father of Lies and his angels. It has nothing to do with the gospel of the God of mercy and love preached by Jesus Christ. He has already strongly rebuked his disciples (Luke ix, 54, 55) for suggesting that those who rejected him should come to a fiery end, saying: "Ye know not what manner of spirit ye are of." Obviously implying that they had forgotten their true nature as the sons of the God of Love. Yet this same teacher is represented in Matthew xxv, as condemning all men who will not receive him to the Mithraic lake of everlasting fire. If we are to agree that Jesus's policy of divine compassion was consistent, we must consider this chapter as suspect, as it undoubtedly is; for it was obviously written by the same pen as the completely Mithraic passage already quoted in the last section, from the preceding chapter of Matthew xxiv, 27–31.

It must have often puzzled thoughtful Bible students that Jesus who so emphatically taught that we should not judge one another (Matthew vii, 1), indignantly repudiating the role of Judge for himself while he walked on earth (Luke xii, 14), and who positively declared: "I judge no man" (John viii, 15), should afterwards have been depicted as returning to judge the whole of mankind. Is it possible that the Mind of Christ could change, i.e. be double-minded, and that he should reverse his attitude and decision? What, then becomes of the concept of his manifestation of the *unchanging* Will of God?

Peter would have us believe (Acts x, 42) that it was after the resurrection that Jesus made this complete *volte face*, and announced that he was to be the judge of the quick and the dead; and Paul (in 2 Tim. iv, 1) states that the Lord Jesus Christ "shall judge the quick and the dead".

We are then faced with the problem of whether we shall believe that Jesus did in fact change his mind and character, which would invalidate his claim that throughout his ministry he spoke only those things that the Father gave him to speak: "For I have not spoken of myself; but the Father which sent me, he gave me a commandment, what I should say, and what I should speak" (John xii, 49) and "The words that I speak unto you I speak not of myself" (John xiv, 10), or whether Paul and the writer of the Acts were guilty of inaccuracy and of teaching a later doctrine based upon a Mithraic conception. For, from the first, Mithras was known to be the Judge as well as the Mediator. Cumont writes: "It was Mithra, the protector of truth, that presided over the judgement of the soul after its decease."

M. Darmesteter, in the Introduction to his book on the Zend-Avesta, says that Mithras is a judge in hell; and, as we have already seen, it would be absolutely in keeping with the nature of Mithras to appear in glory in the clouds with his Mazdean angels.

It therefore seems quite obvious that the passage in Matthew xxv is of Mithraic inspiration. Nevertheless, some may point out that Jesus, even while repudiating the role of Judge, seemed to admit that, in some sense, he did judge when he said (John v, 30):

> I can of mine own self do nothing; as I hear, I judge: and my judgement is just; because I seek not mine own will, but the will of the Father which hath sent me.

In this passage he first relegates all judgement to the
Father, but he does imply that, listening to the voice of the
Father, the Son becomes aware of His judgement. Therefore
when he, as it were, relays such judgement, it must be just
since it is the judgement of God. But he still insists that he
is no personal judge, and that his mission is definitely not
to judge men but to save them: "And if any man hear my
words, and believe not, I judge him not: for I came not to
judge the world, but to save the world." (John xii, 47).

From first to last he insisted that it was the Father alone
who judged (John xii, 48): "He that rejecteth me, and
receiveth not my words, hath one that judgeth him."

Nevertheless, in one sense, Jesus Christ was and must
inevitably be the judge of all men. His spiritual stature
"judges" that of lesser men: shows them how far they fall
short of the ideal of the Perfect Man. Comparing themselves
with this great Model, men become aware of their own lack
of spiritual development. To some this "judgement" is an
affront; to others a challenge to follow him and to become
like him. In this sense, and this only, is it true that "the
Father judgeth no man, but hath committed all judgement
unto the Son".

The Son, the Perfect Man, by his own perfection "judges"
all who have not attained to his stature, and shows them the
distance between themselves and the evolutionary goal;
but, at the same time, by his very existence, proves that this
goal is attainable by the aspiring spirit of man, and thus
becomes the Saviour of man from his present imperfections,
by showing how these can be put off and replaced by the
qualities and attributes of the Divine Nature.

6

Mithras in the Apocalypse

GEORGE BERNARD SHAW, evidently unfamiliar with other apocalyptic writings of this *genre*, could only account for the peculiar composition known as *The Revelation of St. John the Divine* by suggesting that it sounded like the ravings of a drug addict. Ernest William Barnes, one time Bishop of Birmingham, in his book, *The Rise of Christianity*, while not going quite so far, referred to the author of the Apocalypse as being "bitter", and explained that he was writing in a state of "half-mad resentment" and fury at the recent persecutions of the Christians in the reign of Domitian. He also points out that the "barbaric Semitic Greek" in which the book is written provides certain proof that it was not the work of the author of the Fourth Gospel, as many have supposed. He also says, "the writer thinks of the Son of God in terms of a solar deity such as Mithra," and then goes on to quote a few of the innumerable passages that abundantly confirm this opinion.

He tells us, too, that the Fathers of the Early Church were hesitant about including this strange work among the canonical writings. The odd thing is that it should ever have occurred to them to do so[1], for not only is it mainly and strikingly non-Christian in tone, but it certainly cannot be considered as a special "Revelation" since it bears such a

---

[1] In his introduction to *The New Translation of the Bible* James Moffatt writes:
"The Apocalypse had a struggle first to gain and then to maintain its place in the New Testament; indeed, what eventually told in its favour was the belief that it had been composed by the apostle John."

striking similarity to passages in the books of Ezekiel and
Daniel.

But, as we have already seen, this type of visionary
writing had been in vogue for about two hundred years at the
time the Apocalypse was written, and was evidently derived
from ancient and esoteric teachings known only to certain
initiates of the Judaic Faith, teachings impregnated with
the imagery and symbols of sun-worship gleaned from
Babylonian, Persian and Chaldean sources.

It will be sufficient for our purpose to compare passages
from Daniel with those of the Apocalypse; but chapters
i, viii, ix, x, xi, of Ezekiel may profitably be studied in
order to confirm the relationship of the Apocalypse with
the Old Testament, and the Mazdean influence on both:

In Daniel vii, 9, 10, we read:

I beheld till the thrones were cast down, and the
Ancient of Days did sit, whose garment was white as
snow, and the hair of his head like the pure wool: his
throne was like the fiery flame, and his wheels as burning
fire. A fiery stream issued and came forth from before him.

The Apocalypse starts with a similar picture:

And in the midst of the seven candlesticks one like
unto the son of man . . . his head and his hairs were
white like wool, as white as snow; and his eyes were as
a flame of fire; and his feet like unto fine brass, as if they
burned in a furnace; and his voice was as the sound of
many waters. And he had in his right hand seven stars:
and out of his mouth went a sharp two-edged sword:
and his countenance was as the sun shining in his strength.

Here is a definitive portrait of the Sun-God as given
by the writer of the book of Daniel. The seven stars are
recognizably the seven Amshaspands of Ormuzd. Whether
the deity depicted is known as Merodach, Shamas, Mazda,
Apollo or Mithras, it is certainly not a portrait of the
Mystic of Galilee.

Then we have the primitive imagery of the four beasts, first found in Ezekiel i, 10, 11:

> As for the likeness of their faces, they four had the face of a man, and the face of a lion on the right side; and they four had the face of an ox on the left side; they four also had the face of an eagle . . . and their wings were stretched upward; two wings of every one were joined one to another, and two covered their bodies.

And then in Daniel:

> And the four great beasts came up from the sea, diverse one from another. The first was like a lion and had eagle's wings . . . and a man's heart was given to it. And behold another beast, a second like to a bear . . . and to another, like a leopard, which had upon the back of it four wings of a fowl; the beast also had four heads . . . and behold a fourth beast, dreadful and terrible, and strong exceedingly; and it had great iron teeth: it devoured and break in pieces, and stamped the residue with the feet of it: and it was diverse from all the beasts that were before it, and it had ten horns.

The version in the Apocalypse runs:

> And I stood upon the sand of the sea, and saw a beast rise up out of the sea, having seven heads and ten horns, and upon his horns ten crowns, and upon his head the name of blasphemy. And the beast which I saw was like unto a leopard, and his feet were as the feet of a bear, and his mouth as the mouth of a lion: and the dragon gave him his power, and his seat and great authority.

As we see, Ezekiel's and Daniel's four beasts have been incorporated into one. Both have ten horns, both rise from the sea. The latter fact suggests that this imagery was of great antiquity. For, as we have seen, it was the Babylonian

Merodach, one of the earliest of the sun-gods, who rose
from the sea and returned to the Father's house each night.
And it was the dragon of night which every evening bruised
the heel of the returning God who each morning bruised
the head of the dragon, an incident referred to in the
following paragraph, Revelation xiii, 3; "And I saw one of
his heads as it were wounded to death." Quite obviously
both writers were drawing on the same source of Ancient
wisdom, as the teachings of the faiths of Antiquity were
called.

Throughout the Apocalypse we find constant reference
to the horned beasts, the horns symbolizing their power,
but in many chapters they appear to have been tamed
and become subservient to the Deity. The most significant
of these passages is the one in Revelation iv, 7, for the
beasts as described here are recognizably those of the
Mithraic degrees: "And the first beast was like a lion, and
the second beast was like a calf," (young bull), "and the
third beast had a face as a man (the Persian), and the fourth
was like a flying eagle."

But the evil Beast is clearly the one equated with the
dragon. And this Beast, in the eyes of the author of the
Apocalypse, was evidently Mithras whose priests and highly
placed followers had been responsible for the persecution of
the Christians. This is perhaps most clearly brought out in
Revelation xiii, when, after describing the Beast who made
war with the saints, he attacked the chief symbol of Mithras,
the Sword:

He that killeth with the sword must be killed with the
sword. Here is the patience and faith of the saints.

He then goes on to describe the worship of the Beast:

And I beheld another beast coming up out of the
earth; and he had two horns like a lamb and he spake as
a dragon. And he exerciseth all the power of the first
beast before him, and causeth the earth and them which

dwell therein to worship the first beast, and he causeth all both small and great, rich and poor, free and bond to receive a mark in their right hand, or in their foreheads: and that no man might buy or sell, save he that had the mark, or the name of the beast, or the number of his name.

We can scarcely doubt that this relates to the worship of Mithras when we learn from Tertullian that Mithras "marks on the forehead his own worshippers," and E. W. King tells us that "a very curious portion of the initiatory ceremony in the ancient Mysteries was the giving of the Mark of Mithras. The Mark was indelible and is said to have been done by a kind of tattooing. Augustine is referring to this practice when he speaks of "a certain Demon that will have his own image purchased with blood." He also speaks of engraven stones that were given to initiates at the end of their probation, tokens of admission into the fraternity and for a medium of recognition between members. These were said to bear the initiate's name and number (Johan. 1. Disc. 7). This would account for not only the last paragraph of the citation from the Apocalypse just quoted, but also for Rev. ii, 18.

To him that overcometh will I give to eat of the hidden manna, and will give him a white stone, and in the stone a new name written, which no man knoweth saving he that receiveth it.

This is without any doubt either a description of the Mithraic initiation or of a Christian innovation taken directly from the Mysteries. For it is the Soldier of Mithras who "overcomes" during the twelve tests, and the manna referred to is almost certainly the honey which Cumont tells us was presented to the Initiate because of its preservative powers. He also says that the Mithraic brotherhoods were organized so that each resembled a large family in which there were no social distinctions, "the same faith had made the slave the equal, and sometimes the superior of the decurion and the clarissimus" since the conferred Degrees depended not on birth but on successfully passing the tests of endurance. Weigall writes of the Mithraists, "they recognized no social distinctions, both rich and poor, freeman and slaves, being admitted into the Army of the Lord." Hence: "He causeth all, both small and great, rich and poor, free and bond, to receive the Mark."

With this closely-knit freemasonry among all classes, aristocracy, militarists, merchants and slaves, with a sense of brotherhood so keen that it transcended human ties, nepotism of the kind that is found in Freemasonry was inevitable, and it may often have seemed literally true to the persecuted and repressed Christians that no man might buy or sell save he that had the mark, or the name of the beast, or the number of his name.

The crown of life, so conspicuous a feature in the Mithraic Mysteries, but never referred to in the Gospels, is mentioned in Revelation ii, 10, and again in Revelation iii, 11, "Hold thou fast which thou hast, that no man take thy crown." "My crown is Mithras" being the ritualistic declaration of the Soldier of Mithras.

The Babylonian influence on the thought of the writer of the Apocalypse is particularly marked in the reference to the war in heaven, which reads:

> And there was war in heaven: Michael and his angels fought against the dragon; and the dragon fought and his angels, and prevailed not; neither was his place found any more in heaven. And the great dragon was cast out. . . .

It is interesting to compare this with the following passage by Canon George Rawlinson in his essay "The Religion of the Assyrians":

> The Babylonians and Assyrians believed that at a remote date, before the creation of the world, there had

been war in heaven. The hosts of heaven were assembled together, and were engaged in singing a psalm of praise . . . when suddenly discord arose . . . Asshur was invoked to put himself at the head of the rebels, but refused to go forth with them. Their leader . . . took the form of a dragon, and in that shape contended with the God Bel, who proved victorious in the combat and slew his adversary by means of a thunderbolt, which he flung into the dragon's gaping mouth. Upon this the entire host of the wicked angels took flight, and was driven to the abode of the seven spirits of evil, where they were forced to remain, their return to heaven being forbidden.[1]

Seven, as we have seen, is Mithras' number, and the Apocalypse opens with a reference to the seven Spirits which are before the throne of God. It has already been noted that the seven Spirits which were before the throne of Ormuzd were the seven Amshaspands of which Mithras was at one time considered to be the chief. Reference is again made to these in Revelation viii, 2, 6, and again xv, 1, 6. The seven Spirits are also likened to lamps of fire burning before the throne (Revelation iii, 1, and iv, 5); while in Revelation v, 6, they become the seven horns and seven eyes of the slain Lamb.

Yet another plagiarism from Daniel is that of the sealed book which, in the Old Testament, reads:

And at that time shall Michael stand up, the great prince which standeth for the children of thy people;

(Michael, the warring angel being the Hebraic equivalent of Merodach, Shamas and, eventually, Mithras)

and there shall be a time of trouble such as never was since there was a nation . . . and at that time thy people shall be delivered, every one that shall be found written in the book . . . and they that shall be wise shall shine as

---

[1] *Religious Systems of the World.* (Sonnenschein.)

the brightest of the firmament; and they that turn many to righteousness as the stars for ever and ever. But thou, O Daniel, shut up the words and seal the book, even to the time of the end.

We hear no more of that book until the theme is elaborated in the Apocalypse in the words:

And I saw in the right hand of him that sat on the throne a book written within and on the backside, sealed with seven seals. And I saw a strong angel proclaiming with a loud voice, Who is worthy to open the book, and to loose the seals thereof? And no man in heaven, nor in earth, neither under the earth, was able to open the book, neither to look thereupon. And I wept much because no man was found worthy to open and to read the book, neither to look thereon. And one of the elders saith unto me, Weep not: behold the Lion of the tribe of Juda, the Root of David, hath prevailed to open the book, and to loose the seven seals thereof. And I beheld, and, lo, in the midst of the throne and of the four beasts, and in the midst of the elders, stood a Lamb as it had been slain, having seven horns and seven eyes, which are the seven Spirits of God sent forth into all the earth.

Here undoubtedly are the Amshaspands who mediate between Ormuzd and the lower spirits to whom they serve as models of perfection.

The writers both of the book of Daniel and the Apocalypse had identical views as to the appearance of the Son of God. In Daniel x, 5, 6, we read:

Then I lifted up mine eyes and looked and behold a certain man clothed in linen, whose loins were girded with the gold of Uphaz: his body also was like the beryl and his face as the appearance of lightening, and his eyes as lamps of fire, and his arms and his feet like in colour to polished brass, and the voice of his words like the voice of a multitude.

In Revelation i, 13, as we have already seen, his eyes were described as "a flame of fire and his feet like unto fine brass" and, in the following chapter (Revelation ii, 18) this is positively stated to be a portrait of the Son of God:

These things saith the Son of God, who hath his eyes like unto a flame of fire, and his feet are like fine brass.

The writers of the books of Ezekiel and Daniel might be excused for portraying the Sun-God, as the true Messiah had not then come, but the author of the Apocalypse is writing after the event, yet it seems that his idea of the Perfect Man has remained unchanged since he was described at the time of the Babylonian Captivity.

And what could be less like the gentle and compassionate Teacher of Galilee than John the Divine's description in Revelation xix, 11–16:

And I saw heaven opened, and behold a white horse; and he that sat upon him was called Faithful and True, and in righteousness he doth judge and make war. His eyes were as a flame of fire, and on his head were many crowns; and he had a name written, that no man knew but he himself.

(The distinctive mark of the Soldier of Mithras).

And he was clothed with a vesture dipped in blood: and his name is called The Word of God. And the armies which were in heaven followed him upon white horses, clothed in fine linen, white and clean. And out of his mouth goeth a sharp sword, that with it he should smite the nations: and he shall rule them with a rod of iron: and he treadeth the winepress of the fierceness and wrath of Almighty God. And he hath on his vesture and on his thigh a name written, KING OF KINGS, AND LORD OF LORDS.

Here surely we have the exact antithesis of one who sought to rule by Love and taught the worship of a wholly and unchangeably good, merciful and compassionate God?

As we have seen, both the Old and New Testament writers speak of four beasts, the fourth being the embodiment of all evil. In the case of Daniel's vision, these symbolized four kings who should arise out of the earth (Daniel vii, 17). But in the case of John the Divine the Fourth Beast is undoubtedly Mithras.

To the Christian and others outside the Mithraic fold, Mithraism, with its bull-slaying God who was also identifiable as the Bull, in whose regenerative blood the Faithful bathed; with its animal masks of Lion and Bull, Horse, Eagle and Gryphon, and its eschatological teachings of metempsychosis, evidently seemed to be the worship of the Beast, even as Pure Christianity has always been the worship of the Perfect Man.

And, in a sense, this was a correct diagnosis, for its militarism, its emphasis on the male attributes, on stoicism, brute courage and endurance, its initiatory trials and Tortures, its Taurobolium reveal it as a religion of violence, a cult of the jungle, the supreme law of which is the survival of the fittest. If it occasionally restrained the animal in its demand for continence it was only that the self-disciplined man should use his conserved energies for world-conquest. It was a means of taming the animalistic man, and not, like Christianity, the means of putting him off and attaining to a higher, more harmless and compassionate species, such as that attained by Jesus of Nazareth. It was, as Cumont says, "a doctrine that deified the whole of physical and tangible reality." It was the Westernized form of nature-worship, and sought, like the modern materialists, not to transcend but to conquer and re-make the world. It was, like all exoteric forms of Sun-worship, the deification of nature, as Christianity and the highest Gnosis in all Faiths is the transcendence of nature. To the Sun-worshipper the outward universe is the creation of that "Majesty on High"; to the Christian, God is Spirit, and all unlike this invisible and eternal Reality is temporary and illusory, or, as the Hindus and Buddhists describe it, *Maya*.

Between these two points of view there must ever be an

unbridgeable gulf, for they not only lead to incompatible ways of life but to the development of a totally different kind of a man, the best description of these two probably being Arthur Koestler's Yogi and Commissar, the latter clinging to his animalism and jungle habits, usually degenerating further into the brutish state, the former evolving to a higher species in the degree that he is able to put on the higher Mind and nature found in the Perfect or Whole Man of his faith; in the case of the Christian, Jesus Christ; in that of the oriental, such rishis as Gautama, Shankhara, or even the modern Gandhi.

Renan in his *Lettre à Berthelot* puts the matter succinctly when he writes:

> Before religion reached the point where it proclaimed that God should be sought in the absolute and the Ideal, that is to say, outside the world, one cult only was reasonable and scientific and that was the cult of the Sun.

But it was to this cult that the writer of the Apocalypse, even though he called himself a Christian, obviously belonged. All his symbolism is in the phraseology of a Sun-worshipper.

What appears to be the most likely explanation is that before what he believed to be his conversion to Christianity, which was, in fact, merely his pre-conceived idea of what Christianity taught, he had been a Kabbalist, an Hebraic occultist of the same school of thought as the writers of the Books of Daniel and Ezekiel upon which he had drawn so freely in the compiling of his so-called "Revelation", which also has echoes of other apocalyptic writings, such as the Book of Enoch.

Like the Church Fathers he was enraged against Mithraism, not only because of its persecutions of the newer Faith but because of the astonishing likeness of many of its rites, beliefs and symbols to those of that Faith, explicable only, at that time, as being the result of devilry in the priests and worshippers of the Beast, who, as Paul so forcefully put it, sat in the place of God "telling himself that he was God".

He is quite evidently unaware of the completely in-compatible nature of the Mysteries of Mithras and the Creed of Christ, and seems only anxious that his new deity should usurp all the glories and privileges of the Sun-God; should, in fact, totally replace the pagan God who, as the Beast, was to be cast in to the bottomless pit (Revelation xx, 1, 2, 3):

> And I saw an angel come down from heaven, having the key of the bottomless pit and a great chain in his hand, and he laid hold on the dragon, that old serpent which is the Devil, and Satan, and bound him a thousand years. And cast him into the bottomless pit, and shut him up and set a seal upon him, that he should deceive the nations no more.

History has proved this to be not good prophecy but wishful thinking on the part of the writer, for the Mithraic Beast has continued to deceive the nations with its advocacy of the cult of violence throughout the centuries, culminating in the supreme violence of today.

He speaks, too, of the false prophet that wrought miracles before the Beast, "with which he deceived them that had received the mark of the beast, and them that worshipped his image. These both were cast alive into a lake of fire burning with brimstone" (Revelation xix, 20)— the Mazdean lake, which leaves us in no doubt as to the origin of the writer's imagery. This is still further emphasized in his description of the heavenly kingdom, so utterly unlike that spiritual realm within spoken of by the Founder of the Christian Faith.

For the author of the Apocalypse "the city was pure gold like unto clear glass. And the foundations of the wall of the city were garnished with all manner of precious stones."

Here, indeed, is the city that housed Mithras' golden mansion, the city of the Sun with its rainbows glittering like jewels: "and the street of the city was pure gold, as it were transparent glass."

It is from this pagan source, and not from the Gospels, that throughout the ages men have gained the impression that heaven is a localized Kingdom whose golden gates open to admit the Faithful after death. It is a purely Mithraic teaching, and has no Christian basis. It is quite obvious that the writer of the Apocalypse had not begun to understand the true nature of Christianity, and had brought his own conceptions of the deific nature and of the character of Jesus Christ into the Church of his adoption, superimposing the Sun-God terminology and symbology on the Creed of Christ.

Nothing more clearly indicates the fact of the Church's syncretism than its adoption of this piece of writing as canonical. It is true that they may not have had all the Gospels with which to compare it. Weigall gives the date of the writing of the Apocalypse as from A.D. 69–93, while Barnes places it a few years later. But there were Q, and the Pauline Epistles, as well as the First Epistle of Peter. And even though, as we have seen, the last two showed a tendency to compromise with the rival Faith, they had certainly not gone completely over into its camp as did "John" of *The Revelation*. Moreover, Barnes tells us that the hesitation on the part of the Fathers to include this writing in the New Testament *lasted long*; in which case we may assume that by the time it was officially accepted all the Gospels were at hand with which to compare it. In which case their decision was more inexcusable than ever. For, as it stands, the Apocalypse is clearly revealed as the wide open gate through which the teachings, symbology and terminology of Sun-worship flowed into the Catholic Church which, far from doing anything to stem the adulteration, deliberately put its seal of approval on it by including it in the canonical writings. It was through this gate that the Sun-God openly entered the Temple of his rival, and through the Apocryphal teachings that which pretended to be the Christian Church became the Catholic Church of Mithras-Christos.

7

Constantine and the Sun-God

CONFRONTED with the historical picture of the Council of Nicaea, with what Eusebius, Bishop of Caesarea, describes in his *Life of Constantine* as its "vast garland of priests, composed of a variety of the choicest flowers," congregated in the great hall of the Emperor's Palace, we realize how very far the organization of the Christian Church had travelled since the days when Paul had found it, an obscure society of sincere, friendly and dedicated people who regularly met together over the simple meal described in the *Didache* to thank God for the advent of Truth brought to the world by His Son, Jesus Christ.

Paul's dream of making what he conceived to be the Creed of Christ the universal religion had come near to being realized. The galaxy of 318 bishops had been assembled from every part of the Roman Empire at the Emperor's invitation and expense. Constantine himself deemed the meeting of sufficient importance to preside over it, and was in sympathy with the teachings of these self-styled Christian Fathers. Paul's plan and powers of organization had undoubtedly triumphed.

Unfortunately, the price that the Church he had championed had paid for its gain of so much of the pagan world was the loss of its soul: the true creed of Christ.

These power-loving, self-willed, stubborn and contentious bishops who so enthusiastically acclaimed a homicide who had conquered the Western world by force of arms as their ally, had little in common with those humanly defenceless, pacific, humble non-violent groups of Christians in the first century who relied on God for everything, including the healing of the sick.

Nor did the difference lie only, or even chiefly in the character of these priests (a creed drawn up by the Arians was described as a "bastard and vile-begotten document," while the Bishop of Myra was said to have inflicted Arius with a punishing blow on the jaw for his heresy) who claimed to be Christians. The Council of Nicaea itself was living proof of how far from the true understanding of the teachings of Christ those who presided over the Christian Church had strayed. The contact with the pagan world and its beliefs, the concessions which the Church had doubtless been forced to make during its persecutions, the worldliness that had crept into its priesthood, had altered the whole nature of the original Gospel of compassion and non-violence taught by a quiet, God-obsessed man to his obedient students on the hills of Galilee.

Now, the Church founded to perpetuate the teachings of the Prince of Peace was split into three violently-contending factions, those who followed Alexander, those who followed Arius, with a small centre party led by Eusebius of Nicomedia.

The Alexandrians, afterwards known as the Athanasians, held to the Homoousian belief that the persons of the Trinity were of one substance. The Arians, according to Canon Bright in *The Age of the Fathers*, contended that "the Son had not existed from eternity and that he differed from other creatures in degree and not in kind," while Eusebius, and also the Emperor Constantine, both thought it was a great pity that the matter had been raised at all, and believed that it should have been left to the individual conscience rather than crystallized into dogma.

All three attitudes proved that the theologians had no real understanding of the implications of Jesus of Nazareth's life and teachings. Not one of them arose to point out the reconciling truth implied by the distinction made in the Gospels between Jesus the man and the Christ-like nature that animated him. Nor was any reference made to his, and Paul's, fundamental teaching of the nature of Reality, which would have illuminated and closed the dispute.

The Nicene Creed which was eventually decided upon as being canonical, commenced: "We believe in one God, the Father Almighty, Maker of all things both visible and invisible," which, while it would be a correct statement coming from the followers of Mithras, or any other nature-God, was a direct denial of Jesus's emphatic teachings that "It is the Spirit that quickeneth; the flesh profiteth nothing" (John vi, 63), and "that which is born of flesh is flesh; and that which is born of the Spirit is spirit" (John iii, 6), and with Paul's forthright declaration: "the flesh lusteth against the Spirit and the Spirit against the flesh: *and these are contrary to one another.*" (Gal. v, 17.)

By enforcing the belief that the most High God was responsible for making these pairs of warring contraries, and so for all misery and evil, and of creating not only the perfect invisible but also the far from perfect visible, they were positing an imperfect First Cause, in complete opposition to the Founder of their Faith who insisted that the Father was perfect; and by act, as well as word, taught, with Socrates, that the Highest Good never sent evil to any man.

While the Creed was correct in its homoousianism, its belief that the persons of the Trinity were of one substance —Spirit ("God is Spirit, and his worshippers must worship him in Spirit and in Reality." John iv, 24. Moffatt's Translation), it was in error if it implied that Jesus of Nazareth, in his physical aspect, was Spirit, and therefore of the same substance as the Father. The Arians were obviously making this distinction. When they spoke of the Son of God, they were thinking of the fleshly Jesus, the son of Joseph and Mary, and in that they were correct in saying that he was of different substance, had not existed from eternity and differed from other creatures in degree and not kind. But Jesus was not, in his physical sense, the Son of God. This "Son" is necessarily of the same substance as the Father, and God is Spirit. It was obviously to his spiritual and eternal nature, his divine sonship, that Jesus was referring when he declared, "Before Abraham was, I am", and "I and my Father are one." These statements clearly implied both his pre-existence and his eternal co-existence with the Father, which rules out any argument as to whether the son was born or begotten of the Father, except inasmuch as a ray may be said to be eternally begotten of the sun.

Eusebius's nervous disinclination for this discussion proved his own uncertainty. Constantine's attitude revealed his indifference, and therefore his very superficial understanding and love of Christianity. In a letter that he had addressed to Alexander and Arius when the controversy was first raging, and the two points of view had been put to him, he chided them for contending with one another "about these small and insignificant questions".[1] Yet the question at issue was no less than the answer to the eternal and vital queries of, "What is man? and what is his relationship to God?" In other words, the very foundation upon which any true religion must be built, and without a correct knowledge of which all religion is useless as an aid to man's salvation, or evolution.

But despite Eusebius's tremendous build-up of the Church's champion in his *Vita Constantini* into a near-saint, and the Emperor's self-righteous declarations, such as that in his letter to Sapor, the Persian, when he wrote: "The God I serve demands from his worshippers nothing but a pure mind and a spirit undefiled" at a time when he had every intention of slaughtering as many of Sapor's subjects as he could, Constantine was never a Christian either in his philosophy or life. And few things could have made this more evident than his attitude to the all-important controversy that led to the assembling of "The Council of the 318".

In his youth and early manhood he is admitted by all to have been a worshipper of the Sun-God. There is no evidence that he ever ceased to worship that deity, despite his interest in Christianity; and a great deal of evidence to prove that he continued to identify himself with that God

[1] *Vita Constantini* by Eusebius, Bishop of Caesarea.

throughout his life, and even on his death-bed, when, lying upon a white bed, in garments of shining white, he is reported to have said: "Now I have confidence that I am a partaker of divine light."

In the eyes of a Mithraist, Constantine, in his youth and early manhood, might, with his military skill and perpetual victory in battle, have been called, with justice, an excellent Prince. In the eyes of a follower of the Prince of Peace, he was, by these same acts, a power-loving homicide, and hardly the man to preside over an assembly which was to decide upon the spiritual teachings to be given to the Christian world. Eusebius describes the entrance of the Emperor into the Council Hall, saying that he passed through the midst of the priestly throng like "some heavenly angel of God clad in glittering raiment that seemed to gleam and flash with bright, effulgent rays of light, encrusted as it was with gold and precious stones."

That heavenly angel of God, so like Mithras in his glorious array and so utterly unlike the simple, unpretentious Teacher of Galilee, was responsible a year later for the slaughter of his eldest son, Crispus, his nephew aged eleven, and his second wife Fausta. Hardly the type of man, it might be thought, to decide on the spiritual pabulum fitting for the consumption of mankind. Yet this was the man that the Christian bishops of the time acclaimed as their champion and friend, obviously deeply taking to heart his directives in his farewell speech to them after the Council, among these being the perilous doctrine that, if bishops sin, their offences should be hushed up, lest their flock be scandalized, or be encouraged to follow their example; and the reminder that, as few people come to religion through their desire for Truth, but for the benefits it promises, "Christians should be like physicians, and prescribe for each according to his ailments. They must not be fanatics; they must be accommodating." In other words, Truth must not be an absolute. To achieve good ends, any means may be employed; advice ardently embraced by the Catholic Church from that time onward, especially influencing the writings and legends of Eusebius, and the policies of those errant sons of Mother Church, the Catholic-born dictators of our present age.

Doubtless after the persecutions that they had endured under his predecessor, Diocletian, Constantine's tolerance and adoption of Christianity may have seemed Christ-like to the Fathers of the Church. But to less prejudiced eyes of the present day, he must be seen as totally undeserving of the title of Christian. From first to last he was an ambitious, extravagant, militaristic pagan, a man of great capabilities and powers, but, above all, of violence, by means of which he achieved and held his Empire. There could hardly be anything less Christ-like than such a life.

By the time he found Christianity, it had, as the Council of Nicaea made plain, ceased to be essentially Christian, and was already, thanks to such innovations as those of Paul and the writer of the Book of the Revelation, so impregnated with the symbolism and philosophy of the sun-worshippers as to make Mithraism and Christianity at times indistinguishable. To a man as wise in this world as Constantine, it must have seemed, as he examined these two systems, a complete waste of time and energy to fight about their labels. To a pagan Emperor, used to the altars of many gods being assembled in his cities, it was just a question of admitting a new God to the Pantheon. And not so very new, as he must have suspected, when noting the likeness of the Christ as presented by Paul and John the Divine to his own Sun-God.

The only religion of which he would have disapproved and refused to tolerate was one that disapproved of him and his ambitions; in a word, Christianity in its original form. The peace-loving, humble, non-violent, good-living, gentle Christians of the first century had been a silent but persistent rebuke to tyranny, violence and worldly power, and so were persecuted by those of whom such an outlook and way of life constituted an intolerable criticism. But Constantine could have detected little or none of this Christ-like spirit in the authoritarian Church with whose fierce quarrels he had to deal, and whose bishops were willing enough to approve of his wars when they were fought against the pagans ostensibly to champion Christendom. In their protector they were willing to shut their eyes to all the crimes forbidden by the Founder of their Faith.

Constantine, who was a born statesman, could not have failed to see that an organization which could command such obedience and devotion in its followers would be an immense acquisition to the State—so long as it upheld the policies of that State. Mithraism might have served for this purpose, but it did not lend itself so well to universalism, had not sufficient appeal to women, and was nothing like so well organized as the newer faith; nor could the followers of Mithras, for all their austerity, equal the fanatical fervour of the followers of Christ, of which he had been an observer under the persecutions of Diocletian. Early in life it must have been apparent to him that the zeal that could make men court martyrdom in the maws of wild beasts could be turned to good account in the cause of the Empire. Such courage and self-sacrifice were even greater than that which inspired the initiates undergoing the Twelve Tortures of Mithras, who had proved to be the bravest and best-disciplined soldiers of his Army.

But, as he well knew, the Mithraist's loyalty to the Emperor, and therefore to the Empire, sprang from the identification of these things with the God they worshipped with such fervour. The Emperor was his representative, his particular care, on earth. A similar connexion must be made if he were ever to win the increasing congregations of Christians throughout his Empire to a like devotion and patriotism, weaning them from their former impractical and foolish policy of non-violence.

This policy had already been modified with the passing of time. What had originally been a refusal to depart from the essential nature of a compassionate God of Love, had hardened into a refusal to take the military oath to pagan Emperors who were enemies of their Faith. But supposing the Emperor were no longer an enemy? Supposing he upheld the God so like his own, and became Christianity's champion and friend? A universal authoritarian Church, able to impose its will, as the Christian Church was doing, upon thousands of people throughout the Roman Empire, could obviously be of the greatest possible assistance to the government of the Empire, and the aim of world-domination, if its will could accord with that of the Emperor.

From the evidence before us it seems possible that Constantine had been thinking somewhat on these lines as early as the time of his invasion of Italy, especially at about the time of the Battle of the Milvian Bridge of which so much has been written by both pagan and Christian authors. The discrepancies between the versions of this event and the marvels that accompanied it are so great, and the inaccuracies of the chief Christian historian, Eusebius, so glaring and undeniable, that it would be futile to hope to come to an approximation of the truth were it not for the slight knowledge we have of the nature of Mithraism and of the Emperor's addiction to that form of worship.

Both pagan and Christian writers are agreed that this battle, which preceded Constantine's triumphant progress into Rome, had been won by divine intervention. On the nature of that intervention they were far from being in agreement. Lactantius, who wrote very shortly after the event, said in his treatise *On the Death of the Persecutors,* that Constantine had been warned in a dream to have his soldiers' shields inscribed with a cross before going into battle next day. In other words, his weapons were to be dedicated to the service of Christ, Eusebius, in his *History of the Church* published in A.D. 326, thirteen years after the battle, said nothing of this dream but merely stated that at this time of trial Constantine "piously called to his aid the God of Heaven and his Son Jesus Christ".

In 337, however, when the Emperor was dead and unable to confirm the legend, Eusebius wrote in his *Life of Constantine,* what is now the official version of the story, of how Constantine, repenting of his worship of pagan gods, when confronted with the heavy task of conquering

Rome, prayed for a sign from heaven which should tell him the name of the true God that he must worship in order to be granted victory. In answer to his prayer, what was afterwards identified by the Christians as a cross of radiant light, was seen in the heavens, with the inscription "Conquer by this". Not only Constantine but the whole army was said to have seen this apparition. That night the Emperor dreamed that Christ appeared to him bearing the sign he had seen in heaven, and told him to copy it as a talisman to carry into battle. (Surely a most unlikely directive from the Prince of Peace?)

The next day Constantine sent for workers to make the sign he had seen, which was afterwards known as the *Labarum*, according to his design. When finished, it was a long, gilded spear with a transverse bar surmounted by a crown of gold, with jewels surrounding a monogram of Christ. From the bar hung a purple cloth embroidered with gold, jewels and the busts of Constantine and his sons.

A third version of the story was supplied by the pagan orator, Nazarius, while delivering a panegyric on the anniversary of Constantine's tenth year of rule, when the Emperor was still alive and able to correct the report had he found any fault with it.

In this version there was no hint of dreams of fiery crosses; but he affirmed that the marvels attending the battle had been such that all Gaul had been awed by the stories about them. Celestial armies had been seen moving across the sky and the eyes of the watching and wondering soldiers on earth had been dazzled by the shining armour and flashing shields of those above. What is more, they had heard the celestial cohorts shout, "We seek Constantine; we are marching to the aid of Constantine." And the speaker's explanation was that it had been the deified Emperor Constantius, father of Constantine, bringing the hosts of heaven to the aid of his worthy son. After all these conflicting versions of the divine intervention that had gained victory for Constantine and instated him in Rome, the validity of all three may well be in doubt. But one solid, tangible factor emerged from this confusion, and that was the famous *Labarum* which was undoubtedly fashioned and used, and was said to be in existence as late as the ninth century.

The story of its fashioning would seem to have been invented in order to explain the existence of this emblem that was continually carried into battle by Constantine and his army; for by its description it was originally quite evidently none other than the Mithraic sword and radiant crown used at the initiation ceremonies in the Mysteries of Mithras, symbolizing world-conquest by the sword and the divinity of Kings. It was certainly by this, and not by the pacific, self-immolating cross of Jesus Christ, that the Battle of Milvian Bridge and all the other battles necessary to the building of the Roman Empire, had been won.

Eusebius assures us that Constantine swore to the validity of the official version of the story, on oath. This may well be true. Constantine was said to have continually sworn on oath in order to be more emphatic, and he is unlikely to have been more punctilious about truthfulness than his priestly chronicler, of whom J. B. Firth moderately says, and abundantly proves, in his book, *Constantine the Great*, "Eusebius is notoriously untrustworthy."[1]

It is quite probable that when, after the murder of his wife and son, the priests of Mithras refused him purification, and the Christian Fathers proved more accommodating, Constantine decided that the embarrassingly obvious Mithraic symbol that had accompanied him to wars, must be "explained away", for no Mithraist could fail to recognize the age-old sword and crown, and they might claim him as their own in future ages on this evidence. Why, therefore, should it not become the cross and crown of those who had won his favour by assuring him of salvation? It is equally possible that both priest and Emperor had come to see, in the course of time, that the synthetic nature of the Catholic Church, especially its connexion with Mithraism, must be disguised from its Christian congregations if their original fervour and loyalty were to be preserved,

[1] *Constantine the Great*, by J. B. Firth. (G. P. Putnam's Sons, 1905.)

for this had always been inspired by what they imagined to be the original Gospel of Jesus Christ.

The addition to this emblem of the initials of Jesus Christ points unmistakably to the early date of Constantine's plan for a religious synthesis, a plan explicitly stated in his previously quoted letter to Alexander and Arius, when he wrote:

> It was my purpose in the first place, to bring the diverse opinions of all nations respecting the Deity to a settled condition, *and a single form* . . .

So, for nine centuries, the bejewelled *Labarum* blazoned forth the unholy syncretism that took place in the reign of Constantine, when the name of the Prince of Peace, the most gentle, tender, compassionate and loving man who ever trod the earth, was used to sanctify the violence, ambition and worldly power of those protégés of Mithras, the Emperors of Rome, and their successors in tyranny.

The Edict of Milan, issued soon after the conquest of Rome was another open avowal of Constantine's intention. Having made himself master of the West, he not only wanted to consolidate his conquest by gaining the friendship of the people, his Christian as well as his pagan subjects, but he also realized that, for a truly united Empire, there must obviously be a uniformity of fundamental beliefs and a common ethic, in order to avoid wasteful internal conflict such as had occurred in the reign of Diocletian. To ensure this, a symbiosis of paganism and Christianity must be established. He was also anxious to keep on the right side of the gods who had so far ensured him victory. He wanted the approval, and never the enmity, of any and every god. Therefore, they should all be allowed their devotees, even the Christian God who was so accommodatingly like his familiar Sun-God that in worshipping the one he was also worshipping the other. So long as the Christian Church could be relied upon to perpetuate the Mithraic values, and uphold the God's imperialistic character, what did it matter what one *called* the State Church? It was the spirit that mattered, the name profited nothing.

Therefore, shortly after his victorious entry into Rome, he went to Milan, and joined with his pagan ally and co-Emperor, Licinius, in issuing the Edict of Milan, the chief clauses of which ran as follows:

Inasmuch as we, Constantine Augustus and Licinius Augustus, have met together at Milan on a joyful occasion, and have discussed all that appertains to the public advantage and safety, we have come to the conclusion that, among the steps likely to profit the majority of mankind and demanding immediate attention, nothing is more necessary than to regulate the worship of the Divinity.

We have decided, therefore, to grant both to the Christians and to all others perfect freedom to practise the religion which each had thought best for himself, that so whatever Divinity resides in heaven may be placated, and rendered propitious to us and to all who have been placed under our authority. Consequently we have thought this to be the policy demanded alike by healthy and sound reason—that no one, on any pretext whatever, should be denied freedom to choose his religion, whether he prefers the Christian religion or any other that seems most suited to him, in order that the Supreme Divinity, whose observance we obey with free minds, may in all things vouchsafe to us its usual favours and benevolences.

Wherefore, it is expedient for your Excellency to know that we have resolved to abolish every one of the stipulations contained in all previous edicts sent to you with respect to the Christians, on the ground that they now seem to us to be unjust and alien from the spirit of our clemency.

Henceforth, in perfect and absolute freedom, each and every person who chooses to belong to and practise the Christian religion shall be at liberty to do so without let or hindrance in any shape or form.

We have thought it best to explain this to your Excellency in the fullest possible manner that you may know that we have accorded to these same Christians a free and absolutely unrestricted right to practise their own religion.

And inasmuch as you see that we have granted this indulgence to the Christians, your Excellency will understand that a similarly free and unrestricted right, conformable to the peace of our times, is granted to all others equally to practise the religion of their choice. We have resolved upon this course that no one and no religion may seem to be robbed of the honour that is their due.

This document by no means proves, as the ecclesiastical historians have insisted, that Constantine was converted to Christianity at this time. It merely ensured that Christianity should have the same privileges as the pagan religions, and that Christians should no longer be persecuted for their beliefs. Why should they, now that neither their beliefs nor their Church's policies conflicted with those of the Emperor? And so the pact was tacitly made. Constantine would protect the Church, and the Church would uphold him and his policies. This was very evident in 335 when the Emperor made the bishops aware of his plans for war against the Persian pagan, Sapor. Their enthusiasm for what they saw as a war against paganism was so great that, according to Eusebius, they declared their intention to accompany Constantine into the field, which so pleased him that he had his tent made in the shape of a church! This sanctifying of murderous campaigns for the protection or propagation of the Faith was now the policy of Christendom.

The Edict of Milan could certainly not have been termed a Christian document, for the deity was referred to in it only vaguely as "*Summa Divinitas*", and the even vaguer, "*Quicquid est Divinitates in sede caelesti.*" Certainly not the terminology of a convert to the God of the Hebrews.

A further indication that Constantine's conversion to the new Faith was inspired by expediency rather than deep conviction, lies in the recorded fact that when Eusebius of Nicomedia and two other bishops, hesitated about signing agreement to the Creed of Athanasius, they were warned by Constantia, the Emperor's sister, not to refuse lest Constantine should throw over Christianity in disgust at the dissensions among the Christians.

Furthermore, when, in the year following the Council of Nicaea, Constantine became responsible for the murders of his son, wife and nephew, the attacks of conscience he subsequently suffered led him to apply in the first place, not to the Christian bishops but to the priests of the Sun-God who refused firmly to purify him from such crimes. It was then that he turned to Christianity, and, as J. B. Firth puts it, "was promised full forgiveness at the price of repentence and baptism". Yet even so he made no haste to accept the terms for the salvation of his soul, and postponed the purification of baptism until he was on his deathbed.

Nevertheless, it may well have been a sign both of repentance, and gratitude for the promise of salvation that induced him to build such a great number of churches all over his empire for the propagation of what the Christians believed to be Christianity, but which he must certainly have suspected of being the cult of Mithras-Christos, which he could rely on these churches to perpetuate.

It is quite obvious that, until the last, he identified himself with the Sun-God, in the manner of his co-religionist, Augustus Caesar, and all the other Kings and Emperors who had accepted the patronage and anointing of Mithras.

J. B. Firth writes of this imposed Emperor-worship:

> The Emperor was no longer essentially a Roman Imperator, a supreme war-Lord, a soldier chief of State. He had become a King in a palace, secluded from the gaze of the vulgar, surrounded by all the attributes and ornaments of an Eastern monarchy, and robed in gorgeous vestments stiff with gold and jewels. Men were taught to speak and think of him as super-human and sacrosanct, to approach him with genuflexion and adoration, to regard every office, however menial, attached to his person as sacred.

A few of his titles were, Your Majesty, Your Eternity, Your Divinity. In a word, the age-old Mithraic King, but by no possible effort of the imagination a follower of one who dwelt with humble working men and had no place whereon to lay his head.

His culminating and most blatant self-identification with the Sun-God was made during the building of Constantinople, when the Column of Constantine inscribed at its base with a dedication of the City to Christ, and supposed to contain such relics as the adze employed by Noah in building the ark, Mary Magdalene's alabaster box, and the crosses on which the two thieves were hanged on Calvary, was surmounted by the statue of the Sun-God from which the head had been removed and replaced by the head of Constantine wearing the radiant crown of Mithras. The relationship of the Emperor to the most High God was proclaimed in the pagan inscription: "To Constantine shining like the sun."

Throughout his life, whether he called himself a Mithraist or a Christian, Constantine worshipped the Most High God who was symbolized by the light of heaven.

Professor Bury says of him: "The evidence seems to show that his religion was a syncretistic monotheism: he was content to see the deity in the Sun, in Mithras, or in the God of the Hebrews."

This opinion was evidently shared by the pagan orator and writer, Symmachus, living in the reign of Theodosius the Great, who said of Constantine that he had belonged to both religions.

What has not been so evident is that the same might be said of the Church he championed and whose policies he so very evidently influenced. The world of violence that we see about us today is the direct result of the syncretism effected by Constantine and the Church of his adoption, the unholy alliance of the Gospel of Peace with power-politics, the impossible fusion of violence and non-violence, the Cult of Mithras with the Creed of Christ.

8

Mithras' Other Hiding Places

THE peril to the Christian Church was not, however, finally overcome at the time of the adoption of Christianity as the State religion by Constantine. It still had to reckon with a foe so formidable that, had he not been cut off in his prime, the positions of the two religions might once again have been reversed, and Mithraism, under the transforming, syncretizing powers of Julian the Apostate, and his wise friend and adviser, Maximus of Ephesus, have been instated as the official religion of the Roman Empire.

Flavius Claudius Julianus (born A.D. 331), nephew of Constantine, and known afterwards to the Christian world as Julian the Apostate, was a very remarkable young man, combining the qualities of writer, religious eclectic and idealistic philosopher with those of a courageous warrior; his aims and capacities being remarkably like those of Mithridates VII, which perhaps is not so surprising since they were both devoted followers of the same god.

As one of Julian's biographers writes: "In his private observances and dominant thoughts he was a follower of Mithraism, or the philosophy of Solar Monotheism," of which, she adds, "he was the most notable exponent."[1]

His passionate devotion to Mithras had an obverse side in his contempt for and detestation of Christianity, which was probably aroused in the first place by the horrible massacre of his near relations, including his eldest brother,

---

[1] *Julian*, by Alice Gardener. (G. P. Putnam's Sons, 1901)

at the instigation of one of the "Trinity of Princes" so flatteringly referred to by Eusebius of Caesarea, his Christian-bred cousin, Constantius, after the funeral of Constantine. Julian was only seven at the time, but the tragedy seems to have affected him psychologically and led to a blind and fanatical hatred of Christianity.

Another reason given for his attitude to the new Faith was the fact that his training into it was undertaken by the Arian Bishop of Nicomedia, Eusebius, and that Christianity was therefore presented to him in his youth in the form least likely to appeal to his mystical nature. But the most obvious reason for his dislike of the usurping Faith was that he identified it with his detested uncle who must have inspired him with intense fear as a very young child for having so gratuitously "liquidated" another young nephew. As an adult Mithraist, he also resented and despised Constantine for having, nominally at least, abandoned the imperial God.

Julian being, according to his lights, a man of character and integrity, deeply religious and with a single-minded devotion to his deity, could have had no sympathy with the tolerance that came from Constantine's essential indifference. It seems probable from his satire, *The Caesars*, that Julian fully recognized the significance of the *Labarum*, and that he despised his uncle not so much for being a Christian but for not having been loyal to any one God. This was the nature of his indictment in the satire he wrote for the Saturnalia in which he assembles all the Emperors of Rome, making each gravitate to the God of his choice, and the one, therefore, that he most resembles. But Constantine is found to have no such affinity. No God will own him as his "image and likeness". And he is eventually adopted by the Goddess of Luxury who afterwards passes him on to the Goddess of Extravagance, to which inferior deities, Julian suggests, Constantine was alone faithful.

It was his lack of integration and fidelity that his nephew so much despised, constituting, as they did, an insult to their mutual God.

Julian practised the austerity and self-control that

Constantine in his later life so conspicuously lacked. He was an example of the best type of Mithraist, and upheld a standard which, though primitive compared with the original Creed of Christ, had many considerable virtues, including those of truthfulness and personal integrity. He was also an intellectual and mystic.

Like all great religions, Mithraism operated on many levels, from the basest superstition to the highest metaphysical understanding. Mithras was the bull-slayer, but also the Sun-God; and while the bull-slayer continued to have his Tortures and bloody baptisms, devotions to the Sun-God might range from pure nature worship to the loftiest metaphysical and mystical heights. And Julian's concept of his Faith, after his initiation by Maximus, appears to have been at times so transcendental that it could not only be identified with its original form in the monotheistic system of Zoroaster, but also with the philosophy of Plotinus of whom he was a great admirer, as well—although he did not, apparently, realize it—as with the mysticism of Paul, from whence it would have been but a step to the exalted teachings of the Kingdom of God. But as he regarded Paul as a charlatan, probably believing that he had deliberately filched his teachings from Mithraism, he doubtless gave the origins of the new Faith very little attention.

Yet, as an advocate of mental purity, he could have found no fault with the apostle's instructions to think on "whatsoever things are true . . . honest . . . just . . . pure . . . lovely, and of good report." (Phil. iv, 8.) As a despiser of the body, and one who wished to be delivered from its fetters, he must have agreed with Paul's statements that "flesh and blood cannot enter the kingdom of God," (1 Cor. xv, 50), and that "the things which are seen are temporal: but the things which are not seen are eternal." (2 Cor. iv, 18.) He would certainly have echoed his assurance that "if our earthly house of this tabernacle were dissolved we have a building of God, an house not made with hands, eternal in the heavens. . . . Therefore we are always confident knowing that, whilst we are at home in the body, we are absent from the Lord." (2 Cor. v, 1, 6.) Indeed this last conviction was the basis of Julian's personal courage and non-attachment. Yet, in spite of these fundamental aspects of agreement between the two Faiths, he concentrated only on the differences that existed between Mithraism and the adulterated Christianity of his era. Probably from a dis-inclination to make as deep and sympathetic study of the Christian Gospel as he had accorded to other Faiths, he failed to detect the high ideal and aim of the Creed of Christ, although its innate pacificism would certainly have been alien to his nature, and so he was incapable of viewing Christianity apart from the imperfections of those who professed it as a Faith.

Nevertheless, had he and Paul lived in the same era, and been able to meet, they would have discovered that they had a great deal in common. Not only must they have noted the likeness between their two creeds on their highest level, and seen evidence therein of a common genesis or Gnosis, but they would also have recognized their mutuality of purpose. For Julian wished to do for Mithraism precisely what Paul had desired to do for Christianity: establish it as a world-religion in a form of synthetic Monotheism. To achieve this purpose both zealots were willing to take from the rival Faith any elements that would help to further the popularity and interests of their own. Julian was, in fact, the potential Paul of Mithraism.

Gregory Nazianzen, a Christian and fellow-student of Julian's in his more obscure days at the university, wrote of the Emperor's attempt to organize Mithraism as the State religion, and his adoption of Christian customs:

> He (Julian) also, having the same design (as that of Sennacherib), was intending to establish schools in every town, with pulpits and higher and lower rows of benches, for lectures and expositions of the heathen doctrines, both of such as give rules of morality and those that treat of abstruse subjects, also a form of prayer

alternately pronounced, and penance for those that sinned proportionate to the offence, initiation also and completion, and other things that evidently belong to our (the Catholic) constitution. He was purposing also to build inns and hospices for pilgrims, monasteries for men, convents for virgins, places for meditation, to establish a system of charity for the relief of prisoners, and also that which is conducted by means of letters of recommendation, by which we forward such as require it from one nation to another:—things which he had specially admired in our institutions.

In other words, Julian was planning to adapt the organization he admired of the ideology he loathed to his own world-faith, even as Paul had introduced the most popular beliefs of Mithraism into the worship of Jesus Christ.

Both these men were Gnostics in the sense that their knowledge of spiritual things far exceeded that of any one creed. Both believed that this Gnosis could be incorporated in the worship of their chosen God. Both believed that this God was the perfect manifestation of the Divine Good whence he proceeded, and that the "one thing worth having in life was the consciousness of a close relation to the Divinity". Both, in fact were mystics; both insisted upon the all-importance of moral purity, the need for philanthropy, the overcoming of the flesh and the cleansing of the mind, but neither of them seems to have seen how inconsistent were such ideals with their sectarian beliefs such as, in Paul's case, the doctrine of vicarious atonement, and even more startlingly in Julian's case, his satisfaction (expressed in a letter to Maximus) at being able to sacrifice publicly hecatombs of oxen; the entrails of these unfortunate beasts being believed to divulge prognostications, like tea-leaves in a cup! and his willingness to allow the people to practise the often obscene rituals of the Mithraic Mysteries based on repellent stories of the ancient Gods, and incorporating those of Cybele the Great Mother.

This dichotomy which is unhappily all too often a feature of the human mentality, resulted, in Julian's case, chiefly from the fact that there was no place in his philosophy for tenderness and compassionate love. Stoical austerity, non-attachment and courage being the Mithraic ideals.

While believing in a universal brotherhood based on the fact that all men proceeded from the same Source, and in general philanthropy, his militaristic outlook left no room for belief in the sanctity of life either of man or beast. He believed that death was not an evil but rather a special favour from the Gods, and this personal non-attachment rendered him insensitive to the suffering of others. His character and outlook were directly derived from his religion which it was his life-long ambition to universalize, believing that this was the mission ordained for him by Helios-Mithras who would protect him and ensure his success in such work. Miss Gardener writes:

> In many passages of his work Julian shows by apparently voluntary ejaculations or by express statements how constantly and habitually he expressed himself as the servant of . . . Mithras, and the idea of his special mission from that deity is worked out in the form of a fable in one of his *Orations against the Cynics*.

In another of these orations he affirms his basic belief in the essential unity of all philosophy, stating that its practical aims should be, "the obligation to live above-board and to have no secret corners in the soul wherein unworthy desires and thoughts may lie concealed and beyond all, the need of an infinite aspiration after a Divine Life to enable men to live purely and bravely on this earth." (*Ibid.*)

In his ambition to establish a world-wide cult of Solar Monotheism, he was helped and encouraged throughout his life by Maximus, the Magician, who had initiated him into the Mithraic Mysteries, and taught him numerological and astrological lore. Immediately he came to power, he summoned this revered and well-beloved *Guru* to his side, and shocked the members of the Senate over which he was presiding when Maximus arrived, by rushing out to greet him, and bringing him into the august assembly.

At the time of his death Maximus was by his side, sustaining him, and doubtless helping him to make his, often described, dignified and philosophical departure from this life.

Whether he personally had a hand in it or not, it was certainly men of Maximus's school of thought, the Gnostics, who managed to protect and preserve the teachings so dear to him and his pupil at the times of the great persecutions which started after the death of Julian, and thereafter broke out periodically and with great ferocity in countries whose policies were dominated by the Roman Church. These persecutions were directed at the Gnostics who throughout the ages, have always claimed to know the esoteric Truth which lies behind, and is often perverted by, the exoteric teachings of the orthodox churches. C. W. King writes of this higher knowledge:

We ask what *Gnosticism* is, and what it professes to teach. What is the peculiar *Gnosis* that it claims to itself? The answer is, the knowledge of God and Man, of the Being and Providence of the former, and of the creation and destiny of the latter. While the ignorant and super-stitious were degrading the glory of the incorruptible God into an image made with hands, and were changing "the truth of God into a lie, and worshipped and served the creature rather than the Creator", the ancient Gnostics held purer and truer ideas.

Nevertheless, there were many grades of Gnosticism, from the highly philosophical and metaphysical to the magical, and it was evidently the latter that perpetuated Mithraism. For Windischmann cites Jerome as saying that the Gnostics adopted Mithras, making his name into a mystic charm, from which they got the number 365, as from the mystic name *Abraxas*.[1]

And it was evidently these persecuted wise men, or wizards, who succeeded in concealing the Mithraic Mysteries in occult hiding places where traces of them can be found even today.

Possibly the most successful of these were the secret societies that have persisted down the ages in a direct line from the Knights Templars to the modern Freemasons. Of the initiation rites of the earlier societies, E. W. King tells us:

> The strange and obscene ceremonies observed on the admission of neophytes into the various secret societies that flourished under the Lower Empire and in the Middle Ages are all of them no more than faint traditions of the penances or "Twelve Tortures" that purchased admission into the cave of Mithras.

He suggests that the continued existence of the Gnostic symbols and signs, despite the bitter persecution of Mithraism by the Christian Church after the death of Julian when everything that could be found pertaining to the Cult was destroyed, may be explained by the fact that they were in the first place preserved by the Sufis of Persia, passed on to the Templars, and from them to the Rosicrucians, or Brothers of the Rosy Cross. Of this preservation through many occult channels, he writes:

> From the very nature of things we may be certain that their signs and symbols, after the esoteric doctrines were forgotten, passed into the repertory of all "who used curious arts", the alchemists, astrologers, and wizards of the Dark Ages, and then became the property

[1] In Comm. in Amos, v, 9, 10. Jerome writes:
"Basilides gives to the omnipotent god (Mithra) the uncouth name of Abraxas, and asserts that according to the Greek letters, and the number of the cycle of the year this is comprehended in the sun's orbit. The name Mithra, which the Gentiles use, gives the same sum with different letters."

of the Rosicrucians who were truly the parent *stock* and not a recent brand (as is now pretended) of the present Freemasons.

Undoubtedly one of the means used to preserve the Mithraic Mysteries was the incorporation of a number of their symbolical figures in that curious set of playing cards known as the Tarot, the origin of which has always been a subject of debate.

In Éliphas Lévi's book *Dogme et Rituel de la Haute Magie,* we read that in the dark ages when the wise men, or wizards, were persecuted and their secrets threatened with extinction, they decided to have the sacred, magical signs depicted in a pack of playing cards since no one would think of looking in such a place for Divine Wisdom; and vice, in the form of gambling, which perpetuates itself from age to age, would ensure that the cards and their signs were never lost to humanity since they would be kept in continual use. Many of the symbols on these cards are today clearly recognizable as being of Mithraic origin. Among them we find the Crown, the Emperor and Empress, the Pope or Father of fathers, the chariot of Hermes which is Mithras in his Sun chariot, the Judgement, the Hierophant, the Baphomet, or Head of the Goat of Mendes, the Burning Star and Eternal Youth (Mithras having always been alluded to as the brightest orb in the firmament, and represented as being eternally young), the Radiant Sun which is the Sun-God or Prince of Heaven himself, the Fool who is also the Juggler, wearing the cap that identifies him with Augustine's "Fellow", and finally, the Pentacle, the Mithraic symbol which ensures the soul free passage in its ascent to the Supernal Light. The prayer which is said to be offered with it almost certainly refers to Mithras whose number has always been seven since we first hear of him as the Seventh Amshaspand:

O first and seventh one, born to rule with power, Chief Word of the Pure Intelligence! Perfect work in the sight of the Father and the Son (Timeless Being and

Ormuzd); by presenting unto thee in this seal the *sign of life*, I open the gate which thy power hath closed to the world, and freely traverse thy domains.

Now the Pentacle is said to be Solomon's Seal, and Éliphas Lévi received his knowledge of the Tarot from the Kabbalah, of which King writes that many authors erroneously date it later than Christianity whereas its teachings belong to a far more remote antiquity, as is evident from the Book of Daniel with its Kabbalic symbolism. Furthermore:

> The idea of Emanation is . . . the soul, the essential element of the Kabbalah; it is likewise . . . the essential character of Zoroastrianism. We may therefore consider that it was through their very intimate connexion with Persia that the Jews imbibed that idea. According to the Kabbalah, as according to the Zend-Avesta, all that exists has emanated from the source of the Infinite Light . . . all is an emanation from this Being; the nearer . . . that any approaches to him, the more perfect is it, and the less so does it become, as it recedes from him: this idea of gradation is eminently Persian.

This connexion of the Kabbalah with Mithraism would suggest that we may have stumbled on the explanation of yet another historical mystery—the reason for Julian's wish and attempt to restore the city and temple of Jerusalem. Both he and Ammianus refer to this in their writings, and of how it was prevented in what seemed to be a supernatural manner by the appearance of alarming globes of fire which killed some of the workmen. This phenomenon was considered to indicate the disapproval of the Gods and the project was abandoned. But many historians have been puzzled by Julian's attitude to the Jews in that he not only took deliberate measures for alleviating the oppressions felt by them but should also wish to rebuild Solomon's Temple, the monument to an alien Faith. Our present evidence would seem to point to the fact that on its esoteric side, its Kabbalic teachings, the Faith was not alien, but so akin to that of Maximus and his pupil that they might well have visualized the rebuilt Temple of Solomon as providing yet another repository for their secret doctrines, a fitting shrine for the wise King's Seal. Moreover the Jews shared Julian's repellent proclivity for animal sacrifices, their altars being as blood-washed as Mithras' Taurobolium.[1]

C. W. King suggests the possibility of the Knights Templars having been responsible for the plan of the Tarot Cards at the time of their persecution and dispersal in 1307. This Fraternity is believed to have been the Ancestor of modern Freemasonry. Lessing writes of them:

> The Lodges of the Templars were in the very highest repute during the twelfth and thirteenth centuries; and out of such a Templars' Lodge which had been *continually kept up* in the heart of London was the Society of Freemasons established in the seventeenth century by Sir Christopher Wren.

This would appear to endorse Michelet's supposition that some of the Templars who escaped formed secret societies. He tells us in *Histoire de France* that all except two disappeared in Scotland from whence the highest mysteries of Freemasonry have come, the highest grades being called the Scotch.

It appears that the degrees in Freemasonry have one very strong similarity to those of Mithraism in that the first three do not denote illumination or true initiation, and the neophytes are only admitted into the Mysteries, thus becoming *Illuminati*, when they reach the Fourth Degree of Scottish Novices; the Fifth Degree being Scottish Knights.

---

[1] In this connexion the following citation from *The Sibylline Oracles*, translated from the Hellenistic-Jewish Texts by the Rev. H. N. Bate, M.A., is of interest:

"Thereafter shall there be a holy race of God-fearing men . . . who will pay honour to the temple of the great God, with the fat and savour of holy hecatombs, with sacrifices of fat bulls and rams without blemish, the first-born of sheep and fat flocks of lambs making holy oblations upon the great altar." (Book iii, 573–9.)

King writes that: "the most important division of French Freemasons style themselves Parisian Templars and say they have kept up the succession of Grand Masters unbroken. François I was said to have burnt alive four men convicted of being Templars. If true this suffices to prove the existence of that fraternity down to a period but little removed from the public manifestation of the Rosicrucians."

This savagery on the part of a Catholic King would suggest that the vigilance of the church against the survival of any form of the Mithraic cult was still unrelaxed in the sixteenth century. But it was evidently unable to prevent the renaissance of the Mysteries a century later by the Lutheran Mystic, J. V. Andrea, the Founder according to Nicolai, of modern Rosicrucianism.

This man, who was almoner to the Duke of Württemburg, used the Knights Templars badge of the Rosy Cross for his own fraternity, which aimed at fusing all Christian sects into a universal brotherhood. It is interesting to note that Martin Luther's seal was a Rose and a Cross.

Mithraism may also be traced in modern occultism, especially in astrology and numerology which were prominent features of the Mysteries, and of Babylonian origin. Cumont points out that even before the Roman Emperors had forbidden the exercise of idolatry "their edicts against astrology and magic furnished an indirect means of attacking the clergy and disciples of Mithra". He also says:

> Astrology . . . owes some share of its success to the Mithraic propaganda, and Mithraism is therefore partly responsible for the triumph in the West of this pseudo-science with its long train of errors and terrors . . .

But when we have cited all the external, unorthodox hiding places of the Fellow in the Cap from which he has continued to sway the minds and hearts of men, we must not forget that his chief and most dangerous hiding place is in those very minds and hearts. While they harbour his spirit, while the mind craves for dark mysteries and secret doctrines, and is not content with the clear, clean-cut and simple teaching of the Man of Galilee, and while the heart secretly loves and clings to the natural world and all that is in that world proving that the love of the Father is not in it; while it admires and applauds the militaristic virtues, the world-conquering spirit, instead of loving and enthroning the pacific, world-transcending spirit of Jesus the Christ, there can be no real Christianity on earth, nor in the policies of the world. For what is secretly loved must inevitably be manifested. Men may profess to be Christians but their behaviour will always betray them. The nationalism, materialism, violence of the present age clearly reveals not the worship of the Christ but of Mithras.

It is from this final hiding place—the soul of man—that the pagan god must be ejected, and once this is done the search for him may cease. There would be no need to seek through the ages in orthodox and unorthodox places for evidence of his presence and worship in order to dislodge him, for without our hearts and minds through which to function he could not live for a moment. It is our hearts that give him life, our minds that give him power. Withdraw them and enshrine in them instead the compassionate Christ and the real victory over Mithras believed, falsely, to have taken place in the fourth century, would at last, and in our time, be achieved.

9

Magna Mater

As we have seen, the undiluted masculinity of the Fellow in the Cap, in his occidental guise, was partially concealed in his earlier history by his connexion with Cybele, who, in Rome, was worshipped as the Magna Mater. In this way, the male-female balance was preserved in the Eleusinian Mysteries.

But the original Creed of Christ stood in no need of a goddess to provide the female equipoise, for the Perfect Man of the Christian Faith incorporated in himself, like Adam-Kadman of the Kabbalah, the perfect balance of male-female attributes. In him, mercy and Truth were met together, Love and power were inseparable, compassion tempered justice, and tenderness accompanied strength. There was no need of a Magna Mater to restrain the stern Father of fathers, for, in Jesus, the perfect Father-Mother, the guide, protector, provider and healer, were constantly manifested. The nature of the Ideal Good was expressed by the Ideal Man. To this ideal concept of God E. W. King refers in quoting the Kabbalah according to the Zend-Avesta:

All that exists has emanated from the source of the Infinite Light. Before all things existed the Primal Being, the "Ancient of Days", the eternal King of Light who is the ALL: the real cause of all existence, the Infinite. He alone is He; there is in him no Thou. All is an emanation from this being; the nearer therefore that any approaches to Him, the more perfect is it, and the less so does it become when it recedes from Him. Into the void He let forth his first emanation—a ray of Light, which is the source and principle of all existence, uniting in itself the generative and conceptive forces; being both father and mother in the sublimest sense, pervading all and without which nothing can for an instant subsist. From this Double Force, designated by the first two letters of the name Jehovah (Yod, He) emanated the first-born of God, the Tikkun, or Universal Type (Platonic IDEA) . . . Inasmuch as he has received what he gives, the light and the life, he is considered as equally a generative and conceptive principle, as the "Primitive Man"—Adam-Kadman.

It was this ideal concept of male-female that Jesus Christ embodied; therefore the Christian Faith had originally no need of another impersonation of Womanhood. But by the time the Nativity stories began to circulate such a need had arisen, by reason of two elements that had entered the Church: in the first place, Paul's racial attitude to women which subordinated them both as a sex and a spiritual influence. As a Jew he evidently subscribed to the Talmudic prayer:

Blessed art thou, O Lord, that thou hast not made me a Gentile, an idiot or a woman,

for he writes:

I would have you know that the head of every man is Christ, and the head of every woman is the man (1 Cor. xi, 3). I permit not a woman to teach, nor to have dominion over a man, but to be in quietness (1 Timothy ii, 12). Let the woman keep silence in the churches; for it is not permitted unto them to speak, but let them be in subjection, as saith the Lord. It is shameful for a woman to speak in the church (1 Cor. xiv, 34).

It might also be very embarrassing to the Mithraists, as the mothers of sons might be the first to rebel against the domination of the warrior-God. And it was the Lord Mithras, not the central character of the Gospels who kept women in a state of subjection and regarded them as unworthy of initiation into the Mysteries and therefore of immortality.

The second element, closely connected with the first, was the infiltration of the unbalanced masculinity of the occidental Mithras.

It was evidently in order to remedy this dangerous bias that a story was built up on the assumption of the sanctity and semi-divinity of the mother of Jesus, who thereafter became not the wife of Joseph and the mother of a considerable family as depicted in the Gospels, but the Virgin Mary, the Goddess of Mercy, the female Mediator between man and her holy Son, the Supreme Mediator, while the Church mediated between man and the Holy Mother, so that God was relegated further and further from His children, separated from them by a hierarchy of Mediators who were relied upon to use their influence with him— a far cry from the realization of the mystic: I and my Father are one.

In their task, the authors of the myth had little or no help from the canonical writings then extant (E. W. Barnes puts the date of the beginning of the Nativity stories at A.D. 90, although they were incorporated much later into the Gospels of Matthew and Luke); for the mother of Jesus and the supposed circumstances of his birth are not mentioned either by Paul or the writer of the First Epistle of Peter, while the original gospel-writer, Mark, far from noting in the Master's mother any sign of great spirituality, represents her, in his first reference to her, as attempting to interrupt her son's ministry (Mark iii, 31–35). He then records the Master's repudiation of any human relationship that is not based on a mutual and integrated submission to the will of God. The only other two references to Mary in Mark are where he emphasizes that she was the mother of James the less and of Joses and Salome and records that she stood with other women during the crucifixion "looking on afar off", adding, in parenthesis "who also when he was in Galilee, followed him and ministered unto him" (Mark xv, 41); and finally tells us that she was one of the women who "bought sweet spices that they might come and anoint him", and found the sepulchre empty. Surely if anything had been known or even hinted of a miraculous birth at the time of writing (A.D. 70–100) such an unusual and significant event would have been recorded? The reason it was not recorded was obviously that Mark had no authority for it in the sources available to him: Q. and the Epistles of Paul and Peter.

Even if we accept the account in Luke ii, 40–51 of the questioning in the Temple, as valid, Mary is found here referring to Joseph as Jesus's father and definitely not understanding what he meant when he said that he "must be about his Father's business":

> They understood not the saying which he spake unto them.

But Mary would have perfectly well understood had she really experienced the angelic visitation and virgin birth ascribed to her. Yet all that could be said of her was that, like any other woman whose child shows signs of originality, she "kept all these sayings in her heart"; pondering them, wondering what they might mean. Furthermore, in what has already been shown to be the suspect wine-miracle, Jesus is reported as having rebuked his mother for an untimely suggestion (John ii, 4). Only in the account of the Crucifixion given in John xix, 25–27 is any special tenderness and sympathy evidenced by Jesus for his mother, and this account contradicts the one in Mark when, with the other women, Mary was said to have stood "afar off". Now she is said to have stood by the cross, the account being:

> Now there stood by the cross of Jesus his mother, and his mother's sister, Mary the wife of Cleophas, and Mary Magdalene, when Jesus therefore saw his mother,

and the disciple standing by whom he loved, he saith unto his mother, Woman, behold thy son! Then saith he to the disciple, Behold thy mother! and from that hour that disciple took her unto his own home.

This was a natural and loving provision for the two nearest to him in his human life, but neither this account nor any of the others ascribe to Mary the spiritual stature that would have been hers had she been so evolved as to have annulled the lower law of birth—as strong and binding as that of death of which it is the counterpart—by the higher "law of life in Christ Jesus".

Undiscouraged, however, by this lack of evidence, and even by the chronological tables in both Matthew i and Luke iii, that firmly trace the ancestry of Jesus from David through Joseph (Mary being of the house of Aaron), the Church historians got on with their task of representing the mother of Jesus as being something between one of the many virgins who throughout the ages had given birth to demi-gods after the visitation of some pagan deity, and one of the equally numerous nature goddesses, enabling any pagan converts to the new Faith to be able to recognize their Cybele, their Isis or Magna Mater in the features of the Holy Mother.

The corner-stone on which this fabrication was laid is the prophecy contained in Isaiah vii, 14, which, unfortunately for the hypothesis, has been found by later scholars to contain a mis-translation of the key-word "Virgin" on which the doctrine was based. The word originally used, it is now discovered, should have been "young woman", and an intelligent reading of the context proves without shadow of doubt that the prophecy made by Isaiah was a wholly contemporary one. It is clear that he was merely telling the menaced King Ahaz that in quite a short period—the time it would take for a woman to conceive, bear a son and rear him to the point where he could choose between right or wrong—his enemies would have been dispersed: "For before the child shall know to refuse the evil and choose the good, the land that thou abhorrest shall be forsaken of both her kings"—those of Syria and Israel.

By no possible feat of the imagination could this prophecy honestly be made to apply to an event supposed to have taken place hundreds of years later. Yet the impossible was done; and later, much later—it was only made dogma in the last century—the doctrine of the immaculate conception of the Virgin's mother was imposed upon the credulous members of the Catholic Church.

By this means not only was the Founder of the Christian Faith raised to the position of demi-god, a being so different from ordinary humanity that he could not possibly be accepted as a model for the common man who was hampered by the fact of his animalistic birth, and so for ever at a disadvantage before his exalted Example, but Mithras was reunited to his Cybele. The Magna Mater took her place by the side not only of the Sun-God, but of the Son of God who, in his personal life, had overcome her by resisting her lures, and had shown mankind the way out of the animal kingdom over which she and her male counterpart, the Fellow in the Cap, presided.

Thus the Mystic of Galilee, the transitional man in the process of spiritual evolution, who, by his very kinship with other men, became the hope of the world, since he proved by his example that they could go and do likewise, became "very God" with a near-goddess for a mother, and thus passed so far out of the reach of common humanity that it is not surprising that men gave up the unequal struggle of trying to "follow him".

The cult of the Virgin Mary has, of course, evolved throughout the ages, and the modern Mariolatry found in the Roman Catholic Church today, is derived from many other sources beside Mithraism. The Madonna may be said to be a composite of most of the pagan goddesses; but she triumphs most noticeably as the Queen of Heaven who, centuries before the birth of Jesus Christ, sought, under many names, to lure the monotheistic Jews from their single-minded devotion to Jehovah. As Ashtoreth, and by means of one of his favourite wives, she succeeded temporarily in seducing Solomon, as we read in 1 Kings i–viii. And the prophets were continually deploring her influence and worship, as we see from Jeremiah vii, 18; xliv, 16–22; xvii, 25, as well as Judges ii, 13; x, 6, and 1 Samuel vii, 3, 4, and xii, 10, and in Kings xxiii, 13. She was the Goddess of the Zidonians and also of the Hittites. In "The Religion of the Hittites"[1] Thomas Tyler tells us that, in a treaty between Ramases II and the Hittites (*circa* 1000 B.C.), a list is preserved of the gods of the land of Khita, which includes the name of Ashtoreth. He goes on to say:

> The treaty with Ramases shows . . . that Ashtoreth was a Hittite Goddess. She was also a principal deity of the Phoenicians, though the origin of the name is to be traced to the Mesopotamian and Chaldean Ishtar. She comes before us in the Old Testament as The Queen of Heaven, that is, the Moon.

As Ishtar, the Babylonians and Assyrians depicted her as descending into hell, and slowly being deprived of her starry jewels by the envious Queen of those regions.

She certainly appears to have been resurrected when we gaze on the image of the Queen of Heaven and Mother of God, in Roman Catholic shrines, adorned with jewels, as the simple mother of Jesus could never have been. And she has not merely been resurrected, for, according to the New Dogma of the Bodily Assumption of the Virgin Mary promulgated by the Pope in 1950, she has now ascended into her native spheres; while the crowning of the Madonna Statue in London in 1954, by the Roman Archbishop of Westminster, suggests the final triumph of paganism so long resisted by the Jews of the Old Testament.

As Mithras instated Cybele as a Goddess in Phrygia, so has the Church, supposed to be preserving the teachings and monotheism of the Mystic of Galilee, instated the assiduous "Queen of Heaven", purged of all sins save the incitement to idolatry.

[1] *Religious Systems of the World.* (Sonnenschein.)

The Sun-King

THE Dark Ages were the result not only of the Church's attempt to combine imperialistic Mithraism with the other-worldly policy of the Creed of Christ, but also of her own bad conscience at having attempted such an impossible compromise. It was obvious from the first that her authority, if not her very life depended upon this perilous syncretism not being discovered; therefore she must do everything to prevent enlightenment. Every door must be watched against the entrance in some form of the forbidden doctrines. Hence her ruthlessness to all that was not orthodox, her witch and heresy hunting, and her determination to allow no unexpurgated versions of the Bible, especially the Old Testament with its obvious Mazdean echoes, to reach the general public. Only by keeping the people ignorant of the sources of their religious beliefs could the church-compiled dogmas, agreed by the priesthood to be necessary, if not for salvation at least to the maintenance of the power and authority of Mother Church, be imposed.

The majority of the priests were, of course, almost as ignorant and uneducated as their congregations, but the intellectual hierarchy, the makers of dogmas, the learned bishops who decided the policy of the Church, must have known very well what had happened, and evidently hoped that the security measures they had taken to keep their secret would be sufficient until they had time to establish a system of universal thought-control on spiritual matters so absolute that it would be proof against anything, even the revealed word of the sacred Scriptures. The Faithful must be taught that the interpretation of Holy Writ was "beyond" them, and must be left to the initiates, the priests. The sinfulness of doubting or questioning must be emphasized, so that even if by some unfortunate chance they ever had access to the sources of their Faith, the well-trained congregations would not dream of attempting independent research. It was not of course possible that these early intellectuals could have visualized a state when education had become as general as it is now. And by and large their optimism as to the possibility of keeping their secret was justified, for it was not until nearly the end of the last century that the connexion between Mithraism and Church-Christianity began to be suspected by scholars. The black-out of the Dark Ages, a period of thought-control more intense than any in man's history until the advent of Marxism, provided the essential screen.

But while this produced a temporary internal order and a great strengthening of the power of ecclesiasticism, it could not entirely hide from view the effects of the unholy compromise that was being attempted, even though the true nature of that compromise was unknown. Crusades and "holy wars", however plausibly justified and explained, remained irreconcilable with the concept of God as Love, and the instructions in the Sermon on the Mount to love one's enemies and practise non-violence. But the uneducated, who always find it difficult to argue, were taught that to believe and obey the Church teachings was their only chance of avoiding hell's fire, or Mithras' fiery lake.

A far greater menace than the questionings of a mainly uneducated laity were the genuine and sincere Christians within the Church, the saints, seers and mystics, the spiritu-ally educated, whose lives were dedicated to the Christian Truth. These were almost invariably an embarrassment to the hierarchy of their times while they lived, and were often only canonized a very long time after their death when their unorthodoxy, or heresy, had been forgotten, and their goodness could not be denied. For the genuine mystic achieves the aim of all true religionists—direct communion with the object of worship. A priesthood exists only to aid the votary to reach this high realization. Therefore if all men were mystics the Church would become redundant, which is why the priest so dislikes the prophet who aims at making all men mystics in the manner described in John xvii, 11, 21–23, and distrusts anyone who claims to have reached this state, banishing them from the fold as heretics if they become too recalcitrant, or shepherding them into monasteries and nunneries where they will be firmly disciplined, when they insist on living the life of the Founder of their Faith. For the priest is concerned chiefly with those who go the way of the world and therefore desire the mediation and vicarious forgiveness dispensed by the priesthood whereby that institution maintains its authority, prosperity and power.

The ritual, initiation, penances and divine mysteries of the so-called Church of Christ, all savour strongly of the cult of Mithras, while the self-perfectioning of the saint and mystic, the single-minded desire to achieve at-one-ment with the ideal of perfection—that which the Spanish mystic Teresa of Avila described as holy wedlock with the Divine —remains the way of the Mystic of Galilee who declared: "I and my Father are one."

Such an utterance would make him as unacceptable to the modern Christian Church as it did to the Churchmen of his day. It will always be unacceptable to an institution that exists to shrive miserable sinners and inspire them with the hope that they will be better some day; in spite of the fact that they cannot fully realize that hope without first dispensing with the services of the priesthood.

We have one very clear historical example of the dichotomy between mystic and priest in full swing in the ecclesiastical battle royal that took place between Bossuet and Fénélon in the reign of Louis XIV, known to the world, curiously enough, as *Le Roi Soleil*; and who was indeed the last notable example of a Mithraic King in the West. As Cumont tells us: "The priests of Mithra . . . had been the first to teach in Occidental parts the doctrine of the divine right of Kings."

Louis was brought up on this doctrine by the Romish authoritarian, Mazarin, who, with Anne of Austria followed the tradition laid down by that absolute monarchist, Richelieu. Throughout his life Louis, to whom the doctrine was congenial, was encouraged to conform to it by such worldly members of the Gallic Church as Bossuet, Harlay, Bishop of Paris, and, later, his Confessor, Pére de la Chaise. Although these men would have been put to shame by a true Soldier of Mithras, such as the Emperor Julian, by their lack of austerity, self-purification, honour and non-attachment, they yet succeeded in building up Louis into the supreme example of an Occidental Sun-King, the would-be Universal Monarch whose rule on earth is the reflection of the heavenly rule. Louis was the logical and inevitable effect of the teaching of the Divine Right of Kings, the authoritarian who had none above him but God who was so identified with him that the worship of the one was included in that of the other. His victories in war, aided by the support of the Church, raised him to a pinnacle of power which made him seem, to the aristocracy, and ruling classes at least, as a veritable manifestation of the giver of all good gifts. Honour and glory could come only through his favour. Therefore he was surrounded by the ceremonial and ritual of a deity. His daily carriage drives that he took during the latter part of his reign with his family and courtiers adorned with glittering jewels were all part of the mystique carefully built up throughout his reign to show the peasantry that kings are not as other men.[1] He was the autocrat *par excellence*, and even his beloved Madame de Maintenon dare not oppose his will.

Nevertheless, his early training had engendered in him a deep respect for the Church which stood for him in the place of God. A born authoritarian himself, he knew the value and power of vested authority. He recognized the inter-

---

[1] It is interesting to compare descriptions of the Toilet Ceremonies performed by the deified Pharoahs of Egypt with those of the Grande Levee, first introduced into the French monarchical ceremonial by Henri II—possibly at the suggestion of the learned Diane de Poitiers—but immensely elaborated by Louis XIV who made his Toilet in full view of his assembled nobles.

dependence of Church and Monarchy as clearly, perhaps
even more clearly, than Constantine had done. He knew
that one depended upon the other and that in a crisis each
must support the other. He had no knowledge of Mithras
but he sensed his influence within the Church, and was
aware that that influence invested him with power and
authority. Therefore, although he often revolted against
them, he always eventually bowed to the rulings of the
Church. He was not interested in its metaphysics. Idealistic
philosophy was beyond him; but he respected and was
interested in maintaining its authority and power which
was finally one with his own, and he was a zealous cere-
monialist. Therefore, when he began to understand the
nature of the cult of Quietism which found its way into his
Court, via the handsome and fashionable Abbé de Fénélon
and his teacher, Madame Guyon—and this was not until
long after it had first arrived and been received with open
arms by the devout ladies of St. Cyr, including its Foundress,
Madame de Maintenon—there was no question of his
tolerating it. It was a heresy which, in the Church, was as
bad as a rebellion within the State.

In point of fact the Quietest teachings followed the
tradition of the great Spanish Mystics, who, by that time,
had been approved by the Church, and stood for the
esoteric teachings of Christianity, for world-transcendence
as distinct from world-domination. Left to herself Madame
Guyon might have laboured in vain to make such teachings,
so alien to the thought of the King and the climate of
opinion at his Court, widely known; but they attracted to
her circle the well-born already socially successful protégé
of Bossuet, l'Abbé de Fénélon, who recognized in Quietism,
as displayed in Madame Guyon's most famous work *Le
Moyen Court*, a means of attaining direct communion with
God which the mystic in him so ardently desired. And soon
he was bringing it to the notice of his titled followers, and
through them to Madame de Maintenon who introduced
it into her educational establishment, St. Cyr, where it was
welcomed not only on its own merits but by reason of the

fact that its mother superior, Madame de la Maisonforte, was a relative and devoted disciple of Madame Guyon.

It was therefore Fénélon's interest in Quietism, and the many activities that resulted from that interest which brought it to the notice of the Churchman, Bossuet, who had no doubts whatever about the danger of Mysticism to the exoteric Church; and he persecuted it and its founder fanatically, with the backing not only of his own but of the Romish Church which could condone mysticism in the past—in the long-dead Teresa of Avila and John of the Cross—but would never tolerate its challenge in the present, even when offered, as it was, by one of the Church's most favoured sons. For Fénélon was always recognized by Rome as an adornment of the Church even when he wrote his *Maxims of the Saints* in defence of Madame Guyon's cult and the teachings of the *Moyen Court*, which was by then the favourite reading of the ladies of St. Cyr and of its devout Foundress who carried the precious book about in her apron pocket.

But Fénélon although a sincere champion of Madame Guyon and her way, and with all the makings of a mystic, writing in his *Treatise on the Existence of God*: "Before You I am as though I were not. I plunge into Your infinity. Far from thinking of Your permanence in terms of my continuous flowing, I can no longer find myself, I begin to see in everything that which it really is, I mean Yourself," was not an integrated man. In fact there existed within him the same division, the same dichotomy as that which existed in his Church, as was inevitable with such a loyal son of the Church. The mystic in him for ever warred with the Churchman; the aspirant after higher Truth was impeded by the Traditionalist; saintliness frequently bowed to expediency. And it was because of this division, not because of the weakness of his and Madame Guyon's outlook and beliefs, that he and his Cause suffered defeat at the hands of the single-minded, worldly Bossuet and his party.

To a lesser degree, Madame de Maintenon also suffered from this inner tension. A deeply devout woman whose marriage with the Sun-King had disillusioned her about finding happiness through worldly honours and high position, she was attracted both to Fénélon personally and to his Quietism which opened up to her for the first time the possibility of attaining to direct communion with God. In addition, Fénélon's interest in the education of young women was equal to her own, and she considered him the good genius of St. Cyr. But when it came to the choice— after the publication of the *Maxims* when Louis became so terrifyingly aware of the state of affairs—she chose Ortho- doxy, which included her King and his continued protection and power (for she knew quite well that he was not suffi- ciently spiritually evolved to follow her to the mystic heights), in preference to what even she recognized for a time as being a purer form of Christianity than that taught by the Church.

But much as she and Fénélon suffered through this spiritual tug-of-war, which in his case led to his banishment to Cambrai and the ending of his tutoring of the King's grandson, the Duc de Bourgogne, and in her case to near- disgrace and the one time in her life when she was out of favour with her illustrious husband, the chief sufferer from the Abbé's double-mindedness was certainly his young pupil who adored him and readily assimilated his idealism. Fénélon undoubtedly tamed what had once been the ungovernable nature of the young Duc and had written for him his famous book *Télémaque* which gave a picture of how a truly Christian Prince should behave and was a refutation of the Mithraic teaching of the Divine Right of Kings, since it strongly condemned the theory that the King could do no wrong, but, on the contrary, recommended the strictest obedience to the law of God. In this sense the book was a definite criticism of Louis and his policy.

Although his loyalty to the Church prevented his open declaration of the fact, Fénélon was by nature a pacifist, and his convictions on this subject were conveyed to his followers; yet when war broke out, he could advise his nephew to fight for his country, a betrayal that his hitherto devoted sister-in-law, who had been converted to his pacifist point of view and brought up her son accordingly,

never forgave. His destestation of war was certainly apparent
to his royal pupil, which was all very well until the Duc de
Bourgogne became direct heir, through the death of his
father, to the throne of France, when Fénélon was obliged
to see the situation with the eyes not of the idealist but of
the Churchman who must uphold the Mithraic policy of
his Church. The Prince who aspired to stand in the shoes
of the Sun-King must be trained to behave as that King had
behaved, in order to make France and the Catholic Church,
the greatest powers in Europe. It was quite plain to the
tutor that his idealistic teachings must be not only modified
but, if necessary, reversed. But the guileless boy was not
prepared for such a *volte face*. The earlier teachings held,
and he could not understand the change that took place in
his education and was probably only able to retain his
hero worship of Fénélon because soon after the change of
policy, the Abbé and his *Maxims* were condemned by Rome,
and his tutorship ended. Quietism and some of its implications came to the notice of the King. *Télémaque* was
recognized as a subversive attack on his state-policy, and
the author was banished to his archbishopric at Cambrai,
while the Duc de Bourgogne's education was put in the hands
of one who could be relied upon to teach him the necessity
of following in his grandfather's victorious footsteps.

The vacillating, unsatisfactory character of this unfortunate young man undoubtedly resulted chiefly from the
double-mindedness of the man who had the greatest
influence over him. He loved and admired Fénélon until
the end of his short life, but he had to be trained into the
idea of Kingship, and taught that perpetual warfare for
the aggrandizement of the nation was a Divine Right.
The ideal Soldier of Mithras was still the model in the days
of the Sun-King.

What often seemed to be in Fénélon a lack of courage
was actually a lack of integration, his highest sense of
Truth for ever warring with his deep loyalty to the Catholic
Church. On the heights he wrote *Télémaque* and instructed
his royal pupil into idealism, on the heights he humbly

followed and courageously defended the doctrines of Madame Guyon; in the depths he conformed to the Mithraic policy of the church and felt himself obliged to uphold its teachings of the Divine Right of Kings.

But at times he powerfully reacted against this dangerous and often disastrous theory which throughout the ages had caused the Western world to be continually ravaged by the sword. And it was in such a moment that he wrote Louis the letter which, being intercepted by the discreet Madame de Maintenon who wished to retain Fénélon at St. Cyr, the King never received, and which, although it is well known, deserves quoting in part to illustrate the practical effect of Emperor-worship on an occidental King and the fate of Europe:

For nearly thirty years your chief Ministers have reversed all the old maxims of the State to raise your authority to the highest point. Neither the State nor its laws are any more spoken of, only the King's good pleasure. They have carried your revenue and expenses beyond limits, lauded you to the skies for having, as they say, surpassed the greatness of all your predecessors. In reality the whole of France has been impoverished in order to introduce at Court an outrageous and incurable luxury. They have accustomed you to receive constant and exaggerated flattery carried to idolatry, which for your own honour you should have indignantly rejected. They have rendered your name odious and all the French nation insupportable to our neighbours. The war with Holland was undertaken solely from motives of pride and vengeance, from whence it follows that the extension of the frontiers which you have gained from it are unjustly acquired. The treaties of peace signed by the vanquished were not signed freely, but with the knife at the throat. . . . This is enough, Sire, to prove that you have passed your entire life far from the paths of truth and justice. So many dreadful troubles have desolated Europe for more than twenty years, so much blood has been shed, so many scandals committed, so many provinces ravaged and towns and villages reduced to ashes—fatal results of the war of 1672, undertaken for your pride and the confusion of the Dutch. This is the true source of all the evils France is suffering. Since this war you have always insisted on granting peace and imposing your conditions as the Master instead of conducting them with equity and moderation. For this reason it could not last. Your enemies, shamefully crushed, have thought only of rising and uniting together against you. Is it surprising? You have not even kept within the terms of this peace imposed by you with so much arrogance. This conduct has united all Europe against you. Even those who have not dared declare it desire with impatience your defeat and humiliation as the sole means of gaining liberty and repose of the nations.

The allies prefer war with losses to concluding a peace with you, because they are certain from their own experience that it would not be a true peace, and that you would keep it no more than the others, and would make use of it to crush each of them separately as soon as they were disunited.

Meantime your people die of famine. You live with your eyes fatally bandaged. God will certainly at last rend the veil. For a long while His arm has been raised against you, but he is slow to strike because He has pity on a Prince who has been all his life besieged by flatterers. You do not love God; you only fear him with a slavish fear. Your religion consists only in superstition and superficial practices. You refer everything to yourself as though you were God upon earth and everything upon it created only to be sacrificed to you. . . .[1]

This letter and the state of Europe at the time of its composition illustrate the cumulative result of allowing the warrior-god to take precedence, in what was said to be Christendom, of the Prince of Peace; the inevitable effect of the unholy compromise still being maintained in the Catholic but certainly not Christian Church.

[1] Lavallée. Correspondance Générale, 111–334.

It should be noted that while the Churchmen of his time backed Louis up in his policy of self-aggrandizement, and made no effort to stop the perpetual wars that made such a shambles of Europe, ruined the country and directly resulted in the downfall of the Monarchy, they were most severe on the subject of the King's personal morality. His liaison with Madame de Montespan was sternly condemned by them, although having driven him as a young man into a loveless State marriage, the Church might be thought to have had some responsibility for his moral lapses. In fact, throughout its history, the Catholic Church has concentrated on the seventh commandment almost to the exclusion of the sixth, except in the narrow sense of personal murder. It has even gone so far as to re-arrange the decalogue of Moses so that two commandments stress the forbidden crime instead of one. By telescoping the first two commandments and so slurring over the clause so embarrassing to a partly pagan church of bowing down to graven images, the seventh commandment becomes the sixth in the Catholic catechism while the tenth is split into two, the ninth reading: Thou shalt not covet thy neighbour's wife—standing starkly on its own.

Such an obsession with carnal lust is not apparent in the Gospels, but continence was a very prominent feature in the Mithraic Mysteries, on account, as we have seen before, of its energy-preserving powers. While the reason for it was probably forgotten, the practice was perpetuated in the Catholic Church. So long as the two commandments relating to personal morality were kept intact, Louis and his soldiery could lay waste to Europe without being in danger of Mithras' lake of fire. Such values are nowhere found in the Gospels which record throughout a life of compassionate love which released an adultress from the legal penalty attached to her crime, and a consistent policy of non-violence; but they are in complete accord with the Empire-building and Empire-sustaining Mithras.

Like the celestial orb, the Sun-King rose, reached his zenith of militaristic glory and regal splendour, and then inevitably set, and vanished into darkness, only on his

death-bed recognizing his complete impotence and the
fallacy of the doctrine on which he had been persuaded to
base his life. His last words to the infant heir to the throne
of France, whose father, the miserably confused Duc de
Bourgogne, was already dead, bear witness to the change of
heart and outlook which, as he lay sick and helpless, must
have been an exceedingly dark night of the soul:

> My child, you are going to be a King. Do not imitate
> me in the taste I had for magnificent buildings and war.
> Strive on the contrary to be at peace with your neighbours.
> Try to be a comfort to your people, which I unfortunately
> have not been.

A death-bed repentance, perhaps, but possibly more
sincere than that of Constantine; the sword at last lain
aside for the Cross, a Mithraic King's conscious submission
to the Prince of Peace.

But neither on his death-bed nor during his life did the
Sun-King even begin to understand the deep and immense
significance of the spiritual battle between the two priests
of his Church that took place in his memorable reign. He
was, as Madame de Maintenon often regretfully observed,
spiritually immature; very much a man of this world. To
him the whole tiresome business was a lot of unnecessary
fuss about two unreadable books. He had found the *Moyen
Court* "quite incomprehensible" even when read to him by
his wife; and as head of the Gallic Church, he had greatly
resented the intervention of Rome and the public rebuking
of his priests. He had no idea of the importance both to his
country and to Christendom in general of the outcome of that
battle which was, in a very real sense the conflict between the
way of Mithras and the way of Christ brought into the open.

Although Madame Guyon's system was far from perfect,
far from being the complete presentation of the original
teachings taught on the hills of Galilee, inasmuch as it was
the mystic approach, teaching immediate communion
between man and his God, selflessness opposed to self-
assertion, and passivity and Love as opposed to compulsion

and violence, it was far nearer to the Creed of Christ than the Mithraism of Orthodoxy. And had Fénélon been the victor in the battle with Bossuet, and had the Church set its seal of approval upon his and Madame Guyon's system, the way of the mystics, the non-violence of the Christ, might have permeated the policies of the Catholic Church. The Pope of the day was sympathetic both to Fénélon and his views, but felt he must keep on the right side of earthly power in the form of the French King who demanded denunciation of the *Maxims*. But had Truth triumphed over expediency, and spirituality over ceremonialism and Tradition, the Creed of Christ over the cult of Mithras; and had the young Duc de Bourgogne continued under Fénélon's tuition and influence—and lived, there is no doubt that the history of the Western world would have been very different since the reign of the Sun-King.

With a truly repentant pacifist King insisting on justice for the people, lightening the burden of taxation, remedying social wrongs, there would have been no Voltaire and his Encyclopaedists, for there would have been no hypocritical Church or autocratic State to criticize and condemn. And without them and their influence there would have been no revolution to set a vogue for unlimited violence and and rule by the lowest elements, that culminated in the tyranny of Stalinism and the whole levelling down process of an atheistic, socialist age. The Creed of Christ has always called men to go higher in the evolutionary scale. The way of Mithras, or materialism, is to keep humanity at its present level and govern it by force and thought-control. And it was this latter policy that won the day when Bossuet and his authoritarian King triumphed over Fénélon and Madame Guyon.

It was useless for Louis to advise his youthful heir to renounce war when Church and State were still geared to the Mithraic policy of Imperialism and violence. The Monarchy struggled for survival through two more difficult reigns and then the unfortunate symbol of an autocracy that had for generations lived by the sword was mercilessly killed by the sharp sword of the guillotine.

The Mark of Mithras

MISLED by their false God the Emperors with their empires have vanished from the face of the earth. History has abundantly proved the truth of the words of the writer of the Apocalypse who, for all his paganism, understood the futility of physical violence and depicted his Lord as using only the sword of the Word (Revelation xix, 15).

Of the Mithraic sword he truly foretold: "He that killeth with the sword must be killed with the sword."

But the God surveys the empty thrones of his one-time devotees with Olympic indifference. He has, as we have seen, always been adaptable. His genius is now bestowed on the dictators and power-states who serve him well. Never at any time in his history has he had more worshippers. His cult is particularly suited to a scientific age which asks for the endurance, self-immolation and non-attachment that he so well knows how to supply. The young airman offering himself for experimentation at the aeronautical schools, and undergoing the torments necessary in order to condition men for space-travel and an eventual visit to the moon, is a true Soldier of Mithras approved by his God, as is also the radiologist who quite literally burns himself up in order that the weapons of Mithras may be worthy of the Invincible One.

As we look about us today with a tutored eye, we see everywhere the Mark of the Beast, the result of two thousand years of the worship not of Christ, but of Mithras. The external world is plainly the creation of the warrior God.

More than ever are the words of the Christ seen to be true: My kingdom is not of this world.

How could it be?

His was the kingdom of Love. This is the world of violence. His kingdom was ruled by Divine Wisdom. This world is governed by human knowledge. The inhabitants of his kingdom were men of selflessness and compassion. The inhabitants of this world are men of self-indulgence and curiosity. The God of his kingdom was Spirit. The god of this world is matter. The Mark of the Beast is materiality and physical force. The Mark for the Christian must ever be: "the prize of the high calling of God in Christ Jesus." (Philippians iii, 14.)

Nowhere in this world can the Christ find a place to lay his head; but Mithras is perfectly and triumphantly at home in the modern climate of thought. It calls for all his attributes and powers, and flatteringly worships them. The ideal man, the hero, of today, even though he works in a back room and never dons a uniform, is a Soldier of Mithras. Even the women have hastened to assume the qualities of the more than ever popular God. The Service-woman, the sportswoman, the Gun-moll has taken the place of the gentlewoman. As for Love and compassion, they are mere sentimentality, and, even worse, reactionary.

There is much talk of brotherhood in Mithras' world, but when examined closely it is found to refer merely to Brother Ant, the co-worker, the fellow-cell. The poor things have no Father, only a directing communal mind whose demands are so curiously like those of the Fellow in the Cap.

Even outside the Totalitarian States, the brother man of other countries is only tolerated when he conforms. Intransigence leads at once to the discipline of Mithras' sword; not only in the West but everywhere: Kashmir, Korea, and, more recently, Egypt and Hungary. This is not surprising. Brotherhood without the link of a common Fatherhood must always remain artificial and unreal, for where then is the ethical, moral and spiritual criterion?

Mithraic worship may have had to adapt itself to modern conditions, but it exists more strongly than ever. We must go to Spain or Portugal to find the Taurobolium, but the same spirit may be found in the teeming abattoirs of the world and at the altars of the medical research laboratories where animals are slaughtered by the thousand in order that perhaps one day, through their sacrifice, the gods will bestow health of body if not of soul on mankind. Wherever we look we find the pagan belief in the efficacy of and necessity for bloodshed in the world created by Mithras, the world bearing, so unmistakably, his Mark.

And that irreverence for life, which inevitably results when men come to place the importance of a community, a brotherhood, an ideology, scientific research or the nation before that of the individual, is everywhere in evidence.

True Christianity has always emphasized the importance and value of the individual, since the individual alone can attain to spiritual at-one-ment with a higher ideal of Good than that of this world, and spiritual evolution must therefore ever depend on the personal efforts of the individual man. It cannot be achieved by force, legislation, indoctrination, soul-engineering, human policy or any other external means. Yet if it is not achieved, if the reverence for life which based the original Creed of Christ is not instated in the human heart and evidenced in the policies of the world, man as a species is doomed. But how few seem to have recognized this fact!

In *The Golden Bough*, under the heading of *Oriental Religions in the West*, Sir James George Frazer, quite unwittingly, gives the opposite, far more popular Mithraic viewpoint when he writes:

> Greek and Roman society was built on the conception of the subordination of the individual to the community, of the citizen to the State; it set the safety of the commonwealth as the supreme aim of conduct, above the safety of the individual. . . . Trained from infancy in this unselfish

ideal the citizens devoted their lives to the public service and were ready to lay them down for the common good.

This "unselfish ideal" which permitted in its exponents no thought for the victims of such unselfishness, who would with luck be killed before they, usually most unwillingly, laid down their own lives, has led inevitably and inexorably to a series of ever-worsening wars that have culminated in the present situation wherein men realize that another outbreak of Sir James's brand of unselfishness would almost certainly obliterate humanity and possibly disintegrate the earth.

Sir James deplores the fact that during the Middle Ages this unselfish attitude was set aside, and goes on to say:

> All this was changed by the spread of Oriental religions which inculcated the communion of the soul with God, and its eternal salvation as the only objects worth living for, objects in comparison with which the prosperity and even the existence of the State sank into insignificance. The inevitable result of this selfish and immoral doctrine was to withdraw the devotee more and more from the public service, and to breed in him a contempt for the present life which he regarded merely as a probation for a better and an eternal.

This despisal of the way taught so positively by the God-obsessed Jesus of Nazareth—although Sir James prefers to use the term "Oriental religions", and quite untruthfully implies that such an attitude was ever general in the West—has usually been a feature of non-conformist Christian reformers, and never more so than today when what passes for Christianity (but is in fact pure Mithraism which, as we have seen, always taught that *good dwelt in action*), insists that serving the creature is more important than worshipping the Creator, and that social work is a higher service than self-perfectioning.

But where in the Gospels do we find Jesus concerning

himself with social work or the affairs of State? Where do we find him instructing his followers to build hospitals, make armaments, join the military forces or be otherwise "public-spirited"? His explicit instructions were that they should heal the sick and the sinning by spiritual means alone, and preach the Gospel of the invisible Kingdom of God. To fit themselves for such tasks it was essential that they should keep their thought as single-mindedly God-pointed as their Example had done, thinking and speaking perpetually of the things of the Spirit.

This concept of Christianity has been lost because it has seldom if ever been taught since the days when it was practised by the Master and his immediate disciples.

Mithraism, on the other hand, has been quite explicitly taught, and Sir James, who would probably have indignantly denied the charge, clearly reveals himself as a Mithraist, and the mouthpiece of millions of Mithraists, by his despisal of the saint and the recluse, and his admiration of those who, forgetful of self, are willing to live or die for the good of their country. He ends his diatribe against the spiritual hypothesis on what is, for him, a more optimistic note:

> The revival of Roman Law (of the Aristotelian philosophy of ancient art and literature at the close of the Middle Ages) marked the return of Europe to native ideals of life and conduct, to saner and manlier views of the world.

And these saner and manlier views of the world led directly to a series of wars which wrecked Europe and ruined France, and eventually resulted in what, by Sir James's standards, was the supremely sane and manly Hitler, and a steady increase of physical force which today has culminated in nuclear fission, scientific domination, and an age of previously unimaginable violence which is rapidly getting out of human control.

By their fruits ye shall know them! Sir James's opinions, the direct result of the occidental teachings of Church and State, are as clearly anti-Christian as they are Mithraic.

So, at the end of our quest, we find ourselves confronted with the question not of "What has become of Mithras?"—that is now obvious enough—but "What has become of Christ?"

His name has lent sanctity to the shrine in which his rival has been preserved, and his doctrine propagated, for nearly two thousand years. In the Catholic Church Jesus of Nazareth has remained just where his enemy consigned him—nailed to the Mithraic sword, unable to detach himself or his Creed from the Roman emblem, the use of which by so-called Christendom makes his teachings a mockery and of no effect.

In the eyes of the world he has failed. As a teacher he suffered the ignominious death of a common criminal. As a Prophet he has been discredited, since after two thousand years we see no more of the Kingdom of Heaven which he said was at hand than was observable when he spoke of its imminence. As a model he has proved too difficult. As a God he has been defeated by the subtlety and wiles of his more popular adversary. On all sides we hear the condemnation: Christianity has failed.

But such a verdict comes from those who have never known Christ, but only Mithras. Their judgement is therefore based on Mithraic values, whereas Christ's kingdom is not of this world.

If we turn to the cross of the non-conformist we find that the figure has disappeared, in accordance with Paul's realization: "henceforth know we no man after the flesh: yea, though we have known Christ after the flesh, yet now henceforth know we him no more." (2 Corinthians v, 16.) The promise of the empty cross, the abandoned sword, is that he has risen. What is left is the invisible Christ. And in the world unperceived by the senses, the kingdom of Heaven within which is his kingdom, the seeing eye perceives that he truly lives. Even in the world ruled by his rival, there are a few precious outward signs of the inward rule of the Christ: in the resistance, for instance, which is gradually but inexorably gathering momentum in the human spirit to violence; in the passionate desire to secure justice for the under-privileged; in the indignation which is aroused when the rights of others are violated, as, recently, in Hungary and Egypt; in the increasing longing for a peace that is something more than a few years between wars; in the non-violent attitude of the Quakers and Gandhians; in the Tolstoian conception of the Kingdom of God; in the influence that is wielded by a mere handful of pacifists, quite disproportionate to their numbers, an influence so great that they have been absurdly accused of having been one of the causes of the second world war, since Hitler believed that they voiced a majority opinion in England; in the increase in the number of humanitarian groups in the West that insist on the rights of the inarticulate lesser creatures; in the spreading of the idea of a harmless diet through the vegetarian societies of the Occident; in the idea of loving service and social justice that lay behind the founding of the Welfare State, although it has now been twisted into the shape of a stepping stone to materialistic totalitarianism.

All these are the signs recognizable by those with eyes to see that, despite the perversion of his Creed, despite the earthly triumph of his foe, the Christ still reigns, and will always reign so long as there is a human heart willing to receive him. Like Mithras, he can only appear in our experience when men give him mind, heart and tongue through which to manifest himself. But, unlike Mithras, he does not force himself into these sanctuaries at the point of the sword. His method is, and always has been, tender persuasion: "Behold, I stand at the door and knock."

He is there. He has risen. He stands without. But only men like you and I can let him in. Only through Love-regenerated hearts can the Saviour be seen to function and to save.

And until each man and woman undergoes that deep spiritual experience of opening the door of his being to the gentle Christ-Spirit, his rival and antithesis will continue to dictate the policies of this world. All about us we shall see the evidence of his rule even as we do today. Until he is dethroned in our hearts the Mark of Mithras will be upon us. Though his altars lie in ruins, his name is forgotten and he hides behind that of one said to be his conqueror, but who, in this world, is his victim, humanity will never be delivered from its ever-increasing agony of violence from which the Son of God wished to save it by his Creed of Compassion; and if men do not repent, or change their thinking, they may well find themselves consigned to that Lake of Fire provided by the God of their choice, hearing in their death throes the mocking challenge:

Soli Deo Invicto Mithrae!

BIBLIOGRAPHY

Old and New Testaments

The Golden Bough by Sir James George Frazer. (Macmillan.)

The Rise of Christianity by Ernest William Barnes. (Longmans Green and Co.)

Harmsworth Encyclopaedia.

A Classical Dictionary by J. Lempriere, D.D. (George Routledge and Sons Limited.)

Gospel Light by George M. Lamsa. (A. J. Holman Company, Philadelphia, U.S.A.)

The Paganism in Our Christianity by Arthur Weigall. (Hutchinson and Co. [Publishers] Ltd.)

Religious Systems of the World. (Sonnenschein.)

Standard Dictionary of Folklore and Mythology. (Funk and Wagnalls.)

The Gnostics and Their Remains by C. W. King. (David Nutt.)

The Mysteries of Mithras by Franz Cumont. (Kegan Paul, Trench, Trubner and Co. Ltd.)

Dogme et Rituel de la Haute Magie by Eliphas Lévi.

Julian by Alice Gardiner. (G. P. Putnam's Sons. 1901.)

Constantine the Great by John B. Firth. (G. P. Putnam's Sons.)

Virgil by the Rev. E. Lucas Collins, M.A. (William Blackwood and Sons)

The Poems of Virgil, translated into English verse by James Rhoades. (Oxford University Press.)

Suetonius, The Lives of the Caesars, with an English Translation by J. C. Rolfe Ph.D. (William Heinemann Ltd.)

The Teaching of the Twelve Apostles, a Translation with notes by Canon Spence, M.A. (James Nisbet and Co.)

The Nature and Function of Priesthood by E. O. James. (Thames and Hudson.)

The Authentic New Testament, Edited and Translated from the Greek, by Hugh J. Schonfield. (Dennis Dobson.)

Plotinus: The Enneads, translated by Stephen MacKenna. (Faber and Faber Ltd.)

INDEX

(excluding Preface and Notes to this edition)